scraptherapy™

Cut the Scraps!

scraptherapy™

Cut the Scraps!

7 Steps to Quilting Your Way through Your Stash

IRRESISTIBLE
20
PROJECTS

Joan Ford

The Taunton Press

The Taunton Press
Inspiration for hands-on living®

The Taunton Press, Inc.,
63 South Main Street, PO Box 5506,
Newtown, CT 06470-5506
email: tp@taunton.com

Editor: Erica Sanders-Foege
Technical editor: Linda Turner Griepentrog
Copy editor: Nina Rynd Whitnah
Cover design: 3&Co.
Interior design: Carol Singer
Layout: Laura Lind Design
Illustrator: Joan Ford
Technical assistance, illustration: Tinsley Morrison
Photographer: Burcu Avsar, except for quilts on back cover and
pgs. 11, 47, 53–189: Scott Phillips © The Taunton Press, Inc.

The following names/manufacturers appearing in *Cut the Scraps!* are trademarks: Aurifil™,
Cut for the Cure™, Korner Radial Rules™, Mary Ellen's Best Press™, Nifty Notions®, Paintstiks®,
Q tools™, Quiltsmart℠, ScrapTherapy™, Tucker Trimmer™, Wing Clipper™.

Library of Congress Cataloging-in-Publication Data
Ford, Joan, 1961-
  Scrap Therapy cut the scraps! : 7 steps to quilting your way through your stash / Joan Ford.
    p. cm.
  Includes bibliographical references and index.
  ISBN 978-1-60085-333-3 (alk. paper)
  1. Patchwork quilts. 2. Quilting--Patterns. 3. Rags. I. Title. II. Title: Cut the scraps!
  TT835.F667 2011
  746.46--dc22
                    2010047873

Printed in the United States of America
10 9 8 7 6 5 4 3 2 1

A few years back, when I mentioned to my husband that I was considering leaving my "real" job as an accounting executive recruiter to pursue a career as a quilt designer, Dave only flinched a little. Then he said, "Why not?!" Thanks, Dave!

ACKNOWLEDGMENTS

I often say, "It's not about the quilt," because, to me, making a quilt is so much more than sewing together a collection of fabric pieces. It's about the connections made between quilters where they gather. It's about creating something incredible from random pieces of fabric. It's about memories and stories. It's about a feeling of accomplishment when the task is complete and the quilt finds a home.

Similarly, the book you are holding is a compilation of extraordinary skills and resources. I extend special thanks to the many creative talents at The Taunton Press. The efforts of countless dedicated individuals made the daunting task of creating this book seamless and enjoyable. Most especially, my sincerest "thank you" to my editor, Erica Sanders-Foege, who is simply an amazing, multifaceted person.

Thanks also to technical editor Linda Griepentrog, whose sense of humor made fact-checking fun. As the voice of experience and reason, she provided the appropriate level of encouragement to this first-time book author.

Thanks also to the quilt shops and quilt teachers worldwide who believed in the ScrapTherapy™ program and offered it to their customers with such enthusiasm. And to all my dear friends at Brewer Quilting and Sewing Supplies, especially Barb Sunderlage and Rose DeBoer, who turned a breakfast meeting into an incredible journey.

Special thanks to shops, teachers, and quilters in the Syracuse, New York, area, especially Janet Lutz and the staff at Calico Gals, who have supported the Scrap-Therapy program and me from day one.

Finally, it's not about the book in your hands. It's about the desire to own every single project in it, even if it means never sewing a single stitch! It's about the quilter who seeks a solution to a seemingly overwhelming stash of scrap fabrics. It's about you! Thank you for appreciating quilts and the quilt-making process.

contents

PART TWO
The Projects to Make 50

The Challenge Ahead

So many quilters' stories begin with sweet reminiscences of childhood sewing lessons at their grandmother's knee. Not mine.

Mine started with a central New York December. It snowed every single day. I was so depressed that I stockpiled several sweaters' worth of yarn to knit Norwegian sweaters all winter. Yes, I know what you're thinking: This woman needs to get out more. That December, I received an inexpensive sewing machine as a gift. It sat in the corner for two months because I didn't know how to use it.

FEBRUARY 8, 2003

On February 8, 2003, I took my first quilting class. Before I even got to class I read and reread, cover to cover, the twenty-page soft-cover book on beginning quilting. I kept that book on my nightstand. I practically slept with it. I could not wait.

On February 8, 2003, I became a quilter. I started making quilts with a vengeance. Later that same year, my first entry in the New York State Fair won a blue ribbon in its category. I finished several quilts a month, while working a full-time job. I'm a "finisher," so these weren't tops, they were finished quilts, bound and labeled.

I received lots of advice from friends who are quilters. One person said, "Save all those leftover pieces of fabric from your quilts; you may want to make scrap quilts some day!"

AND MY THERAPY BEGAN

An accountant by training, I pride myself on my organizational skills. I found some clear plastic boxes, shoebox size, and stored my leftover pieces of fabric. The fabrics were all sorts of odd shapes and sizes, folded so they fit vertically in the box, fold-end up so I could see the colors. The boxes were color-coordinated. One box for warm colors: reds and oranges. One box for cool colors: blues and greens. Floral prints, novelties, darks, lights were all perfectly stowed away on the bottom shelf next to the washing machine in my basement. Ready to use...someday.

As time went by, my quilt habit intensified. I started teaching, making samples, and designing easy quilts to promote fabric lines. And the basement stash continued to grow, neat and tidy, and safely stored. Thank goodness I'm so organized.

Then I went to a quilters' guild meeting. A local woman had passed away, and she had been a quilter and garment-maker. No one in her family wanted her fabrics. The family members brought several huge bins full of her scrap fabrics in all shapes and sizes to the guild, hoping someone could use them. Not surprisingly, the guild members were thrilled! Free fabric! And I stood back and watched as the carefully stowed stash was plundered, soon to become gorgeous quilts made by guild members, most projects donated to local charities.

And there I stood. I must be the most selfish person on the planet, because all I could think about was my own stash. Bits and pieces of my favorite colors, my favorite prints, my memories. Folded, lovingly stored away, in color-coordinated piles, neat and tidy *for someone to use when I'm dead!*

It was at that very moment that I knew I needed a better plan. I needed ScrapTherapy!

A QUILT CAN BE MORE THAN A QUILT

At first, I never considered myself to be a scrap quilter. I love buying new fabric. It has a certain never-before-touched feel and smell. Oh, the possibilities...matching colors and prints, coordinating solids and accents.

As I made more and more scrap quilts, I found that I could satisfy the itch to purchase new fabric and use it in a scrappy quilt project to combine the best of both worlds. In a way, making a scrap quilt can be similar to having a diet soft drink with a decadent dessert—using leftover fabric pieces while indulging in a new fabric treat—the two go very nicely together.

To begin any quilt, not just scrappy quilts, the quilter selects fabrics, then works with each piece intimately—pressing, cutting, sewing, sandwiching, and quilting. Every part of the quilt is touched over and over again by its creator, adding personality and energy at every step. As a quilt is used, it generates warmth. All that good energy wrapped into making the quilt gets wrapped around you! Like a reusable hug.

Scrap fabrics add one more dimension to a quilt's personality. Each scrappy piece of fabric with memories attached to it—a leftover from a graduation gift, a scrap remaining from a wedding quilt, fabric pieces from a holiday runner—is selected with care and sewn into the project. The positive memories and energies multiply.

TIME FOR A CHANGE

But there is a dark side. The fabric scraps accumulate. Using them seems complicated at first, then over-whelming as the scrap stash grows. Where to begin, how to begin? And still, the bag of scraps remains. Lurking.

It's a shame for quilters to feel badly about any aspect of this special hobby, but I see it all the time. Quilters roll their eyes when they consider all the pieces of fabric stored away in bags and boxes, unused, the guilt nearly overwhelming.

By presenting a logical method to organize and use perfectly wonderful leftover fabrics, I hope to inspire and motivate you. Quilters who love their craft can create from their own scrap stash, stress-free! The task may seem daunting at first, but it can be simple, and it can make sense—all in seven basic steps.

The ScrapTherapy concept is about sorting, cutting, and storing scrap fabrics using a simple, sensible, and logical process, and then using the sorted scraps in inspiring patterns that incorporate varied techniques. It's fun and functional. Scrap fabrics in a wrinkled wad aren't keeping anyone warm. They aren't satisfying the urge to create. They aren't lifting spirits as a finished quilt would.

The process works. The ScrapTherapy method started with my own stash. Neatly cut and stored scraps take tons less space than the wrinkled bins full of messy fabrics. Thousands of cut-up scraps from my stash have been repurposed into numerous quilted projects, some on the pages that follow. Locally, I teach the ScrapTherapy program at guilds and at a nearby quilt shop to quilters who are looking for fresh ways to use their stash. In 2007, the ScrapTherapy program became a popular class offering at independent quilt shops across the country and around the globe. The program continues to be a solution for many customers who say, "I can't buy one more piece of fabric until I use what I have!"

Now, it's in your hands! What do you have to lose? I challenge you to create irresistibly scrappy projects from your own stash! Are you ready to accept the challenge?

After all, they're only scraps!

PART ONE

The 7 Steps

CHAPTER 1

Fixing the Scrap Problem

STEP ONE: GETTING STARTED

Determine that it's your turn to take action. It's time to turn your scrappy fabric pieces into something else. Realize that change doesn't happen overnight, but it happens in small steps, one fabric scrap at a time. Start small, and stay focused. Set minigoals. Set new goals as the goals are reached. Celebrate small successes—like reaching the end of a bag of scraps or filling a box with scrap squares. A glass of wine, a cup of tea, a small fabric purchase, an outing to the quilt show—pick your pleasure!

It all starts with a satisfying hobby. Quilters love to make quilts with care for special events, gifts, and charity. A trip to the quilt shop can take several blissful hours of careful fabric selection for the next project—a focus fabric, coordinates, accent fabrics, binding, and backing. "I'll take a little extra of that fabric, it's so pretty!"

Soon the cutting and sewing produces results, and the quilt is complete. Then the challenge—what to do with the leftover pieces of fabric? It's too much to throw away. Save the last few inches of a strip here, an extra square there, a small piece remaining from the focus fabric. Set them aside to use later and start a new quilt. Create another beautiful finished project and stow the leftovers in a bag under the table or in a trunk or drawer. It's a vicious cycle—wonderful and terrible at the same time!

I GOTTA, GOTTA, GOTTA GET ORGANIZED!
Show any quilter a basket of messy scrap fabrics and it's an image they can understand. Most will say, "Oh, honey, is that all you have? I'm so sorry! I can beat that, hands-down!"

But behind the boast, there's the guilt. Echoes from childhood remind us: Eat everything on the plate, don't let anything go to waste, you paid good money for that—don't throw it away! It's the same thing with our fabric stash. Those voices warn: Don't waste, save the leftovers, you might need that someday, be frugal. But the scrap piles continue to grow. Unused, the scraps accumulate in bags and boxes and seem to take on a life of their own, invading every empty space.

Then it comes to a breaking point. Something must be done to use these scrap fabrics, we say.

And so we find a pattern or a book that will help with the task at hand.

Find the perfect pattern, open it to the supply list. Inevitably, we're directed to start collecting scraps in various sizes and shapes—twenty 4-in. x 8-in. rectangles, fifteen 6½-in. squares, etc. To find the appropriate scraps, we must then dive into the tangled scrap mess. This piece is too small. This piece is missing a corner. That piece is all wrong. With some determination, eventually, the scraps are identified in the correct quantities and shapes. Only then can the project begin in earnest. More often, it seems, the project is abandoned in despair, and the scraps continue to accumulate. Quilting is a hobby; it should be fun and relaxing, not a source for frustration.

Sure, there's advice about organizing your stash in more efficient ways. Bloggers and periodicals offer complex arrangements to store virtually any shape in all sizes of fabric leftover pieces. For many, like myself, the storage space required to house such a system isn't practical. And the storage variations are overwhelming.

The advice varies. One month, it's throw away every scrap fabric piece that's smaller than 6½ in. The next month, it's keep everything larger than ½ in. Put the scraps in a brown paper bag and grab randomly. Arrrghh!!

Often, only a small handful of patterns to use the stored fabric scraps are offered to go with each system. With each new magazine, a new piece of advice. All valid, but concepts go unmatched from one issue to the next.

Where to begin? The ScrapTherapy method encompasses it all—a simple, straightforward organizational scheme and a plan to use the newly organized scrap pieces in an endless array of scrappy projects.

I SAID, "ENOUGH IS ENOUGH!"

The ScrapTherapy program started with my own stash. I'm an organized person. I kept my leftover scrap fabrics neatly organized in shoebox-size bins and organized by color. I stored the boxes far away from my sewing space. When a scrap of red was needed for an appliqué berry, or a piece of yellow for the center of a flower, forgetting my scrap stash, I went to the fabric store for a fat quarter, never touching the scraps in storage.

I am a "finisher." Some quilters like to make only the quilt tops. I find joy in every aspect of making the quilt—piecing, layering with backing and batting, and quilting. Beautiful quilted projects came from my sewing studio. With every finished quilt, more scraps were added to the basement storage. These unused scrap fabrics haunted me, making me feel incomplete and unsatisfied, a failure at frugality.

When I finally hit a breaking point, I realized that my system wasn't working for me. I needed simple. I needed it to make sense. I needed practical. I needed to make something and finish it. And I needed to feel the energy of success!

I grabbed my scrap bins from the far reaches of the basement, took my scraps to a weekend quilting retreat, and got down to business. One piece at a time, the scraps came out of storage and were pressed and cut into three sizes that played well together—5 in., 3½ in., and 2 in. (more on the sizes in Step Two). I discovered

THE VERY FIRST SCRAPTHERAPY QUILT

Here is the retreat quilt that started the ball rolling.

The classic **Summer Winds** block is one of my favorites and was made with dark background fabric and 5-in. scrap squares. If you look closely, the bright scrap elements of the block include squares, half-square triangles, and quarter-square triangles. The small squares in the corners of the block are made by simply cutting a 5-in. scrap square into quarters. The scrappy triangles are cut from 5-in. scrap squares that have been cut in half, then cut into triangles using half-square and quarter-square triangle specialty rulers. The finished block is 12 in. square.

The borders and sashing fabrics came straight from my stash. The backing is oh-so-soft polyester plush fabric, layered, sewn, and turned for a finished edge without binding.

that these sizes fit beautifully back into the storage bins and took much less space as cut-up scraps than as messy pieces. A bonus!

Working diligently into the evening at that retreat, I felt euphoric when I started to see the scrap squares stacking up, neatly organized and ready to sew. Once I had a nice collection of brightly colored scraps, I put the uncut scraps aside for another cutting session at another time, and started playing.

In my retreat bag, I packed some specialty rulers—rulers that offer an easy way to make half-square triangles and quarter-square triangles from strips—and some stash fabrics in larger quantities.

By midnight, using the tools in my bag, I had a scrappy quilt block. By 3 a.m., I had a small quilt top made only from items in my stash. Eureka! I was on to something, and it felt great.

I looked up from my work, ready to "show and tell." Lost in a sense of accomplishment, I failed to notice the late hour. Needless to say, everyone at the retreat except me had gone to bed.

A BASIC, LOGICAL STRATEGY

From this one evening, the ScrapTherapy program evolved and grew. One piece at a time, my scrap fabrics were converted to usable squares and the squares became quilts. One quilt became two...and then three... and it kept going. I found existing patterns that worked with the three sizes I decided to cut. I created new patterns that used one, two, or all three of the sizes. And the scrap stash waned, and waxed, and waned again.

It works.

Now, it's your turn. Have you had enough of tangled scrap fabrics? It's time to find the treasures hiding in the scrap heap, one step at a time.

CHAPTER 2

The Cutting Workshop

STEP TWO: CUTTING

Get down to the business of cutting up your scraps. Set small, attainable goals and reward your efforts with positive reinforcement—like sewing time! For example, 10 minutes of cutting earns you 30 minutes of sewing time. Make it into a game and watch your messy scraps become tidy stacks of usable pieces. Feel the guilt lift away as your scraps take the first steps to ScrapTherapy projects!

The decision is made and it's time for your therapy to begin. The enormous bin overflowing with scrap fabrics is in front of you and you feel your stomach start to churn. "This is going to take forever!" you lament. However, you know that a small investment of time can have a big payoff. Memories are waiting in your tangled scraps. Your tangled scraps are waiting for you to make them into something wonderful!

DEFINE "SCRAP"

Everyone will have his or her own definition of what constitutes a "scrap" piece of fabric. While there are exceptions to every rule, and the rule of thumb may vary from one person to the next and from one piece of fabric to another, for me, it's a scrap if the piece of fabric is less than $1/4$ yd. by width-of-fabric—9 in. x 42 in. Usually, my fabric scraps are much smaller than that: leftovers from a fabric strip, an extra rectangle or square, odd shapes remaining from mitered borders, and long, skinny strips of backing leftovers. These pieces are tossed into a basket as I work on the latest quilt project.

In my mind, if the fabric is more than $1/4$ yd. and is completely intact (no Swiss-cheese holes where an appliqué piece has been cut away), it goes back into the stash to wait its turn as cornerstones, a small border, an accent fabric for blocks, or one of many more possibilities.

My stash also has dedicated space to fat quarters (18 in. x 21 in.) and large, but odd-shaped fabrics—usually leftovers from backings. Running yardage is stored on several shelves, folded edge out for easy access. When the basket of scraps is full, it's time to get focused on cutting.

GATHER CUTTING TOOLS

Cutting the fabric isn't my favorite part of quilt-making, but it's an important part as this is where accuracy begins. As a result, for my cutting sessions, I like to make the cutting task as easy and efficient as possible without giving up accuracy. To begin, I gather some of my favorite tools. Here's a short list of some of my favorite must-have cutting essentials.

RULER

Let's face it, we've got a lot of cutting to do and we want it to be fast and accurate, so we want the best tool possible for the task ahead. Any straight-edge acrylic ruler used for quilting will work. Consider a ruler that has strong, distinct vertical lines typically used to cut strips, so lining up fabric is fast and accurate. Also, make sure it shows dimensions clearly in whole inches and ½ inches (so there are fewer ½-in. mishaps). Sixteenth-inch marks are an excellent added feature for increased accuracy and speed.

Consider a ruler that has a smooth bottom—no textured dots or lines to catch on the fabric and slow down the cutting process. For most cutting sessions, I start with a 7-in. x 14-in. ruler, or a similar size, but it's not about any one brand of ruler. It's about how comfortable you are with its accuracy and speed to get the job done. My favorite is the Nifty Notions® Cut for the Cure™ Rulers. For a typical cutting session, I keep these sizes handy: 7 in. x 14 in., 4 in. x 14 in., 7 in. x 7 in., and 4 in. x 4 in.

SEE-THROUGH STORAGE BINS

See-through, shoe-box size bins allow the cut-up scraps to be stored neatly in stacks. In addition, with the see-through sides, you can tell where a certain color and size fabric piece might be lurking in your organized scrap stacks. Shoe-box size fits the scrap sizes nicely. The stackable bins have removable lids for storage and stability. While plastic bins aren't optimum for long-term fabric storage, our goal is to use the scraps in the near term, not store the scraps for the long haul. The bins are reusable, and the scrap fabrics have a better chance of getting used if they are visible.

ROTATING CUTTING MATS

A 12-in. rotating cutting mat has an even cutting surface that turns or rotates. This is especially nice for smaller pieces of fabric, since you can easily turn the mat instead of the fabric after each slice. This helpful tool keeps the cutting task fast and accurate, plus it is portable and convenient for cutting sessions on the go!

45MM ROTARY CUTTER AND FRESH BLADE

A fresh blade at the beginning of a big cutting session makes the job so much more pleasant. A fresh blade

PALMING THE RULER

Many quilting classes teach us to place the ruler on the mat with thumb and three fingers on the ruler and the pinky just off the edge of the ruler to keep it from slipping. Add a little pressure during an extended cutting session, and your fingers are going to be tired, causing the potential for the ruler to shift while cutting. Instead, consider forming a new habit.

As shown in step 3 of the "Cutting from Yardage" sidebar on page 18, place your hand on the ruler as before, then drop your palm onto the surface of the ruler. Immediately, you'll notice the pressure on your hand and fingers is much more comfortable and the energy to hold the ruler in place comes from your shoulder rather than the muscles in your fingers and hands. You'll find you'll tire less quickly and therefore can extend your cutting sessions.

Additional products are available that add a handle to the ruler via suction cups. These are very popular, but I feel that too much of the surface of the ruler is covered up by the suction mechanisms. With the lines on the ruler hidden from view, fast and accurate cutting is more difficult.

also allows you to cut through more layers of scraps with confidence. More layers equals more scraps, faster. More scraps equals getting down to sewing sooner. Getting down to sewing sooner equals a happy quilter!

> With a fresh blade, it's tempting to start whacking away at layers of scraps but I try not to cut more than six layers of fabric at a time. Additional layers may cause the fabric to shift, which, in turn, jeopardizes accuracy.

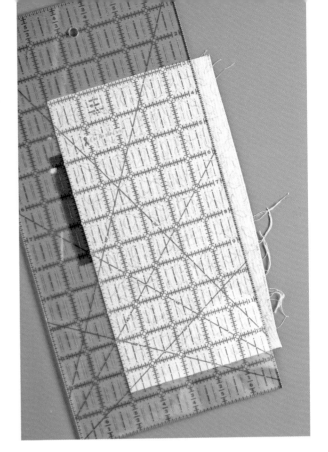

VINYL FABRIC GUIDE

These orange vinyl strips are just one more factor in the "fast and accurate" equation. Put one on the bottom of the ruler, precisely on the correct cutting measurement line. The vinyl clings to the ruler without leaving sticky residue. The thickness of the vinyl creates a guide that stops the ruler right at the edge of the fabric and makes the cutting process nearly thought-free. I like to use the Qtools™ Cutting Edge.

LIQUID SPRAY STARCH ALTERNATIVE

This stuff is magic! It comes in a pump bottle. You spray a small amount on wrinkled fabric, then iron out the wrinkles with ease without leaving starchy stiffness in your fabric. I'm particularly fond of the starch alternative because my scraps get bunched up and have stubborn creases from being stored in a crumpled heap in the scrap basket. I use Mary Ellen's Best Press™.

SET REACHABLE GOALS

It's said that "Rome wasn't built in a day"; along the same logic, your scrap fabrics will not magically turn into organized cut-up stacks overnight. It's discouraging to set huge goals and miss them.

Set smaller goals and **meet** them. Grab a small handful of scraps from your messy basket or bin and take them to your ironing board. Press them flat and make a small stack of pressed scraps. Place the pressed stack on or near your cutting space. If you're like me, that gets annoying because the stack is in the way. With just a short cutting session, that small stack can be cut and stored. Ten minutes and it's out of the way. Then you're ready to start over with another small handful of scraps.

You'll be surprised how motivating it can be to meet these mini-goals and feel progress as the cut scrap piles accumulate.

SCRAPTHERAPY SIZES

The ScrapTherapy sizes are 2-in., 3½-in., and 5-in. squares. Every ScrapTherapy quilted project starts with scraps cut into one, two, or all three of these sizes. Why these sizes? The logic starts with squares, not strips or triangles. Truth be known, I had the storage bins.

I needed scrap sizes that fit well in the bins, and these sizes fit nicely—two stacks of 5-in. scrap squares fit nicely into one bin. Three stacks of 3½-in. plus five stacks of 2-in. scraps fit nicely into a second bin. Amazingly, the fabric stacks don't topple around once they're in the bins! I've traveled with the bins tucked in the bottom of my suitcase; as long as the bin is full or nearly full of scraps, the stacks stay neat.

I also needed the sizes to make sense, with the ultimate goal being to use the scraps in projects. The 5-in. scrap size was the first to be decided; it's a versatile size with lots of potential. As a bonus, shortly after I decided to cut my scraps into 5-in. squares, the fabric manufacturers started making "charm packs"—a pack of 5-in. fabric squares that included one square for each style and color in a fabric collection. With charm packs came charm patterns—more ways to use up the 5-in. scraps.

Next, I decided on the 2-in. size. A 2-in. square was about as small a piece of fabric as I wanted to fuss with, in terms of stacking and storing. I felt that if I needed a smaller scrap piece, I could always trim it down.

I needed something in between the two sizes. Then it came to me—a 2-in. scrap will finish to 1½ in. (subtract ½ in. for seam allowances). If I made a four-patch out of the 2-in. scraps, the four-patch from 2-in. squares would finish to 3 in. (1½ in. plus 1½ in. equals 3 in.), which is 3½ in. unfinished. That's how 3½ in. became the third ScrapTherapy size.

With just these two scrap sizes, I could make four-patches and sew them next to 3½-in. scraps alternately in rows. Add a border or two and a completely scrappy top is all done, no pattern, just plain sewing, using nothing but scraps from the bins.

With the same logic, make nine-patches from 2-in. scraps and the nine-patch will finish to 4½ in. (1½ + 1½ + 1½ = 4½). A 4½-in. nine-patch (finished) is 5 in.

unfinished. With limited planning, just make scrappy nine-patches, sew them alternately in rows with 5-in. scraps, add a border, and you've got a scrappy quilt, perfect for a fast-finish project!

This is a terrific method to make quilts for charity projects in a hurry and at minimal cost. Once your bins are full, all you have to do is start sewing squares together and add a novelty focus print for a border and some backing. Done!

The three ScrapTherapy sizes make sense; they "play" well together—it's as simple as that.

IT'S OKAY TO THROW AWAY

There's just one problem. What if a scrap is smaller than 2 in. and you can't get a 2-in. scrap square from it? I'm here to tell you, it's okay to throw it away. Yep, you read it right.

I know what you're thinking: I paid for it, I'm going to keep it. We've all been trained to be frugal and save everything. However, if there's no chance that you'll ever use it, why are you keeping it? Where are you keeping it—in another basket that you have to dig through? Yes, there are plenty of uses for smaller pieces of scraps—snippet quilts, miniatures, appliqué. But if you don't do these types of projects requiring small fabric pieces, why do you think you might start now? You might be surprised how liberating it can be to get rid of stuff you know, deep down, you won't use. You're making an effort to organize larger, logical pieces so you can find them quickly in see-through bins. The larger pieces can be cut down for smaller projects, and they'll be easier to find and more efficiently stored.

Still not convinced? Get a gallon-size zip-top bag. With a permanent marker, put the current month and year on the bag and place all the small pieces in the bag, starting a new one each month. Stow the bags in a specific place in your stash. In one year, if you have used the scraps from the bins before even considering using the scraps from the bags, *it's okay to throw away!*

And here's one more feel-better idea. Place all the too-small fabric scraps in an old pillowcase. When the pillowcase is full, topstitch it closed and take it to the animal shelter. They'll use the pillow in the animal cages.

CUT, CUT, CUT

Cutting scraps can be a little different from cutting from yardage. For starters, the pieces are often smaller. Many of the scraps don't have a straight, trued-up edge. And the grain may not be as easily identified if the selvages are gone. As you cut, you'll find your own efficiencies to reduce effort and increase efficiency. Here are a few tips I find helpful when I cut my scraps:

- Try to avoid cutting fabric squares with bias edges. Hold an odd-shaped fabric in front of a light source like a window to identify the horizontal and vertical lines in the fabric weave.

- Cut multiple layers at once, but try not to cut more than six layers at a time.

- Select fabrics randomly and try not to sort by color or print at this stage.

- Sort fabrics into three stacks as they are cut, one stack for each size.

- Cut the largest size possible from each scrap. Larger scrap squares can always be cut down if needed.

For a scrap that will become a 5-in. square, make a fresh cut a little more than 5 in. away from one raw edge.

Turn the fabric 180 degrees (or use a rotating cutting mat and you won't have to disturb your newly cut fabric), then make a parallel cut exactly 5 in. away from the first cut using the lines on the ruler, not the lines on the cutting mat. You can see how using the orange vinyl strips can make this step easier.

Then turn the fabric (or rotating mat) a quarter turn, and make the third cut perpendicular to the first two cuts and a little more than 5 in. away from one of the raw edges, while lining up the first two cuts with horizontal ruler lines that are 5 in. away from each other.

Turn the fabric (or mat) one last turn 180 degrees and make the final cut to make the 5-in. square.

Now that your scraps are cut neatly into the three ScrapTherapy sizes, stop and take a deep breath. Feel the sense of accomplishment for a moment or two. You're on your way!

1   2   3   4

CUTTING FROM YARDAGE

Cutting from running yardage is slightly different from cutting smaller scrap pieces. I use a somewhat different approach on truing up the edge from most instructions I've seen.

Fold fabric once or twice to accommodate the width in the available workspace. True up the edge by making the first cut, a little more than the desired strip width away, while aligning top and bottom fabric folds with parallel lines on the ruler. For example if you need to cut a 3½-in. strip, cut a 4-in. strip off the rough edge of the folded yardage, then turn the 4-in.

strip upside down to use the freshly cut edge to cut the 3½-in. strip. Cut strips as needed from the running yardage, from the fresh-cut edge. Adjust folds every two or three cuts to make sure folds are still perpendicular to cut lines. Notice I've made no reference to using the lines on the cutting mat as a square-up guide. When cutting fabric, I always use my ruler and a fresh cut as my start point—it's much more accurate than lining up fabric with lines on a cutting mat that can become distorted over time and with use.

STEP THREE: SORTING

Organize the cut-up scraps in your bins by value or type of collection. As you consider how to store scraps in the storage bins, think about how those scraps might be used and plan ahead. It'll be easy to pull out scraps by value or collection type for your next ScrapTherapy project.

I just hate doing laundry! All that sorting: darks, lights, and everything else. Seems you can't escape without at least two or three loads, no matter what. Ironing—ick. Sorting—yikes! Folding—gads! It's funny, I don't mind doing any of these things when it comes to my fabric stash. Why is that?

LIGHTS, DARKS, AND EVERYTHING ELSE!

Step Three has everything to do with sorting your cut fabric scraps. I like to say, it's just like the laundry—darks, lights, and everything else.

As discussed in Step Two, for each minicutting session, I arrange three short stacks at my cutting station. One ministack for each size. Once the cutting session is done, the stacks get placed in the scrap bins by size. But that's not all. As I cut, I also sort, not necessarily by color, but by value. Why? I try to stay mindful of the next step. When I'm cutting, I'm evaluating how I might use what I'm cutting. If it seems I have a growing pile of small scraps and I notice that as I cut, I make a mental note to make the next project heavy in the 2-in. scrap department. It's the same with values. If I've got a building collection of medium-value novelty prints, maybe the next project is something more kid-friendly or novelty-themed.

VALUE

Lots of quilters have difficulty determining value. Dark generally means the scrap piece is darker than 90 percent of the rest of your scraps—dark, dark blues, deep rich purples, blacks with just a bit of print in them. Conversely, light scraps are lighter in value than 90 percent of everything else—white-on-white prints, white with bits of print, pale yellows, pinks, and blues.

If a scrap is not dark and not light, it falls into the "everything else" category or medium value. Brights nearly always fall into the everything else category.

When sewing scrap fabrics next to each other in a scrap quilt, it's important that the value is different. Sometimes it's not enough that the color is different, the value also needs to contrast for the pattern to stand out.

As I place cut scraps into the bins, I have a separate bin for extremely, dark scraps and extremely, light fabrics; these are separate from the everything else or medium-value scraps, which make up the bulk of my scrap collection. The values are determined as I cut.

SORT SCRAPS BY THEME IN THE PRINTS

You may find as you are cutting your stash that there's a recurring theme happening. Let's say every time you reach in to start a new batch to cut, you pull out some holiday themed prints, or '30s, or Civil War reproduction prints, or batiks. If you can see yourself making a scrappy quilt using scraps in these categories, maybe you need a separate bin, in all three sizes for fabric themes. That way, if you decide to work on a scrappy holiday project, for example, you don't have to sort through everything, just the holiday fabric bins to make the project.

SUPPLEMENT YOUR STASH

I love going to quilt shows but when I don't have a plan, too often I end up buying something I don't necessarily need—sound familiar? Wouldn't it be nice to go to these events and be able to purchase a souvenir from the show that you can use? So before I head out to a show or shop hop, I take a look at my scrap bins. What type of fabric seems to be lacking? For example, it seems I am always running out of light-value scraps in all three sizes. Or I've got some fabric scraps set aside to make a '30s-era scrappy quilt, but I want to supplement that theme a bit more so the quilt has enough variety.

Take this mental list with you on your fabric adventure. Select fat quarters that fill in the holes in your scrap stash.

GETTING THERE

Once you generate a healthy stack of neatly cut and sorted scrap fabrics in a variety of values and prints, it's nearly time to start sewing!

CHAPTER 3

The Setup

STEP FOUR: SELECTING A THEME

Before you dig in, it's time to zero in on a theme and/or color scheme for your project. Choose a focus fabric, or let your scrap pile decide how your next quilty project will materialize (pun intended). Your theme will be the common thread that pulls all the elements of the project together.

THEME GAMES

Not sure about a theme? Here are some common examples.

- Botanicals—any print, any color, that has a flower or a leaf

- Animals—prints that include dogs, cats, penguins, turtles, ducks, lions, etc.

- Geometric—plaids, stripes, checks, squares, diamonds, circles, triangles, zig-zags, honeycombs, etc.

- Earthy—natural colors, in muted tones, like dusky green, gold, dirty brown, russet, terra cotta, tan, etc.

- Spots and dots—any and all polka dots

- Novelties—dog bones, umbrellas, bon-bons, shoes, sewing notions, jack-o-lanterns, etc.

Now that your scraps are cut and organized into bins, it's time to start using them. You certainly can plop yourself in front of your sewing machine and "have at it," picking scraps randomly from your bins and sewing them together. Postage stamp quilts—sewing rows and rows of the same-sized scrap squares—will work up in a hurry. Add an accent and focus border from your stash and your scraps can become a quilt in no time. Sometimes the easiest approach is just the ticket!

On the other hand, a scrappy quilt plan presents the opportunity to incorporate visual interest as you tackle design challenges.

Choose a pattern and decide on a scrappy theme or color scheme. Focus and background prints found in your stash or at the quilt shop may drive the project theme, or scraps in your bin may be the source of inspiration. Either way, you're ready to dig in and start playing.

CONTROLLED RANDOMNESS

Think of a jigsaw puzzle. You choose the puzzle you'd like to make and dump the box of pieces onto the card table. You sort and gather, collect and coordinate possible matches. You try and fail, and you try and succeed. Soon the pieces match and the picture starts taking shape, and it feels good. When it all comes together and the picture is complete, you feel satisfied knowing that you've accomplished your goal.

Let's explore another approach to the jigsaw puzzle. This time you choose two puzzles, one a serene nature landscape and one a Picasso cubist painting. You like them both so much that you dump both boxes of pieces onto the card table at the same time. You insist that these will make a great picture, all mixed up, even if the pieces don't fit. As you work, the picture starts getting weird, patterns don't match, and it feels like you're struggling to force the pieces together. You give up, unsatisfied and frustrated.

Now, consider making a scrap quilt, do you want a cohesive, interesting collection of varied pieces or a collection of mismatched elements that don't play well together? I believe that scrap quilts can be interesting, filled with variety, and coordinated without being boring.

Scrap quilts make some quilters nervous. Quilt making can be a study in precision. Scrap quilts are about letting go and experimenting with color, scale, and value. In contrast, ScrapTherapy quilts tend to follow a planned scrappy theme. I'm pretty tightly wound by nature, so pulling scrap fabrics blindly from the bins (or randomly from a brown paper bag with the scraps all mixed up inside) and sewing them together makes me uneasy. Most of the quilts I create start with a theme. I select scrap fabrics that coordinate with that theme, then I let randomness take over after the scraps have been selected.

CHOOSE A THEME OR DIRECTION

When you start thinking about your next scrappy project, selecting the theme for that project usually falls into one of four broad categories.

1. FOLLOW YOUR HEART

See a ScrapTherapy pattern that you love? Make it happen—it's as simple as that. Follow the color scheme and value suggestions and select the scraps, background fabrics, and focus prints suggested. Your quilt will be unique to you because it will have your favorite scraps and fabric pieces, but it will look similar to the photograph in the book.

2. USE WHAT YOU HAVE

Stand back and take a look at your scraps. What kind of fabrics do you have in excess? For example, have you been making lots of baby quilts lately, generating a ton of baby prints in your scrap bins? Consider one of the kid-oriented patterns like **Once Upon a Scrap** or **Lucky Chain**. This time, have that baby quilt ready before the baby shower announcement!

Or maybe you've got a lot of earthy prints and colors that will lend themselves well to **In the North Woods** or **Scrappy Trails**. Consider a soft cozy flannel for backing and you'll be ready for the next summer campfire or chilly lazy Sunday afternoon.

Turn scrap overkill into over-the-top quilt treasures and move those out-of-control scraps out of your scrap bins!

3. USE WHAT YOU WANT

I just love blue and purple! When I buy fabric, I almost always go heavy on blue and purple prints. That means many of my nonscrappy quilts are blue, which in turn means blue scraps are always at my fingertips. What to do? Make blue scrappy quilts, of course! **Star Gazing**, for example, started with lots of blue fabric scraps in dark and light values. These scraps were left over from a large basket sampler quilt made entirely from shades of blue and white fabric I'd used the previous year. The focus border print was selected well after the quilt blocks were underway.

What's you favorite color? If you have a lot of one color or type of fabric print, don't worry about select-

ing the focus print, typically used
for the border, right away. Make
a few blocks within your favorite
theme, then take the blocks to the
stash or the quilt shop to audition
some focus or main-player fabric
selections.

4. LET THE FABRIC DECIDE

When using what you have and
using what you want, the focus
print might be decided after several blocks are constructed based
on what they look like. Another
approach starts with selecting
the focus print or inspiration
fabric first, usually reserved for
the border, then selecting the
scrap fabrics around the colors
predominant in that print.

   Tulip Patches started with a
focus border print and a couple of coordinates. I saw the
fabrics on the bolt and simply couldn't pass them up!
The scraps were selected to coordinate with the focus
print. Does that ever happen to you? You see a focus
print, and it speaks to you. The next thing you know,
it's going home with you. When that happens, you can
build a scrappy quilt around the focus print. Projects like

Tulip Patches and **Lightning Strikes Twice** are perfect
examples of projects that can be driven by the colors in
the main-player and accent fabrics.

SELECTING THEME SCRAPS

Once you decide on a theme, it's easy to select scraps
that fall into that category. Dig into your scrap stacks
and ask yourself, "Does this go with my theme?" If the
answer is "yes," pull it out of the scrap bin and set it
aside to begin sewing. If the answer is "no," put that
scrap piece back in the bin and find another scrap
fabric that's a "yes." Continue drawing scraps from
your bins until you have more than enough in the pre-
determined theme to make the quilt.

   For interest, always throw in a few "almost theme"
fabrics. For example, if you are selecting scraps that
follow an earthy theme, choose some gray-blues or
muted purples, or a few brighter greens and browns.
Don't choose just one off-theme scrap, choose a
handful. One off-theme scrap might stand out, several
off-theme scraps, placed randomly throughout your
project, will blend in and belong. For example, notice
that the **Tulip Patches** quilt (see page 150) has several

KNOWING WHAT YOU LIKE

One of my regular ScrapTherapy students has
a wonderful problem. She has never met a
Halloween fabric she didn't buy. At least, that's
how it seems. She has the most impressive
collection of fabrics with pumpkins, skeletons,
witches, and ghosts I've ever seen. I just love
to watch her scrappy creations come together.
Each one is unique, bright, and playful. And she
has such a good time putting her quilts together
with all of her favorite things in one project.

MOST SCRAPS AREN'T SOLID, DISTINGUISHABLE COLORS

What do you do about multicolor print scraps? By all means, include them! For example, if you are using a focus print for your theme, and one of the colors you've chosen to emphasize is blue, choose scraps that create a wide range of blue: solids, prints that read blue but may have some pink and yellow in them, scraps that have a splash of blue. Also include scraps that fall into near-blue categories like turquoise, teal, and bluish purples.

These two blocks are made entirely from scraps. One works well, the other one, not so much.

pink scrap pieces in the appliqué blocks. Pink isn't in the focus print, and most of the scraps selected for the quilt are either blue or brown. Pink was added, scattered randomly into several blocks to add interest.

Once you've selected your pile of theme-oriented scraps, spread them out on your work table and step back. Squint at the scraps for a minute. If you are near-sighted, look in the general direction of your scrap pile without using your glasses (or contact lenses). Does any one scrap jump out at you? Perhaps it's a scrap that's too bright or too dull, too light or too dark, or it just doesn't go. It's okay to see variety, but if one or two scraps stand out dramatically, they'll stand out in your quilt as well and may draw attention away from the overall impact. Consider replacing the stand-outs, or consider adding more similar scraps—that way the "wild child" won't be all by itself in the quilt!

Most importantly, don't forget to consider value—dark and light contrast. For example, if you're choosing scraps that need to be darker than a light-color background print, pull out the background print and place scraps on top of it. Step back and squint at the fabric clump again. Does each scrap appear to be darker than the background fabric? If not, reconsider it. Scraps don't have to be exactly the same value; variety adds interest. However, if you lose the impact of the block pattern because dark and light values are too close, you're doing lots of sewing for limited effect.

Once you zoom in on your scrap theme, something magical happens. All of a sudden, fabric pieces that don't necessarily go together work collectively within the theme. Breaking the rules is allowed, but selecting a theme should come first.

MAKE A TEST BLOCK

Once a theme is decided and scraps are selected, make a sample block. Place your test block on a design wall and stand back and take a good look at it from more than a few feet away. Does the block work? Do the mediums hold up against the lights and darks or the background fabrics? If they do, carry on and make more blocks. If they don't, the completion of one block is the best time to reconsider scrap selections.

It's so easy to get caught up in the excitement of seeing your first quilt block coming together. Try not to wait until each of the quilt blocks is done to step back and evaluate. Often the original test block can still be included in the quilt, even though fabric selection for the remaining blocks is tweaked a little bit.

Don't have a design wall?

Don't worry! Here are a few alternatives to get a better look at your test block:

• Use magnets to stick the block on the refrigerator.

• Tape the block to a kitchen cabinet with painter's tape.

• Use the dartboard in the basement playroom. Darts make great pins!

• Ask your spouse to stand up and turn around so you can use the back of his or her sweater like a felt-board. For a truly realistic assessment, ask your spouse to put on a sweater that matches your focus fabric!

• For more dynamic input, combine the spouse and the dartboard methods. I have found that this may prompt your spouse to make a proper design wall for you to use on future test blocks! (Of course, I'm joking.)

STEP FIVE: GADGETS AND TOOLS TO SAVE TIME

All the patterns in this book can be made with basic quilting supplies—things you'll find in any quilter's sewing studio: acrylic rulers, marking tools, rotary cutters, thread, and a standard sewing machine. Some patterns may suggest alternatives to more traditional methods, incorporating updated processes and tools to make the construction simpler, faster, or more efficient. With so many options available to you, choose the method, tool, or gadget that works best for you. This is a hobby, after all, and it's supposed to be fun!

TOP 10 REASONS TO USE A TOOL OR GADGET

10. More fun

9. Easier to understand

8. Easier to use

7. Math-free!

6. Faster

5. Safer

4. Impressive to your friends

3. Justification for buying it!

2. Your spouse just bought a new gadget for his/her hobby, and you need to even out the playing field/tie up the score/reset the stats (choose one).

1. The "demo" made you do it!

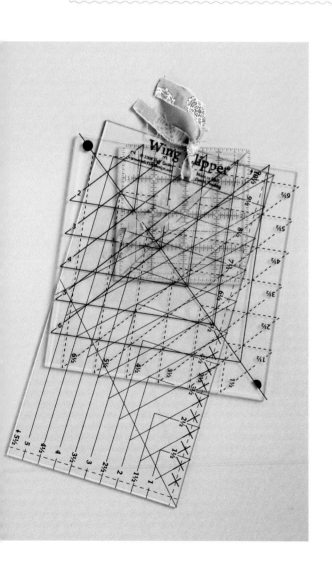

VARIETY IS THE SPICE OF LIFE

Quite a few years ago, I wanted to learn how to knit, so off I went to the yarn store with a clear purpose. The kind woman who sat down with me to demonstrate basic knitting stitches said something I remember vividly to this day. She said, "All of knitting is based on two stitches, knit and purl. Once you learn those stitches, everything else is just a variation of those two."

It's much the same with traditional quilting methods. Quilts start with some basic shapes: squares, triangles, and rectangles. A variety of tools and techniques used to make the traditional shapes keep the quilting craft interesting and ever changing.

In the late '70s, quilting got a big makeover when the first rotary cutter was introduced. No more tedious templates. Fabric pieces needed to make bed-size quilts could be prepared with see-through acrylic rulers, mats, and rotary cutters in a fraction of the time required using more traditional cutting methods. Templates still have their place, as do hand piecing and hand quilting. Old and new methods are equally valid.

GOTTA LOVE GADGETS

I love gadgets and sewing notions. In my mind, buying new tools is simply a required element of the quiltmaking process. If a tool makes a time-honored technique more accurate or simpler, it's a winner! Scrap quilts lend themselves especially well to testing and using the latest sewing notions. Since sewing small fabric scraps can sometimes become tedious, the infusion of sewing notions changes familiar methods, refreshes standard techniques, and improves results.

Some must-have notions for scrap quiltmaking fall into a handful of categories. As you review what you have and what you need from the following suggested items, consider your favorite notions and how those products can enhance your scrap-sewing endeavors.

TRIMMING TOOLS

Trimming tools are rulers with a specific job. Most quilters have a 6-in. or 7-in. square ruler with a bias line. These lined square rulers are the most-used trimming tool in my sewing room!

A tool becomes a trimming tool if it's used to square up a shape after the unit—a half-square triangle, for example—has been sewn and pressed. Some trimming tools have a more specific, single-purpose use like trimming half-square and quarter-square triangle units,

on-point pieced square block elements, or flying geese units (see page 122).

I like to look for trimming tools that come with detailed, easy-to-follow directions. I'm also fond of tools that allow me to cut normal-size fabric pieces—$1/2$-in. and $1/4$-in. dimensions, as opposed to $1/8$-in. or $1/16$-in. sizes—to sew and trim after the units are pressed. Any distortion in the sewing or pressing can be eliminated when the trimming tool is used. The trimming tool designer has done the math, and all you have to do is cut squares or other shapes, sew them, and use the tool to trim. Seam allowances are usually included in the tool's design.

As you contemplate a trimming tool purchase, consider the added value you'll have from using that tool in multiple projects and for trimming block units in a variety of sizes.

FUSIBLES

Printed fusible interfacing and fusible web can add ease and stability to a variety of scrap sewing projects.

TRIANGLE TIPS

With all the tools and gadgets available to make half-square triangles, it might surprise you to learn that my favorite technique is a simple one.

Draw the line on the back of the fabric square, corner-to-corner, sew $1/4$ in. from each side of the line, cut on the drawn line, press, and trim to the correct size, if needed. I like to cut the fabric squares $1/8$ in. bigger than the mathematically correct size needed, then trim the sewn and pressed unit to a perfect square using my square ruler with a bias line. Call me crazy, but I think, even though it can be tedious, this method gets the job done with the most accurate results.

Printed fusible interfacing with a grid format can make sewing small scrap squares a breeze. Place scrap squares on the fusible side aligned with the printed grid. Activate the adhesive using a hot steam iron on the scrap squares, then sew the seam allowances one row at a time. Seams are even, stable, and perfectly matched, and the lightweight interfacing stays right in the quilt. It's perfectly acceptable to skip the interfacing and sew rows and rows of small scraps together to create the border on **Bloomin' Steps**, for example, but the interfacing allows you to evenly distribute similarly colored scraps and stabilize the stitching for more predictable results.

Fusible interfacing is available with a variety of printed grids, patterns, and appliqué shapes—and unprinted as well.

Fusible web is a favorite for machine appliquérs. However, it also makes a quick and easy stabilizer.

Fusible webs usually come with protective paper on one or both sides of the actual adhesive. When applying, be sure to follow the manufacturer's instructions for the specific brand you're using with regard to iron temperature, moisture, press cloth use, etc., for proper fusing. Fusible web is recommended to simplify button hole placement on **Thrown Together Pillow** (see page 66).

FINISHING TECHNIQUES

When you're looking for a special border or finish, such as piping or scallops around a quilt edge, the Piping Hot Binding Tool and the Scallop Radial Rules are examples of tools that help simplify formerly tough-to-master techniques.

EMBELLISHMENTS

A little embellishment can really jazz up a quilt, a tote, or almost any sewing project. A quilt can become a

work of art with a small amount of additional effort. Try a new surface embellishment technique on your next quilted project. Here are some ideas to get you started:

- Fabric paint
- Embroidery (hand or machine)
- Fusible crystals
- Glitter
- Metallic threads
- Couched yarn
- Trims
- Buttons and beads
- Felted wool or wool roving

THE BEST TECHNIQUE OF ALL

Quilting is *your* hobby. The best gadget in the world might be the worst gadget for you. Just because all your friends have it, you don't have to. Quilting creates an opportunity to choose from multiple methods and tools to complete almost any task. I like to try new techniques, notions, and gadgets, but sometimes the tried and true methods are the best.

EXPERIMENT FOR "FREE"

It seems that every time you say, "I've seen it all!" you open a magazine, surf the Web, or visit a quilt shop and the next "gotta have" notion is there for the buying. It solves a problem you never knew you had, and it's so much fun to use, motivating you to make more projects from your scrap fabrics. If you're going to experiment with a new tool or technique, why not experiment while using your scrap stash? It takes a little of the edge off when you know you're not risking that fresh-off-the-bolt yardage.

HOW TO FIND NEW TOYS AND TECHNIQUES

To be the first in your sewing circle to try the latest and greatest sewing notion, stay in the know.

- Become a frequent visitor to your favorite quilt shop. Keep an eye on the notions wall and displays near the cash register; often the newest gadgets get prime space. If you see something that interests you, ask the shop staff to explain how the notion works or give you a quick demo. Never hesitate to ask shop staff what's new.

- Keep up with blogs and other online resources. Sewing notion distributors offer tips and product introductions on their website main pages, blogs, and social networking pages. Become a regular fan or follower and see what's new and how to use the latest tools.

- Read quilt magazines that feature one- or two-page spreads highlighting the newest notions on the market.

- Become an active member in your local sewing and quilt guilds. Most all have a "share and tell" session where you can learn about new tools and techniques from other members or guest speakers.

Tulip Patches
is a heartwarming Quilt
designed and stitched by
Joan Ford
Syracuse NY
Completed May 2010

CHAPTER 4
The Quilt

STEP SIX: PIECING AND SEWING

Here we go! You've had it with the disorganized mess and decided to do something about it. You've been cutting and sorting until it feels as if the only fabric left to cut is the sofa upholstery. You've planned your pattern and picked out the scraps for your next creation. Now it's time to get down to the business of sewing it all together.

LESSONS LEARNED

The first quilt I ever made was a traditional rail fence quilt. There were two block color variations, each made from six different strips. The blocks were $6\frac{1}{2}$ in. unfinished, so the strips were cut $1\frac{1}{2}$ in. wide. Just a few easy steps: piece six fabric strips together, press the seams in one direction, cut into $6\frac{1}{2}$-in. chunks. As I recall, not one of my blocks was $6\frac{1}{2}$ in. square.

I learned some important lessons from that first quilt. Do these lessons sound familiar to you?

- When the pattern calls for a $\frac{1}{4}$-in. seam allowance, it really needs to be $\frac{1}{4}$ in., not $\frac{3}{8}$ in., not $\frac{1}{8}$ in.

- Pressing quilt pieces isn't like ironing a pillow case. When pressed carelessly, long straight skinny pieces of fabric become curved, sometimes even S-shaped.

- Pressed seams can be sneaky! The fabric will play tricks on you. If you don't pay attention, the fabric can get pressed a bit ahead of the seam.

- Being off a little bit in each seam adds up over five seams in one simple block.

- Sewing, pressing, and cutting all eighty blocks needed for the quilt, then measuring them is a bad idea. Better to make a few blocks and then measure to make sure everything's on the right track.

- "Fudge" isn't just a creamy, sweet confection.

As you sew your scraps together, I offer a few friendly reminders and tips to help you make assembling your ScrapTherapy projects fun and uneventful!

SCANT VS. TRUE $\frac{1}{4}$-IN. SEAM

Assuming you've gotten a solid start with accurately cut pieces, most quilts are sewn together using a scant $\frac{1}{4}$-in. seam allowance. A scant $\frac{1}{4}$-in. seam allowance is just one or two thread-widths shy of a true $\frac{1}{4}$-in. seam allowance. As you sew, be sure to place the fabrics right sides together with raw edges aligned. Piecing accuracy starts by simply aligning your fabrics properly. The machine needle should enter the aligned fabric pieces just a little bit less than $\frac{1}{4}$-in. away from the aligned raw edges for a scant $\frac{1}{4}$-in. seam allowance.

A scant $\frac{1}{4}$-in. seam accommodates the thickness of the fabric as the seam is pressed to one side. To be completely confident of your seam accuracy, try a test seam using scraps from your bin. Align and sew two 2-in. scrap squares. Press the seam to one side. For the best results, make the extra effort to press the seam with an iron instead of finger-pressing. Place the pressed scrap two-patch on your ruler. It should be exactly 2 in. x $3\frac{1}{2}$ in. If the test two-patch is larger than $3\frac{1}{2}$ in., your seam allowance is too small. Move the needle farther

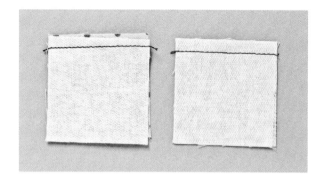

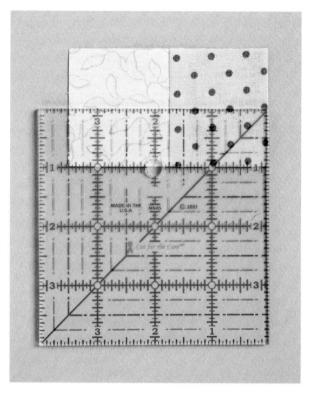

away from the edge of the fabric to make a larger seam allowance. If the test two-patch is less than $3\frac{1}{2}$ in. wide, then your seam allowance is too big. Move the needle closer to the edge of the fabric to make a narrower seam allowance. Continue making test two-patches until you have the most accurate results—or until you run out of 2-in. scrap squares!

If your sewing machine has an adjustable needle position, simply move the needle position to the right (for a smaller seam) or to the left (for a larger seam) to adjust the stitching location. If you can't change the needle position, adjust the fabric positioning under your presser foot to get an accurate seam.

Use the presser foot edge, sticky-notes, repositionable tape, or a seam guide to create a $\frac{1}{4}$-in. benchmark. As you sew, place your fabric against this guide, so your pieces feed into the sewing machine accurately.

Keep a small ruler handy at your sewing table for frequent test measurements as you sew. If you have a sewing table that has a built-in ruler, use it! A quick check early in the sewing process can eliminate frustrations later.

For accuracy, many block elements are sewn larger than needed then trimmed after sewing and pressing. For example, a bias ruler can be a huge help in trimming blocks with half-square triangles to their proper size before sewing into the block. Since I already have 5-in. scraps in my bin, rather than trim each square to $4\frac{7}{8}$ in. to make a finished 4-in. half-square triangle unit, I can sew two 5-in. squares together diagonally, then trim to size. The resulting unit is perfectly shaped, and the triangular dog-ears are trimmed off in the process.

PRESSING BASICS

Pressing seams helps the next seams to have crisp intersections. Follow these basic steps:

1. Place your sewn block on the ironing board just as it came off the sewing machine (right sides together).

2. Position the hot iron directly on the seam and count to three.

3. Lift the iron and gently open one side of the fabric and finger-press the top fabric so that it lays across the seam.

4. If you're pressing the seam toward the dark fabric, the light fabric will remain flat on the ironing board and the dark fabric will be folded over the seam directly at the sewing line.

5. Using only the iron tip, move it across the fold of the fabric. Start in the center and press outward, first one direction, then the other.

6. Lay the iron flat and make one light pass over the seam using the side of the iron. Don't use a back and forth motion, as that can stretch and reshape your piece.

5

7. If you chain-pieced, cut apart your pieces and press each piece individually. Use this opportunity to scramble up your scrappy block units so similar scraps don't end up next to each other. To mix things up, make four or five stacks of pressed units. Add to each stack, one unit at a time, randomly as you press.

8. Get up and move! Place the ironing surface in another part of the room or house, so you have to move to use the iron. It's tempting to keep the iron a twist of the chair away, but it's also nice to stretch your legs between sewing sets.

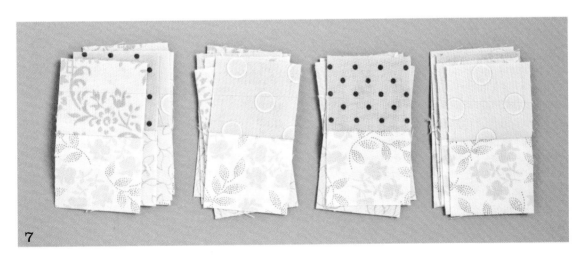

7

UN-PRESSING BASICS

Sometimes a pattern, like **Something Fishy** (see page 87), will suggest that you re-press a seam once the quilt layout is determined. Or, you might discover a pressing error during construction.

1. Place the pressed unit on your ironing board, so the seam lies flat, as if it just came off the sewing machine.

2. Place the hot iron on the seam to flatten the initial pressing fold and to reset the stitches.

3. Turn the unit and refold the seam in the opposite direction from the original pressing.

4. Finger-press the seam in the new direction, then use the tip of the hot iron to fold the new seam into position.

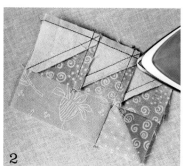

CHAIN PIECING AND PRODUCTION SEWING
Chain piecing is sewing two pieces of fabric together, taking two or three stitches off the edge, then sewing the next set of fabric pieces together. Cut the stitches in between, and press the seams as needed.

Since ScrapTherapy projects work with smaller fabric pieces, not strips, chain piecing is a logical sewing strategy. I suggest sewing a test block first, so any piecing issues or light-dark value questions are worked out. Once you're satisfied with the test block, sew multiple blocks using the chain-piecing technique. This works especially nicely when you're sewing several blocks using similar colors or values of scraps, as for **Star Gazing** or **Lightning Strikes Twice** (see pages 158 and 100). The block units aren't necessarily tied to a single block.

Sometimes, a one-block-at-a-time production line strategy is better, for example in **Something Fishy** (see page 87). For this quilt project, each fish block has a body (3½-in. scrap) and five matching fin half-square triangles. Since it's important that the fins all match in a single fish block, start by sewing two fins together. Sew the two-fin unit to the body; then sew the three fins together; and finally, sew the three-fin unit to the body. Instead of working one fish block from start to finish, jumping up to press at every step, have several blocks started at various stages. For example, sew two fins to start one block, then sew a two-fin unit to a body for a second block, then sew three fins together for a third block, then sew a three-fin unit.

Every time you break to press, you're starting and finishing a block and have some parts in progress. For production line sewing, create little ministacks of each block on your work table to stay organized and try not to get too far ahead with multiple blocks at each stage.

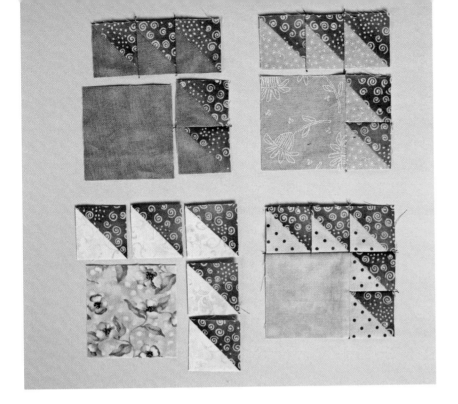

THE "OTHER" PROJECT

"Never say 'never,'" right? When I'm piecing, I can confidently say that I never work on only one project at a time. I keep a little card table next to my sewing machine cabinet reserved for the "other" project.

On that little table near the sewing machine, I keep another, nonurgent project, stacked neatly, ready to sew. The other project might be a smaller project, like a table runner or place mat set or a baby quilt for a newborn who isn't due for a while. Or, it could be a "just for me" project that I'm in no hurry to complete but that needs to keep moving along. Possibly, it's this month's contribution to a year-long block-of-the-month project. Maybe it's a ScrapTherapy project that has lots and lots of piecing.

The other project is all the pieces, cut, stacked neatly, and laid out, ready to sew. The pattern is tucked under the pieces or on a nearby shelf for ready reference. Whenever I work on the piecing for my main project of choice, the other project pieces get sewn together at the end of a chain-piecing string, one at a time. Working on the other project simultaneously does several things:

- breaks up an otherwise monotonous, easy project
- moves a project along that might end up unfinished because it's not on the critical project list
- eliminates long thread ends at the start of a new chain-piecing stretch

Make space for another project near your sewing table and choose a project that doesn't need to advance quickly so it can move along one step at a time, over time. Use this technique as a motivation to finish unfinished projects and keep them going.

NOTE: Make sure the main, active project you're working on and the other project are different so you don't get them mixed up and accidentally sew the dog-lover fabric to the kitty quilt!

TRUING UP FINISHED BLOCKS

You've made your sample block, measured it, and it's the wrong size. Now what? It bears repeating that it's a really good idea to start any quilt, not just a Scrap-Therapy quilt project, with a test block.

The problem almost always comes down to one of three issues: cutting, seam allowance, or pressing. I opened this section of the book with the somewhat bittersweet story of my first quilt project. When I took a closer look at why my blocks didn't measure up, it came down to all three of these problems. Here's how to solve a problem block.

First, from the front of the block, place a small ruler over some of the block elements. If a block center was 3$\frac{1}{2}$ in. (unfinished), what size is it now? In other words, what's the finished size of the block center unit, 3 in. or something else? Is it square or rectangular? Turn the block over. From the back, are there any obvious out-of-shape pieces? Gently unpress some of the seams with your fingers. Measure the size of the cut pieces. Were the fabric pieces cut the correct size?

Next, if a block doesn't measure up, take a close look at the seams from the back. Measure the seams with an acrylic ruler. Get in there and take a close look; one seam that's off $\frac{1}{16}$ in. shouldn't amount to much, but four seams each off by $\frac{1}{16}$ in. adds up to $\frac{1}{4}$ in. Are the seams too wide or too narrow? Review your seam allowance sample and sew another test two-patch from two 2-in. scrap squares. Try making the block again, one element at a time, checking the seam allowance and testing each unit size at each step.

Finally, if the seams appear to be accurate, check the pressing. Turn the block back to the front. Take a close look at the seams. Place your fingernail right up against the seam. Does the tip of your nail disappear under an extra little flap in the seam? Are the seams stretched so piecing threads are showing?

Most likely, by carefully examining each of the three key elements you'll be ready to stitch a second block with renewed interest in the problem area. When my students ask if they should true up their block by trimming the block to the proper size, I suggest that they take a closer look at the block first to determine the problem, so the next blocks will be the correct size without trimming!

TRIMMING BLOCK PARTS

As much as I dislike trimming a completed block to size it down, I feel just the opposite about trimming block elements—like half-square triangles, quarter-square triangles, or flying geese units—after they are sewn as units, but before they're sewn into the block. Let's face it. We piece, we press, and repeat, repetitively. With a big stack of scrap units to press, perfect pressing techniques aren't always the priority.

Half-square triangle units, for example, get sloppy. Fabrics get stretched a tiny bit here and there. Seams aren't always perfect. Try as I might to stay on track, I'm sometimes guilty of sloppy parts. So before I piece my slightly imperfect units into my blocks, I make them perfect with a little trim. Just enough to get things back on track for the home stretch of the block assembly.

When trimming block elements like half-square triangles, be sure to trim all four sides. Place the unit on your cutting mat, line up seams with the chosen trimming tool or ruler, and cut one or two sides, usually along the side and across the top. Then turn the partially trimmed unit upside down, line up the chosen trimming tool or ruler with the appropriate seams, and trim the remaining two sides. Trim carefully when trimming across the top of the ruler.

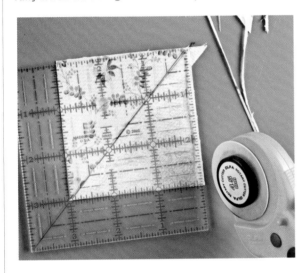

As you work on the quilt projects, you'll notice a variety of suggested notions designed to make the unit trimming process easy. Tools that have a specific trimming job make the quilter's task easier, more accurate, and more fun!

ADDING BORDERS

Many quilts aren't complete until a border is added. For scrappy quilts, it's fun to build in pieced borders to use up more scraps like **Bloomin' Steps** (see page 127), **Runaway Thread** (see page 81), **Wild Salmon Run** (see page 183), or **Feedsack Peaks** (see page 60). However, if you're adding accent and focus borders in strips, it's a good idea to measure the quilt first before cutting the borders to size...or is it?

Some quilt instructions suggest that you measure the quilt top in three places then average the numbers and cut your border to size—a perfectly valid theory. I prefer to skip the math and the rulers and measure the border for larger quilts using the quilt itself as the measuring device. Here's how:

- If you're adding side borders first, take the quilt and fold it in half, so top and bottom edges are aligned.

- Lay the folded quilt flat on a large work surface.

- Find a seam somewhere in the center of the quilt. The seam is a vertical seam on the quilt and will be a line-up guide for the border measurement.

- Fold in half the pieced side border, which has been roughly cut a little larger than the suggested border measurement from the pattern.

- Lay the folded border on the folded quilt, with folds aligned and with the border edge aligned with a center vertical seam on the quilt.

- Hold the fold in place on top of the quilt with one hand, and gently smooth the border across the quilt with the other hand, so there's no extra slack in the border fabric. Be careful not to stretch the border.

- Mark and cut the border even with the raw edge of the quilt.

- Repeat with the second border.

- Unfold a side border strip and place it right side up on a larger workspace or counter.

- Open the quilt and place the quilt top right side down on your workspace over the border. Pin one trimmed border strip to the quilt. Pin each end, then pin the center and ease the fabric in between until the entire border is pinned in place. Use lots of pins (about one pin at least every 2 in.) and remove pins as needed to reposition and ease out any lumpy or stretchy spots.

- Move the pinned quilt to the sewing machine and sew a ¼-in. seam allowance to attach the border. Press the border seam per the pattern recommendation.

- Repeat for the remaining side border and top and bottom borders.

FIXING MISTAKES

TA-DA! Finally! It's done. You've been up late for the last three nights with the end in sight. Your scraps have been obliterated, or at least one or two stacks have been purged from the bins, and they are now part of your newest quilt creation.

You stand back. And there it is—a mistake! A block is sewn upside down, and it's ever so obvious. Disappointed, you put the project away for a few hours and turn to another distraction. After a while, you come back to it, and there it is...again. This time, it's all you see and it's bugging you.

One perfectly fine solution to a mistake is to leave it alone. It's there and it's part of the quilt.

Another solution is to fix the problem. As long as the quilt hasn't been sandwiched and quilted, a misplaced pieced block or block part can be corrected fairly easily.

LET IT BE

A few years ago, I attended a quilt retreat with a large group of women. During one of the "show and tell" sessions, Joanne got up and unfolded a beautiful quilt she'd recently completed. The ladies in the room praised it. It was lovely! Joanne continued to tell the group that there was a mistake in the quilt. She pointed out the mistake so everyone could see it—before that, no one would have noticed it. The block was sewn into the quilt incorrectly. Before she could finish her story, many in the room interrupted to encourage her that the mistake wasn't worth mentioning.

But Joanne continued her story. The quilt, she said, was made over the course of several months, and during the time that she worked on the quilt, her mother passed away. Joanne decided to leave the mistake in the quilt. The mistake was part of the quilt and could very well have been fixed, but the misplaced block needed to stay, as is, to record and reflect the loss and distress that Joanne's creative soul had experienced. It's true that a quilt is a living record of our lives, even if the record reflects a period when we were not at our best. Sometimes you have to let the quilt tell the story.

To fix a piecing mistake in a completed quilt top:

1. Locate and mark the mistake.

2. Turn the quilt wrong side up. With a seam ripper, pull out all four seams connecting the misplaced block or block element, plus at least one or two inches of the seams on adjoining sides, following the original row and block-piecing configuration. This will create a square- or rectangular-shaped hole in the quilt, with adjoining seams unsewn.

3. Adjust the misplaced block to the proper direction—and right sides together—and pin one side of the corrected block into place. Sew a 1/4-in. seam allowance. Pull the extra quilt material out of the way; it will be awkward but workable.

4. Sew the opposite seam in place in a similar manner, using pins and matching or nesting seam intersections as needed.

5. Sew the remaining two perpendicular seams, pinning and nesting seam intersections as necessary.

6. Press the repaired seams, first from the back, then from the front of the quilt top.

MITERED BORDERS

Mitering is a slightly more advanced technique, but the effect can be dramatic. Like everything else, if you break it down into a few basic steps, mitering a border is easy. You might need slightly more yardage than what you would use on a traditional border pieced one side at a time.

When mitering borders, the corner seams form a 45-degree angle. Multiple borders may be sewn together first, then added to the quilt as a single border unit. For multiple borders, like **Scrappy Trails** or **Tulip Patches**, first sew the border fabrics together in sequence, inner to middle to outer. For top and bottom borders, press seams toward the center; for side borders, press seams away from the center so the seam intersections will nest at the mitered seam.

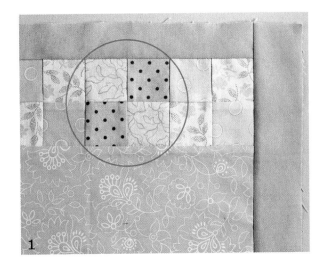

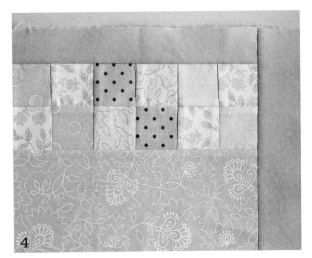

STEPS TO A MITERED BORDER

1. Roughly measure the quilt top width and length.

2. If the pattern doesn't already provide measurements for mitered border lengths, calculate the length of the top and bottom borders: Add the quilt width, plus two times the width of the border, plus 2 in. to 3 in. (for overlap). For example, if the quilt top is 50 in. from side to side and the border is 4 in. wide, the top and bottom borders should each be no less than 61 in. long (50 + 4 + 4 + 3 = 61 in.).

3. Using the same approach as in step two, calculate the length of the side borders. Add two times the width of the border, plus 2 in. to 3 in. to the top-to-bottom quilt measurement. For example, if the quilt top is 65 in. long and the border is 4 in. wide, the side borders should be no less than 76 in. (65 + 4 + 4 + 3 = 76 in.).

4. Measure the border length more precisely as described on page 37. Instead of trimming borders even with the edge, place a pin in the border 1/4 in. from the edge of the quilt.

5. Center and sew the side borders and top and bottom borders to the quilt, starting and stopping 1/4 in. from each edge of the quilt top at the pins. Lock the stitch at the start and stop points. Excess border material will hang loosely at each end. Carefully pull the excess border material out of the way as adjacent borders are added. Do not press.

6. Select one of the corners to miter.

NOTE: Sew and trim each corner one at a time, then move on to the next corner.

7. At the selected corner, fold the quilt top in half diagonally, right sides together. Match the outside edge of the borders in a straight line. Finger-press the seam between the border and quilt top toward the quilt center and lay the corner of the quilt flat on a work surface.

8. Place a straight ruler that has a 45-degree angle on top of the folded quilt. Place the 45-degree line even with the border outside edges and the straight edge even with the diagonal fold on the quilt top.

9. Draw a 45-degree line on the border with a pencil or fabric-marking tool from the end of the seam to the border edge.

10. Secure the borders with pins along the drawn line, matching seam intersections between multiple borders, if applicable. Carefully transfer the quilt to the sewing table and sew directly on the line, starting with a lock stitch at the border seam intersection and sewing outward toward the quilt edge.

11. Trim the seam allowance to 1/4 in. outside the mitered seam.

12. Repeat steps 6 through 11 for the remaining three corners.

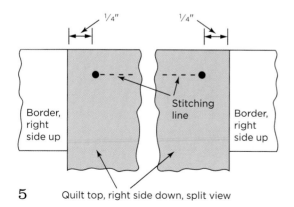

5   Quilt top, right side down, split view

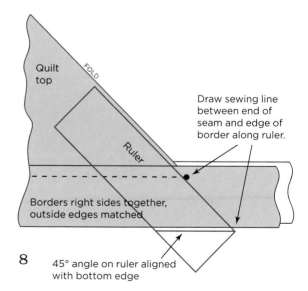

8   45° angle on ruler aligned with bottom edge

13. When all miters are sewn, press the quilt top from the back, pressing the mitered corner seams open and the quilt/border seam toward the border. Press the entire quilt, including the borders, from the front.

"WHY DO I HAVE TO DO ALL THIS PIECING?"

Who isn't busy these days? Patterns that incorporate big pieces of fabric sewn together with a few seams are very popular. Adorable printed panels need only a border or two, then a backing. Projects that go together in a few hours! Terrific!

However, you probably opened this book because you have small scraps of fabric that you're aching to use and cannot bear to throw away. Some of the pieces are small, no question about it. If you want to use small scraps, there's a lot of sewing involved. Sewing those small pieces can be fun, interesting, and rewarding. Stick with it! The rewards are great!

MAKE IT FUN!

With all this talk of planning and organizing, darks and lights, piecing and pressing, stacking and labeling, it almost feels like this ScrapTherapy stuff is choking all the fun out of scrap quilt making! I say, just the opposite! With every single ScrapTherapy project you have an opportunity to create a project filled with memories. As you select fabrics, you'll find that each scrap fabric piece you select will happily challenge you to remember when it was used before. The organizing tips in the patterns will help divert potential problems. You get to use new fabrics too! The gadget suggestions can simplify a tedious or challenging traditional technique. Choosing and sewing fabrics in dark, medium, and light values can present creative problem-solving potential. Each block is like a puzzle and you hold all the pieces. A quilt created from a group of preselected fabrics can be fun to make and allows you to explore and uncover the possibilities right in your own stash.

As with any new habit, the first time through it seems strange. Then you realize that each of the steps makes sense. The cutting and sorting become part of a regular routine instead of a planned commitment. The projects are fun and varied. One quilt leads to another, and to another...and to another.

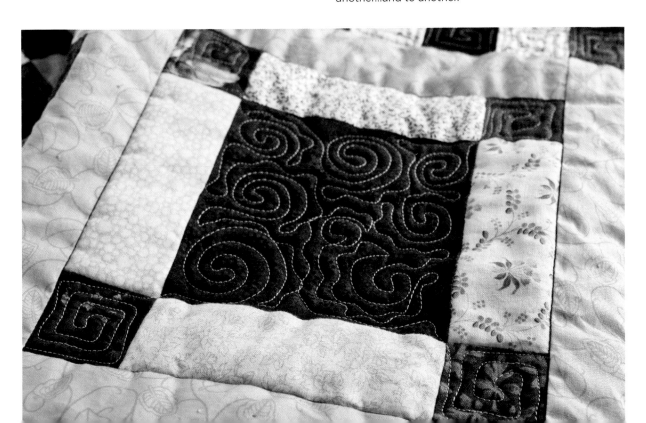

STEP SEVEN: FINISHING THE PROJECT

Time to finish. A quilt top is nice; a finished quilt is even nicer. You've made the effort to piece together a work of scrappy art. The finish line is straight ahead... just sandwich, quilt, label, and take a photograph. You're done! When I finish a quilt, I think that so much of the quilt's personality comes out in the textures, bumps, and lines of the quilting. I don't want to miss one moment of the fun. I enjoy making a quilt, start to finish, from my own creativity and craftsmanship.

Some quilters enjoy the piecing, but not the quilting. Some prefer hand quilting or tying to hold the layers together. Choose your preference and get the job done!

BACKING

Whether you quilt your project yourself or hire someone else to do it, all quilts need backing. As you work with it, the backing should be roughly 4 in. to 6 in. wider than the quilt top in each direction.

Most of the quilts in this book require that you piece the backing with at least two sections, assuming you have standard 42-in. usable fabric width. You can avoid the math and the seams by using extra-wide backing fabrics, between 108 in. and 110 in. wide.

Backing yardage calculations are provided for each quilt. If the backing needs to be seamed, cut the yardage length in half (four yards becomes two two-yard pieces), and trim the selvage off one side of each backing fabric piece. Sew a ¼-in. seam along the cut lengthwise edge and press the seam open. For better wear, avoid having a seam directly in the center of the quilt back. To avoid a center seam on the backing, piece the backing in three sections: one half becomes the center, the other half is cut in half lengthwise. Sew each narrow backing piece to the full-width fabric piece with the selvages removed. **1**

> Long-arm quilters may require additional backing dimensions. If you're sending your quilt to a long-arm quilter, check for specific backing requirements.

Another option to avoid a center seam is to offset one seam so it isn't in the center. If the quilt backing

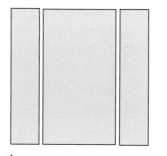

1   2

is between 40 in. and 80 in. wide, leave one backing segment full width and trim the second section to the proper width. The seam will end up offset and you only have to sew one seam! **2**

Challenge yourself to use stash fabrics for your backing. Piece two or three (or more) different coordinating stash fabrics to use up fabric on hand. Keep it simple, though, as you don't want the backing to draw attention away from all the fun and scrappy action on the front.

LAYERING AND BASTING

NOTE: The following steps assume that the quilt will be machine quilted on a standard home machine. The layering and basting process is different for hand quilting and long-arm or short-arm quilting on a frame.

Layering and pin-basting may seem tedious, but they are critical steps in the quilting process. With your work of art so close to being finished, it's easy to short-change these important steps—try to avoid that temptation.

SANDWICHING

Once the backing is seamed and pressed, firmly secure the flat backing right side down to a large work surface like a concrete or tile floor or a very large sturdy table (avoid carpet). Use residue-free adhesive tape, such as painter's tape, to secure the backing to the work surface. Tape liberally, so almost every inch of the backing fabric edge is secured. Begin with one side edge, then tape the opposite edge, gently tugging out any slack in the fabric. Move to the third edge and secure it with tape and then the final edge. If needed, adjust the tape to remove any ripples. **3**

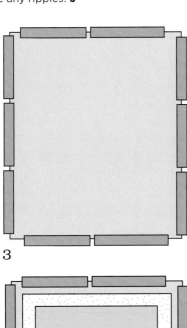

3

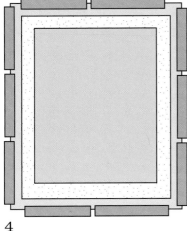

4

Center the batting on the backing and smooth it with your hands from the center out until it's completely flat. Avoid the temptation to trim the batting at this stage.

Place the quilt top, right side up, on top of the batting. Starting in the center and working outward, smooth out any wrinkles, puckers, and folds. Rough-cut the extra batting layer 1 in. to 2 in. beyond the quilt top edges. **4**

PIN-BASTING

Beginning at one corner of the quilt center, place curved safety pins through all three layers of the quilt.

> Since I have a smooth concrete floor in an unfinished basement, I tape the backing directly to the floor, then I sit right in the center of the quilt. I make a game of the basting process, placing pins in straight or diagonal lines, and reversing directions periodically.
>
> Pin-basting allows me peaceful time with the project so I can consider how I might quilt it. Plus, once I get to the sewing machine, pin-basting leaves a record of where I have quilted and where I still need to quilt, as I take the pins out as I've quilted each section. No pins = quilted; pins = still needs to be quilted.

Place a pin every two or three inches. Once the quilt center is pinned, pin the borders. When the entire top is pin-basted, remove the painter's tape from all four sides of the quilt backing, and if there is enough extra backing material, fold the backing edge over the raw edges of the quilt to protect them from fraying during the quilting process. Pin the fold to the edge of the quilt through all layers with another series of curved safety pins. Don't be surprised if you use several hundred pins to baste a twin-size quilt. Fortunately, the pins can be stored and reused over and over again.

SPRAY-BASTING

Another sandwiching option is to spray-baste the layers together using a quilt-basting spray. When you use spray adhesive, stay in a well-ventilated area and be mindful of the overspray on nearby surfaces.

To use basting spray, follow the same sequence detailed above—each layer is sprayed and layered so the batting is firmly held in position between the quilt top and the backing.

THREAD-BASTING

This option is generally reserved for quilts that will be hand quilted so you're not machine quilting over basting threads, making them difficult to remove. It's important to baste starting from the very center of the quilt and working toward the edges in a fairly defined sequence to keep the layers flat.

"QUILT AS DESIRED"

For some quilters, these are the three most dreaded words in pattern instructions. Some want to run and hide; I say, "Bring it on!" If you have a walking foot or an integrated dual-feed foot, you can easily machine quilt your own project on a standard sewing machine. With a little practice and a darning foot, you can add some free-motion quilting. You can also walk away from the sewing machine and do some hand quilting if you want to. The good news is you have all these scraps that you can use to make a practice quilt—or two—or three!

QUILTING ON A STANDARD SEWING MACHINE

Once the quilt is basted, take a step back and decide on a quilting plan. I like to start with some in-the-ditch quilting around borders or blocks. Then spread the quilt out again and take another look before filling in with free-motion quilting. Look for secondary patterns within the play between light and dark. Decide what areas will be quilted lightly so they remain puffy and what areas will be more densely stitched to flatten them.

Consider thread color. Some quilters like to use variegated thread, others like to create contrast. I prefer quilting with a solid-color cotton thread that blends with the main color scheme of the quilt. Truth be known, my most commonly used thread color for quilting is "natural."

Position the sewing machine two to three feet from the left side of your sewing table, so some of the quilt's bulk and weight is supported on the table. Target a block or section of the quilt and remove a handful of safety pins to

free up an area about 8 in. to 12 in. square. Stuff the quilt into the machine with the unpinned area under the foot. Use your fingers to form a pair of parentheses on either side of the needle and gently press outward with the palm of your hand. Gloves with rubber fingertips or palms help maintain control on the quilt as you gently guide the quilt to create the quilting pattern.

You may jump from one block to the next, removing the pins as you go. Unlike with hand quilting, as long as you were meticulous with layering the quilt sandwich and ultrazealous with pin-basting, you don't have to quilt from the center outward, as is commonly suggested. I often move from one spot to another.

When I quilt, I like to create texture. Less quilting creates puffy spots, more dense quilting compresses an area. The quilting can add a whole new dimension to your project.

YOU WIN!

Here's my rule of thumb for machine quilting: You and the quilt are gonna duke it out. And YOU are gonna win! Be bold! It's a pile of cotton and fluff, after all, and it squishes!

It's hard to imagine being able to stuff an entire quilt under the sewing machine arm, and you don't have to. You only have to stuff half of the quilt in there, and only while you're quilting the exact center of the quilt. Quilt one side of the project, then turn the quilt and work on the other side. As you quilt, you remove pins and the quilt gets lighter in weight and easier to maneuver.

I've tried rolling up the quilt and throwing it over my shoulder to support it—that just didn't work for me. I prefer to loosely fold the quilt, almost like an accordion fold, and gently ease the quilt into place for quilting. I find this "squishing and repositioning" process allows me to move around more freely.

TIPS FOR MACHINE QUILTING

Machine quilting can be fast and fun, but sometimes intimidating. Machine quilting classes at your local quilt shop can help you hone your skills. Excellent instructional DVDs and online videos are also available. However, the best way to improve your machine quilting skills is experience. Roll up your sleeves and dive in!

GENERAL QUILTING TIPS

- Refer to the batting package for the recommended distance between quilting lines.

- Change to a darning foot and drop or cover your feed dogs. Consult your machine instruction book for details on inactivating the feed dogs.

- Quilting gloves with rubber fingertips and/or palms are helpful to hold and move the quilt as you stitch.

STRAIGHT-LINE QUILTING USING A WALKING FOOT

- Use straight lines to define the spaces and set the stage for free-motion fill stitching.

- Find end-to-end and diagonal paths for quilting lines.

- Look beyond the blocks and create secondary patterns not necessarily obvious from the piecing alone.

- Your entire quilt may be quilted using the walking foot and straight-line quilting.

FREE-MOTION QUILTING

If you're a novice at free-motion quilting, start with a medium-size meandering line. Practice on a small "sandwich" and strive for smooth lines and gentle transitions from curve to curve. Imagine you're drawing back country roads or Mickey Mouse hands as you move the fabric.

As your meandering improves, try other patterns or just doodle. Swirlies, bishop's fan, leaves, and feathers are some of my favorite filler patterns.

Some quilters wonder why they struggle with free-motion quilting. Here's my theory—often the advice to the aspiring quilter is to draw the desired design on a piece of paper, then you'll feel more comfortable when you quilt it on the sewing machine. I don't agree with this. Think about it—when you draw, the paper stays in one place and you move the pencil around with your hand. When you "draw" the free-motion stitches with the sewing machine, the "pencil" is the needle and it stays in one place, moving up and down making stitches. The quilt moves underneath the needle. No wonder it feels so awkward! In my mind, the best way to learn free-motion quilting is to practice—jump in and do it. Let go. Relax. Remember to breathe!

HAND QUILTING

Hand quilting is traditional, beautiful, relaxing, and perfectly suited for scrappy quilts. Hand quilting can be done with or without hoops and frames. Seek out a local hand-quilting expert and take some classes to hone this time-tested skill.

TIED QUILTS

Tied quilts offer another classic effect perfectly suited to scrappy projects. To tie a quilt, use yarn or heavy thread (like pearl cotton) to make the ties. The finished knots can be on the right or wrong side of the quilt, depending on your preference.

Thread a needle with the thread and insert it straight into the quilt from the side where you want the finished knots. Leave about a 2-in.-long tail. Take a small stitch and bring the thread back up through all the layers. Tie off in a square knot.

Knots should be no more than 3 in. to 4 in. apart across the quilt surface. After the tying is complete, clip all thread tails evenly, about $3/4$ in. long.

LONG-ARM AND SHORT-ARM QUILTING

Some people like to sit and quilt, others like to stand and quilt. Long-arm and short-arm quilting is a completely different process from working on a standard machine, and it requires an investment in equipment.

Long-arm machines are very large and offer about 18 in. of throat space; they work with an attached frame, which can take up an entire room. A long-arm machine incorporates a variety of features to create elaborate continuous free-motion quilting lines; machines can be fully automated or hand guided.

The quilt is rolled onto the rollers attached to the frame. The project is quilted in horizontal segments, and once a segment is complete the quilt is rolled or advanced to the next segment for quilting.

Similarly, short-arm machines are set on a frame and provide a shorter horizontal space on the quilt for quilting, usually 12 in. to 16 in. at a time. A short-arm machine is more likely to be owned by the home user, and a long-arm machine by a quilter for business use.

Another terrific option to finish your quilt is to contract with a professional long-arm quilter. Choose between

MITERING MAGIC

Attach the binding to one side of the quilt with a ¼-in. seam, stopping the stitching ¼ in. before the corner.

Pivot the quilt under the presser foot 45 degrees and sew off the edge; cut the threads. **1**

Place the quilt on a work table, with the sewn binding to the left and the unbound side of the quilt on top.

Fold the unsewn binding to the left at a 45-degree angle so the raw edge of the binding makes a straight line with the upper raw edge of the quilt. **2**

Fold the binding a second time so that the folded edge of the binding is aligned with the left edge of the quilt and the raw edge of the binding is aligned with the top edge of the quilt. Pin to secure the binding in place along the upper edge of the quilt. **3**

Sew a ¼-in. seam to stitch the binding to the quilt. Repeat the same mitering process at each corner.

NOTE: This technique also works to secure the binding to a quilt with an angle other than 90 degrees. Once the binding is secured to the corner, fold the binding away from the quilt to create a straight line along the raw edges of the binding and quilt.

1

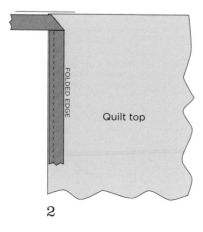

2

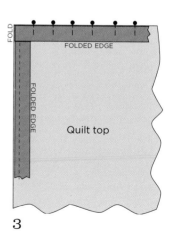

3

pantograph (repetitive quilting designs) or custom quilting. Prices will vary depending on your choices. Try to find a long-arm quilter who is reasonably priced, is located nearby, and has a relatively short lead time. Ask to see samples of their work. Your local quilt shop or guild may be able to refer you to a long-arm quilter in your area. Be sure to talk with them about the process before you layer and baste the quilt, as most long-arm quilters layer the quilt themselves. Some quilters can also supply the batting, but you'll need to bring the backing.

BINDING

When all the quilting is done, it's time to encase the raw edges of the quilt with binding.

Cut the recommended number of 2¼-in.-wide binding strips, either on the crossgrain or bias, depending on the desired look. Join the strips end-to-end using a diagonal seam. Fold the binding in half lengthwise, wrong sides together.

Prepare the quilt for binding by trimming the batting and backing even with the quilt top edges. Beginning along one straight side (never at the corner), sew the binding to the quilt with raw edges aligned. Miter the binding at each of the corners. Fold the binding over the quilt edge and sew the folded edge of the binding to the back of the quilt by hand.

If you have a basket of binding end pieces from quilts past, a scrap quilt is the perfect opportunity to use them up. Connect leftover binding strips end-to-end, and attach to the quilt like any other double-fold binding.

LABEL

How many times have you heard about an heirloom quilt found in an attic or at a garage sale? The quilt was hand pieced, hand quilted, with no history of who made it, when it was made, or where it came from. If only that quilt could talk. The label is the quilt's voice!

Reach into your scrap bin for one more square of light-value fabric. Grab a fabric-marking pen and a piece of fine-grain sandpaper. Place the fabric on the sandpaper for stability and jot down the "important stuff!"

Use the label to detail information about the quilt. Here are a few suggestions for what to include:

- the name of the quiltmaker
- the date the quilt was finished and how long it took to complete
- the pattern source name and designer
- the city, state, and country where it was made
- special care instructions, to accommodate batting fiber content or embellishments
- the occasion it commemorates

The label doesn't have to be complicated; all you need is a square, rectangle, or other shape and enough space to write. Jazz it up with embroidery, computer graphics, cross-stitch, or running stitches. Add a border, print a photo and the information on your inkjet printer, or make a paper-pieced label from scraps that coordinate with the pieces from the quilt top. Get creative or keep it simple!

To sew the label to the back of the quilt, fold and press under a ¼-in. seam allowance around the edges, then pin the label in place with appliqué pins on a lower corner of the backing. Secure the label by hand through the backing with an appliqué stitch.

PICTURE THIS!

It's so rewarding to finish a quilt top. The excitement builds as a quilting plan is finalized. It gets even better when the binding is attached, and then the label.

There's only one more task before the quilt is really and truly done. Before your quilt goes to the lucky recipient, take a picture of it and its label.

Why bother with a picture? One finished quilt leads to another, which leads to another, and another. When one of your quilts is given away, you can easily forget the details associated with it. A printed or digital photo is all you need to keep a record of your projects. You'll be happy you did!

FINISHED SCRAP QUILTS

Scrap quilts are an easy way to justify a gift for someone in need. When the request comes for a quilt for hurricane victims, sick children, or premature babies, it's easy to use perfectly good scraps to make the project. It's nearly cost-free, but filled with heart.

Scrap quilts can be your outlet for new challenges. Justify trying a new technique, like machine quilting, embroidery, paper piecing, or appliqué with a scrap quilt. It's just leftover fabrics after all. If you don't like it, you can move on, guilt-free!

Scrap quilts are unique. When a quilter buys a new kit, it's likely that the quilt made from it is going to be similar to others made from the same kit. Make a quilt from scraps, and another quilter, using the same pattern, will make a quilt that is entirely different. Each scrap quilt has a personality all its own.

Are you ready to sew? Now that you've got a system, it's time to put it to the test. Twenty enticing projects are waiting for your scraps. Your scraps are ready to become new again. Let's get sewing!

CONTINUOUS BINDING CLOSURE

As with many methods and techniques in quilting, several options achieve the same result. Here's how I join the binding ends.

After trimming the batting and backing even with the quilt top, start along one edge and sew the binding to the quilt edges, leaving about 24 in. of the binding unsewn—12 in. at the beginning and 12 in. at the end. Place the unbound section of the quilt flat on your work table. Lay the binding ends evenly along the raw edge of the quilt and fold the binding back on itself so the folds meet and "kiss."

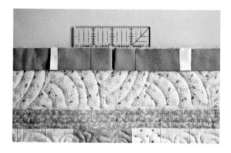

Make two marks on the top binding layer one half the width of the binding from the fold. (I usually cut my binding strips 2$\frac{1}{4}$ in., so one half of that is 1$\frac{1}{8}$ in.) Make two lines on the binding, each 1$\frac{1}{8}$ in. away from the fold. This calculation works for any width double-fold binding.

Fold the quilt onto itself and pin the quilt layers, creating some slack, which allows you to easily work with the binding ends.

Bring the binding end from the left above the quilt onto the work table and open the fold. Place the binding so you can see the marking line, right side up.

Open the crease, and fold the right binding end, wrong sides together, at the marking line.

Place the fold from the right binding aligned with edge of the left binding. At the same time, align the marking on the left binding with the edge of the right binding.

Open the right binding fold and draw a line parallel to the quilt top, from edge to edge as shown. Secure the binding with pins on both sides of the drawn line.

Sew on the line.

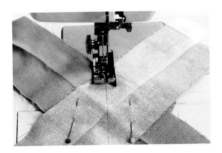

Trim about ¼ in. away from seam (unpin the quilt to test it first, if you like).

Pin and sew the remaining binding to the quilt edge.

It's almost continuous.

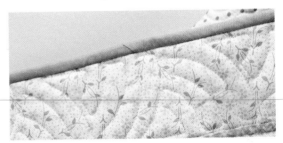

PART TWO

The Projects to Make

Scrappy Trails

The inspiration for **Scrappy Trails** came from a photograph of a two-color quilt made around 1860. For this scrappy version, a small-scale print used in the blocks and the border becomes the inspiration to select the scraps for the pieced blocks and prairie points. The blocks are made two at a time, one in reverse value from the other. When the quilt center is assembled, the blocks disappear and the strong secondary pattern of crossed dark and light "trails" takes over.

The scrappy prairie-point binding is attached to the outside edge of the quilt after quilting for a unique effect. Or you can skip the prairie points and finish with a traditional binding.

Begin by choosing a small-scale, light-value focus print for the main outer border and block background. Then select scraps in medium to dark values to coordinate with the focus print. This project uses seventy-two 5-in. squares for block piecing and an additional sixty 5-in. squares for the prairie-point binding.

FINISHED SIZE: **64 in. x 64 in.**
PATTERN DIFFICULTY: **Intermediate**

FABRIC REQUIREMENTS
1½ yd. focus print for block backgrounds (light-value, small-scale print)
1 yd. focus print for outer border (block background print suggested)
½ yd. inner border, medium value
⅓ yd. middle border, dark value
½ yd. binding, with or without prairie-point option
4 yd. backing
Batting, 70 in. x 70 in.
ScrapTherapy scraps

PREPARE SCRAPS
BLOCKS
Select seventy-two 5-in. squares from various medium and dark scrap prints to coordinate with the block background fabric.

PRAIRIE-POINT BINDING
Select sixty 5-in. squares from various medium and dark scrap prints.

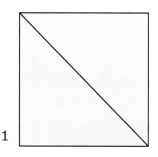

1

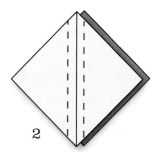

2

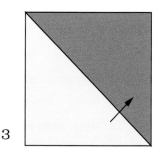

3

PREPARE BLOCK BACK-GROUND FABRIC

Cut nine 5-in. width-of-fabric strips, then cut seventy-two 5-in. squares. Set aside for blocks.

PREPARE BORDER FABRICS

INNER BORDER

Cut six 2½-in. width-of-fabric strips.

MIDDLE BORDER

Cut six 1½-in. width-of-fabric strips.

OUTER BORDER

Cut seven 5-in. width-of-fabric strips.

PREPARE BINDING

For prairie-point binding, cut seven 2-in. width-of-fabric strips for binding. Or, for traditional binding, cut seven 2¼-in. width-of-fabric strips for binding.

> The featured quilt was created with a scrappy prairie-point binding that is applied after quilting. A traditional binding may be applied instead. In either case, binding strips finish the quilt edge.

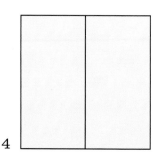

4

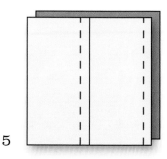

5

MAKE BLOCKS

NOTE: Blocks are assembled two at a time.

Select nine 5-in. scraps and nine 5-in. background squares from the prepared block fabrics. Set the remaining block fabric squares aside for now.

MAKE HALF-SQUARE TRIANGLE UNITS

Using a pencil or fabric-marking tool, draw a diagonal line corner-to-corner on the back of four of the 5-in. background squares. **1**

Pair a 5-in. background square with a 5-in. scrap square, right sides together, and sew ¼ in. on either side of the drawn line. **2**

Cut on the drawn line and press toward the scrap fabric. **3**

Trim each half-square triangle (HST) unit to 4½ in. square. Make a total of eight 4½-in. HST units. Set aside.

MAKE FOUR-PATCHES

Using a pencil or fabric-marking tool, draw a vertical line, centered on the back of the remaining five 5-in. background squares. **4**

Pair a 5-in. background square with a 5-in. scrap square, right sides together, and sew ¼ in. to the left of the vertical line. Then sew ¼ in. from the edge as shown. **5**

Cut on the drawn line and press each two-patch seam toward the scrap fabric. Make a total of ten two-patch units 4½ in. x 5 in. **6**

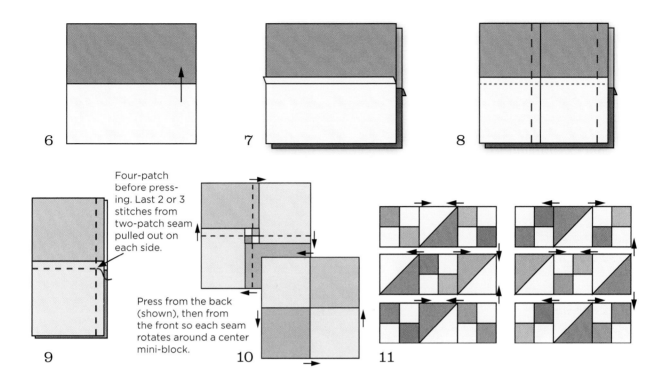

Four-patch before pressing. Last 2 or 3 stitches from two-patch seam pulled out on each side.

Press from the back (shown), then from the front so each seam rotates around a center mini-block.

Select five different two-patch units. Using a pencil or fabric-marking tool, draw a vertical line centered on the back of the two-patch unit, perpendicular to the seam.

Pair each two-patch unit with a different two-patch unit, right sides together and seam allowances inverted and aligned. Important! Be sure the two-patch unit facing you has the scrap fabric on the top and the background fabric on the bottom as shown. **7, 8**

Sew ¼ in. to the left of the vertical line and ¼ in. from the edge. Cut on the drawn line. Furl the seams as described in Quiltmaking Basics on page 191. Make a total of ten four-patch units 4½ in. square. **9, 10**

Furling the seam intersection is a technique borrowed from hand piecing. All four-patch units in each block are pressed with this method to simplify the quilt top assembly.

ASSEMBLE BLOCKS

At this point, you should have eight 4½-in. HST units and ten 4½-in. four-patches made from the nine 5-in. scrap squares and nine 5-in. background squares. Separate matching HST units and four-patches and arrange into two nine-patch blocks as shown. Note the variation in the placement of the HST units and four-patches to make two blocks in opposite light and dark value placement.

Sew each nine-patch in rows and then sew the rows together. Press seams as shown. The pressing direction is different for each block variation. **11**

NOTE: The blocks should now measure 12½ in. square.

Repeat making blocks two at a time until all seventy-two block scrap and background 5-in. squares are used, for a total of sixteen blocks.

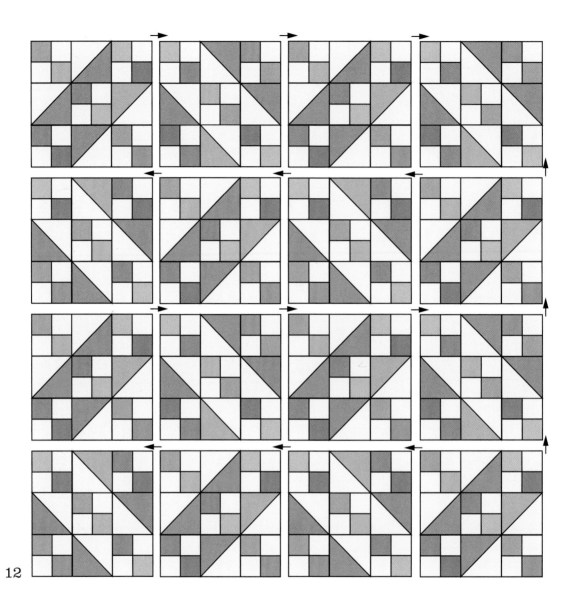

12

ASSEMBLE QUILT CENTER

Lay out blocks randomly in four rows of four blocks, alternating light and dark block variations as shown. **12**

Sew the rows together, alternating the pressing direction in each row. Press block seams in the first row to the right, then press the block seams in the second row to the left, and so on. Then sew the rows together and press the seams in one direction.

BORDERS

Referring to the diagonal seaming method on page 194, sew three 2½-in. inner border strips together end-to-end to create two strips that measure approximately 2½ in. x 120 in.

Double-check your quilt top measurements before you cut the strip lengths, and adjust measurements if needed.

From these strips, cut two inner borders 2½ in. x 48½ in. for the sides and two inner borders 2½ in. x 52½ in. for the top and bottom.

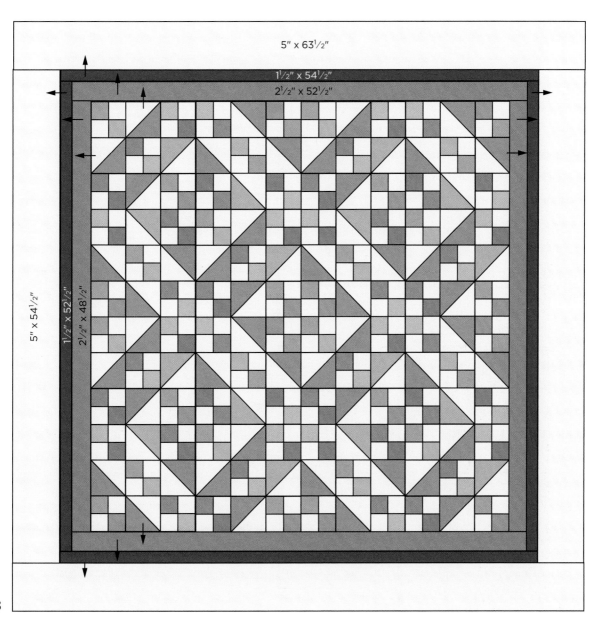

5" x 63¹/₂"

1¹/₂" x 54¹/₂"

2¹/₂" x 52¹/₂"

5" x 54¹/₂"

1¹/₂" x 52¹/₂"

2¹/₂" x 48¹/₂"

13

Repeat the diagonal-seaming process for the middle borders to make two border strips approximately 1¹/₂ in. x 120 in. Then cut two middle borders 1¹/₂ in. x 52¹/₂ in. for the sides and two middle border strips 1¹/₂ in. x 54¹/₂ in. for the top and bottom.

For the outer borders, sew three 5-in. strips together end-to-end with a diagonal seam, then cut two strips 5 in. x 54¹/₂ in. for the sides. Sew two

outer border 5-in. strips together, end-to-end with a diagonal seam, then cut one 5-in. x 63¹/₂-in. strip for the top border. Repeat to make the bottom border.

Starting with the sides, followed by the top and bottom, add each border to the quilt top, pressing seams toward the outer edge of the quilt after each addition. **13**

QUILT

Layer backing, batting, and quilt top; quilt as desired.

TRADITIONAL BINDING

A traditional, double-fold binding may be substituted for the prairie-point binding shown. To make a traditional binding, sew seven 2¹/₄-in. strips together, end-to-end with a diagonal seam. Press the connecting seams open, then press the binding in half lengthwise, wrong sides together. With raw edges aligned, sew the binding to the front of the quilt. Turn the folded edge of the binding to the back of quilt, and hand stitch in place.

PRAIRIE-POINT BINDING

Prepare prairie points Press each of the sixty 5-in. scrap squares selected for the prairie-point binding along the diagonal, wrong sides together. Then press again along the other diagonal without opening the first crease. Use a hot iron for a crisp fold. **14, 15**

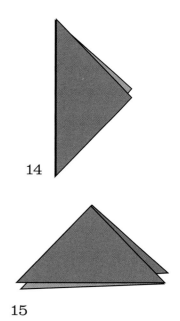

Prepare binding strips Sew seven 2-in. binding strips together, end-to-end with a diagonal seam, and press seams open. Press the strip in half lengthwise as for a traditional binding. Cut the strip into four sections, each roughly 70 in. long.

Secure prairie points to quilt Trim the backing and batting even with the quilt top.

Divide the prairie points into four stacks of fifteen prairie points: one stack for each side of the quilt. **16**

Starting and ending 1 in. from each end, arrange fifteen prairie points evenly spaced along one side of the front of the quilt, raw edges aligned. Reposition the prairie points as needed; pin liberally. Lay one binding strip on top of the prairie points with the starting edge of the binding strip aligned with the quilt top. Secure all layers with pins. Snip the binding strip 1 in. beyond the quilt end.

Using a walking foot, sew the prairie points and binding strip to the quilt top. Stop $3/8$ in. from the end of the quilt. Repeat the process for each side of the quilt, pulling away the end of the binding strip to start sewing the binding to the adjacent side. **17**

Once all four binding strips are sewn, fold the binding to the quilt back so the prairie points lie flat and the binding strip is no longer visible from the quilt front. Hand stitch the folded edge of the binding strip to the back of the quilt. At each corner, fold under and secure the raw edges of the binding strip ends. **18**

IN-SEAM PRAIRIE POINTS

Prairie points may be added to small quilts between the layers before quilting. Follow the directions at right to prepare the prairie points and baste them in place around the edges of the quilt top layer only. Stack the layers in order: batting, backing right side up, and quilt top right side down. Sew around the edge leaving an opening for turning; turn right side out and hand stitch the opening closed. The Prairie-Point Binding method is done *after* quilting for a large quilt like **Scrappy Trails**.

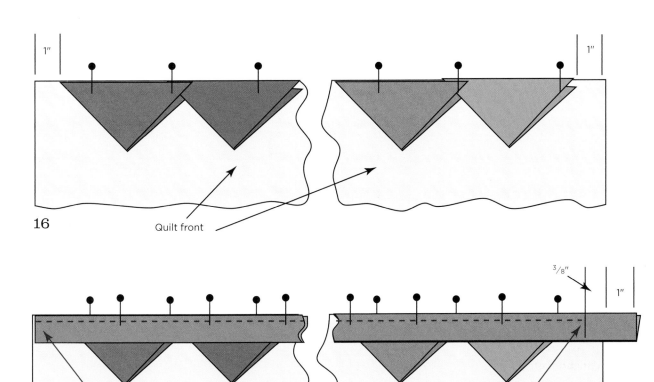

16

1"

1"

Quilt front

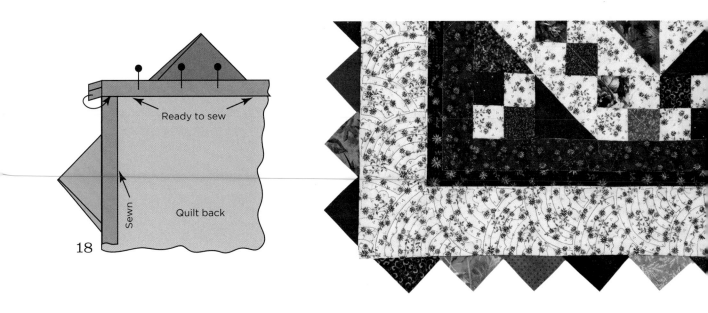

17

1"

3/8"

1"

Start sewing

Stop sewing

Quilt front

18

Ready to sew

Sewn

Quilt back

Feedsack Peaks

Feedsack or Depression-era fabrics have an interesting history, but I chose to make this quilt with '30s scrap prints because they're so cheerful and sunny, especially when paired with white and yellow background fabrics.

Two similar nine-patch block variations make up the entire quilt center. Leftovers from piecing the blocks are used in the inner pieced border, as well as in the **Thrown Together Pillow** on page 66.

Although I used feedsack reproduction scraps, just about any other scrappy theme works nicely. Be sure to choose a background fabric for the blocks with distinct contrast to the medium-value scraps used for the blocks.

I chose medium-value 3½-in. scraps for the blocks, reserving warm colors—red, bubble-gum pink, and orange—for the half-square triangle units. For the outer pieced border, 5-in. scrap squares are paired with yellow squares cut from yardage.

This quilt used three hundred fifteen medium-value 3½-in. scrap squares and thirty-four medium-value 5-in. scrap squares.

FINISHED SIZE: **64 in. x 80 in.**

PATTERN DIFFICULTY: **Intermediate**

FABRIC REQUIREMENTS

1½ yd. white for block background

¼ yd. medium blue solid for inner accent borders

⅔ yd. light blue accent for middle borders

¾ yd. yellow for pieced outer borders

⅔ yd. for binding (consider using same fabric as for inner accent border)

5 yd. backing

Batting, 68 in. x 84 in.

ScrapTherapy scraps

PREPARE SCRAPS

PIECED BLOCKS AND BORDERS

Select one hundred fifty-eight medium-value 3½-in. squares in warm colors for the half-square triangles in the blocks and inner pieced border plus one hundred fifty-seven medium-value 3½-in. squares in multicolors for the blocks. Select thirty-four medium-value 5-in. squares in multicolors for the outer pieced border.

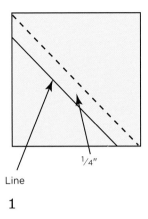

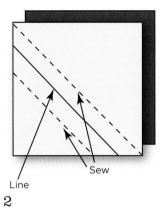

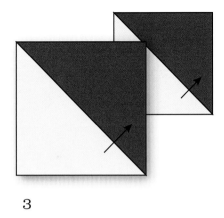

Line   ¹⁄₄″

1

Line   Sew

2

3

PREPARE BLOCK BACK-GROUND FABRIC

BLOCK BACKGROUND

Cut fifteen 3¹⁄₂-in. width-of-fabric strips, then cut one hundred fifty-eight 3¹⁄₂-in. squares. Using a pencil or fabric-marking tool, draw a line ¹⁄₄ in. away from the corner-to-corner diagonal. **1**

PREPARE OTHER FABRICS

INNER ACCENT BORDERS

Cut six 1-in. width-of-fabric strips for the inner accent border.

MIDDLE BORDER

Cut four 3¹⁄₂-in. width-of-fabric strips for the side middle borders.

Cut three 2¹⁄₂-in. width-of-fabric strips for the top and bottom middle borders.

OUTER PIECED BORDER, YELLOW

Cut five 5-in. width-of-fabric strips, then cut thirty-four 5-in. squares from the strips. Using a pencil or fabric-marking tool, draw a diagonal line corner-to-corner on the back of each square.

BINDING

Cut eight 2¹⁄₄-in. width-of-fabric strips for the binding.

MAKE INNER BORDER HALF-SQUARE TRIANGLES

Select one warm-color 3¹⁄₂-in. medium-value scrap square for the block half-square triangle units. Pair it with one white background 3¹⁄₂-in. square, right sides together. Sew ¹⁄₄ in. away from both sides of the drawn line. **2**

Pair and chain-sew all one hundred fifty-eight white and warm-colored squares.

> Sometimes the block point may get pulled into the sewing machine needle plate. To prevent this, change to a straight stitch plate (with a small round hole for the needle) or hold the loose threads as you begin to sew.

Cut each sewn square on the drawn line to make one large and one small half-square triangle (HST) unit. Press each large 3¹⁄₂-in. HST seam toward the darker fabric. Press each

small HST seam toward the darker fabric, then trim to 2¹⁄₂ in. square. Set aside the small HSTs for the inner pieced border. **3**

MAKE FIVE-TRIANGLE BLOCK

Randomly select five 3¹⁄₂-in. HSTs and four 3¹⁄₂-in. scrap squares. Arrange the block as shown. Sew the block parts into rows, pressing the row seams toward the 3¹⁄₂-in. scrap squares. Sew the rows together and press the row seams as shown. **4**

Repeat to make eighteen five-triangle blocks.

MAKE FOUR-TRIANGLE BLOCK

Randomly select four 3¹⁄₂-in. HSTs and five 3¹⁄₂-in. scrap squares. Arrange the block as shown. Sew the block parts in rows, pressing the row seams toward the 3¹⁄₂-in. scrap squares. Sew the rows together and press the row seams as shown. **5**

Repeat to make seventeen four-triangle blocks, which are 9¹⁄₂ in. square.

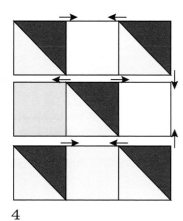

4

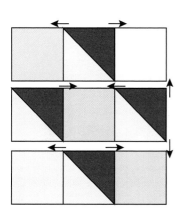

5

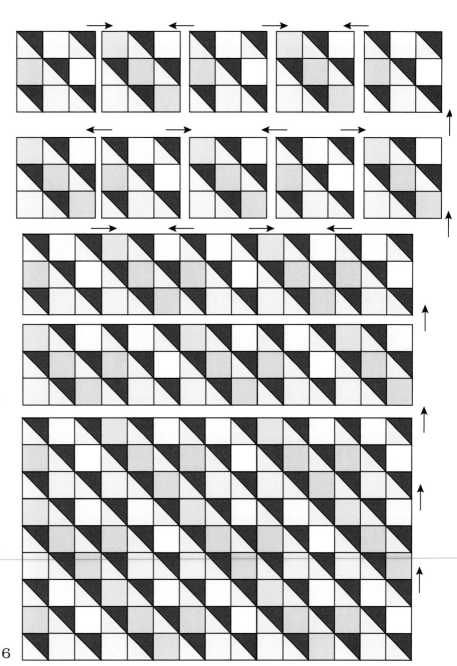

ASSEMBLE QUILT CENTER

Arrange blocks in seven rows of five blocks, alternating five-triangle and four-triangle blocks in each row. Press the block seams toward the four-triangle blocks. Press the row seams in one direction. **6**

Note that the blocks aren't symmetrical. Make sure all the blocks are arranged so each triangle set is oriented pointing "northeast." It's really easy to flip a block inadvertently!

6

BORDERS

INNER ACCENT BORDER

Connect three 1-in. strips end-to-end, using a diagonal seam (see page 194) to make one long strip. Press the connecting seams open. Make two.

From each long strip, cut one $63\frac{1}{2}$-in. side border and one $46\frac{1}{2}$-in. top and bottom border.

Sew the side accent borders to the quilt, then add the top and bottom accent borders, pressing the seam toward the border after each addition.

INNER PIECED BORDER

Sew thirty-two $2\frac{1}{2}$-in. HSTs together as shown for the side inner pieced border. Press the seams toward the dark triangle. Make two, paying close attention to the orientation of the half-square triangle units as you sew the borders!

Sew twenty-five $2\frac{1}{2}$-in. HSTs together as shown to make the top and bottom borders. Press the seams toward the dark triangle. Make two. Notice that one HST is rotated 90 degrees at the corners. **7**

7

MIDDLE BORDER

Sew two $3\frac{1}{2}$-in. strips end-to-end using a diagonal seam to make one long strip. Make two. Trim each to $68\frac{1}{2}$ in. for the side middle borders.

Next, sew three $2\frac{1}{2}$-in. strips end-to-end using a diagonal seam to make one long strip. Cut two $56\frac{1}{2}$-in. lengths for the top and bottom middle borders. Sew the side middle borders to the quilt, then the top and bottom borders. Press the seam toward the border after each addition.

OUTER PIECED BORDER

Select one 5-in. medium-value scrap square. Pair one 5-in. yellow square with the scrap, right sides together. **8, 9**

Sew $\frac{1}{4}$ in. away from both sides of the drawn line. Cut on the drawn line and press each HST seam toward the darker fabric. Trim each HST

unit to $4\frac{1}{2}$ in. square. Make a total of sixty-eight $4\frac{1}{2}$-in. HSTs from thirty-four 5-in. yellow squares and thirty-four 5-in. scrap squares for the outer pieced border. Sew eighteen $4\frac{1}{2}$-in. HSTs together as shown for the side outer pieced borders. Press the seams toward the scrap triangle. Make two, paying close attention to

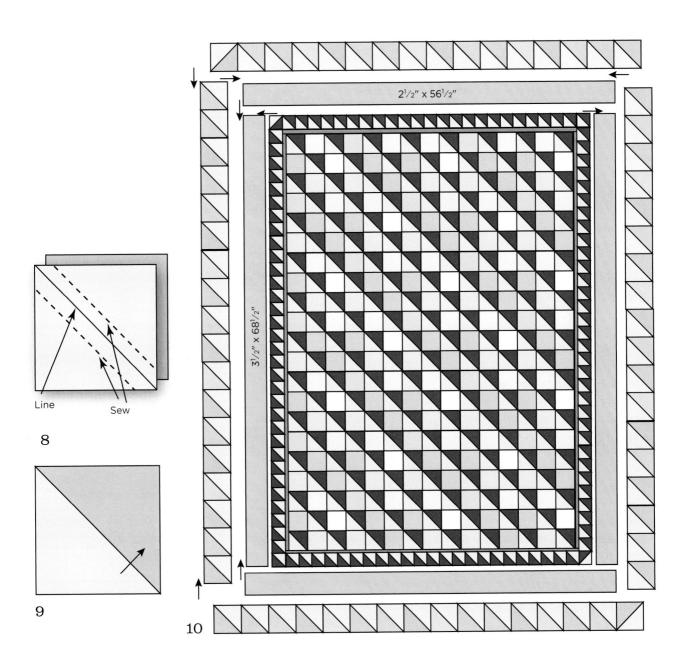

8

Line   Sew

9

10

2½" x 56½"

3½" x 68½"

the orientation of the half-square triangle units as you sew the borders.

Sew sixteen 4½-in. HSTs together as shown to make the top and bottom outer pieced borders. Press the seams toward the dark triangle. Make two. Notice that one HST is rotated 90 degrees at the corners. **10**

QUILT AND BIND

Layer the backing, batting, and quilt top; quilt as desired. Sew eight 2¼-in. binding strips together end-to-end using a diagonal seam. Press the connecting seams open, then press the binding in half lengthwise, wrong sides together. With raw edges aligned, sew the binding to the front of the quilt using a ¼-in. seam. Miter the binding at the corners (see page 46). Turn the folded edge of the binding to the back of the quilt, and hand stitch in place.

Thrown Together Pillow and Pincushion

These two projects use red and white half-square triangle units—exactly the number left over from making the **Feedsack Peaks** (see page 60) sawtooth border. Use up the spare pieces or make a fresh supply, then add some 2-in. scraps for a dimensional effect. Use yardage for an accent border, flange, and the pillow back.

The leftover triangles are paired with 2-in. scraps in green and yellow to coordinate with the pillow border and flange.

Covered buttons (another opportunity to use up scraps!) and buttonholes close up the back of the pillow. If you're not a skilled buttonhole maker, leave a simple flap closure or use hook-and-loop tape.

These projects use forty-four small red and white half-square triangle units (trimmed to $2\frac{1}{2}$ in.)—it takes eight for the pincushion and thirty-six for the throw pillow. If you're not using leftovers, you'll need four red $3\frac{1}{2}$-in. scrap squares plus four white $3\frac{1}{2}$-in. squares for the pincushion, and eighteen red $3\frac{1}{2}$-in. scrap squares plus eighteen white $3\frac{1}{2}$-in. scrap squares for the throw pillow. In addition, you'll need eighteen green 2-in. scrap squares and eighteen yellow 2-in. scrap squares for the throw pillow. If you make covered buttons, you'll need three more 2-in. scrap squares.

FINISHED SIZE: 4 in. x 4 in. pincushion; 14 in. x 14 in. pillow

PATTERN DIFFICULTY: Easy

FABRIC AND NOTION REQUIREMENTS

PINCUSHION
5-in. scrap square cotton, flannel, or felted wool
    for backing
Scrap batting pieces for stuffing

PILLOW
$2/3$ yd. yellow for pillow flange and backing
$1/4$ yd. green for accent border
$1/4$ yd. fusible web
$7/8$ in. covered button kit (3 buttons)
14-in. square pillow form
ScrapTherapy scraps

PREPARE ADDITIONAL FABRICS FOR THROW PILLOW

ACCENT BORDER

Cut two 1½-in. width-of-fabric strips, then cut two 12½-in. strips for the side borders and two 14½-in. strips for the top and bottom borders.

PILLOW FLANGE AND BACKING

Cut two 2½-in. width-of-fabric strips, then cut two 14½-in. strips for the side borders and two 18½-in. strips for the top and bottom borders.

Cut one 12-in. width-of-fabric strip, then cut two 18½-in. panels for the pillow back.

FUSIBLE WEB

Cut two 2-in. x 18½-in. strips of fusible web. If your fusible web isn't this wide, cut multiple strips and abut the ends to make the needed length.

USE LEFTOVERS OR MAKE RED AND WHITE HALF-SQUARE TRIANGLE UNITS

With a pencil or fabric-marking tool, draw a diagonal line corner-to-corner on the back of each white 3½-in. scrap square. Place each white square on top of a red 3½-in. scrap, right sides together, edges aligned.

Sew ¼ in. away from both sides of the drawn line, then cut in half on the drawn line. **1**

Press the seam on each half-square triangle unit toward the red fabric. Trim each to 2½ in. square. **2**

Pair up scraps, chain-sew, cut apart, press seams, and trim to make a total of forty-four 2½-in. red and

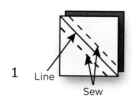

1 Line Sew

2

3

white half-square triangle units. Use eight for the pincushion and thirty-six for the throw pillow.

MAKE PINCUSHION

Select eight 2½-in. trimmed red and white half-square triangle units. Set four aside. Fold each of the remaining half-square triangle units along the diagonal. The seam will be perpendicular to the fold as shown. Press a crisp fold. **3**

Arrange four unpressed half-square triangle units as shown to create a pinwheel block. **4**

Before sewing the block together, arrange the folded half-square triangle units on top of the flat half-square triangle units with raw edges aligned at the block center, alternating color positioning. Pin each folded half-square triangle unit onto its corresponding flat half-square triangle unit as shown. Use extra pins to secure the multiple layers or baste the raw edges together. Sew the

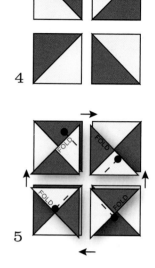

4

5

block, leaving the fold of the half-square triangle units unsewn. Furl the seam intersection, if desired, to reduce bulk. (See "Furling Seams" in Quiltmaking Basics on page 193.) **5**

ASSEMBLE PINCUSHION

Place the 5-in. backing square right side up. Then place the pieced pin cushion top right side down, centered on the backing. Pin to secure the edges. Sew ¼ in. from the pincushion top edges, leaving a 2-in. opening along one side. Trim the backing fabric even with the pin cushion top. Trim the corners to reduce bulk, then turn right side out through the opening. Stuff the pincushion and hand sew the opening closed.

There are lots of stuffing options, including scrap batting (wool batting scraps are especially nice), scrap fabrics, polyester fiberfill, or ground walnut shells (available in pet stores).

6

THROW PILLOW

ASSEMBLE THROW PILLOW TOP

Arrange thirty-six red and white
leftover (or newly created) half-
square triangles into six rows of six,
as shown. **6**

Fold each green and yellow 2-in.
scrap square in half diagonally and
press a crisp fold.

Before sewing the half-square
triangle units together, arrange the
folded 2-in. scrap squares on the
units, aligning the raw edges. Pin
each folded 2-in. square onto its
corresponding unfolded half-square
triangle unit. **7**

Sew the units into rows, then sew
the rows together, leaving the folds
of the 2-in. squares unsewn. The pillow center should measure 12½ in.

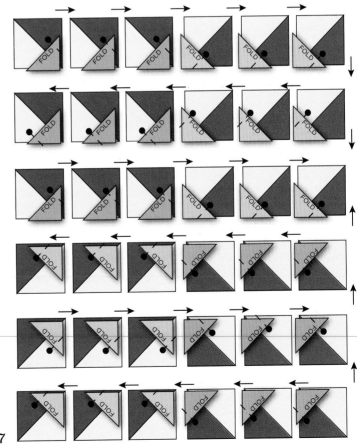

7

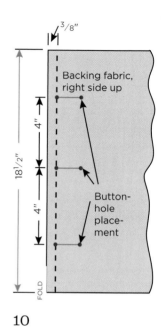

Use a folded 5-in. scrap square and scrap fusible web to practice making button-holes before sewing them on the pillow backing.

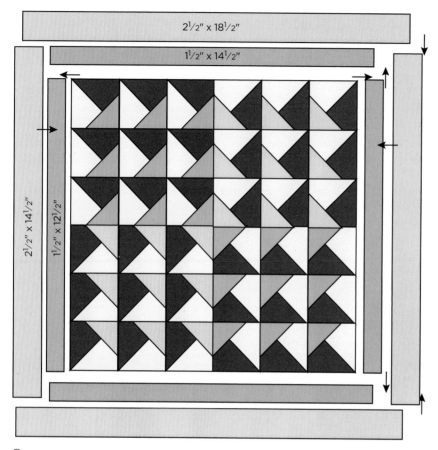

8

Arrange the pieced center and border fabrics as shown. Sew the side pieces, then the top and bottom pieces alternately to the pieced center. The last yellow border strips create the flange. Press the seams as indicated. The pillow top should measure 18½ in. square. **8**

ASSEMBLE THROW PILLOW BACK

Place the fusible side of one web strip on the wrong side of one 12-in. x 18½-in. backing rectangle, aligning it with the long edge. Fuse the web in place, then remove the paper. Fold the fabric 2 in. from the edge and fuse in place. Repeat with the second pillow back section. **9**

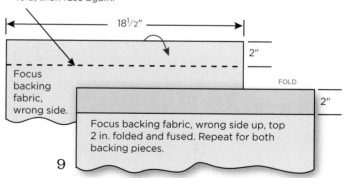

Place fusible web here. Fuse, fold, then fuse again.

9

For buttonhole placement, use a pencil or fabric-marking tool to make three 1¼-in.-long marks on the right side of one backing piece, centered and 4 in. apart, and ³/₈ in. from the fused fold. Stitch the buttonholes on the markings and cut open. **10**

Overlap the backing panels and mark the button locations under the holes, ½ in. from the folded edge. Cover the buttons with scraps and sew one on each marking. **11**

Sew a ¼-in. seam around the outside edge. Turn the pillow right side out through the back opening. Place the pillow right side up. Press the edges flat and place pins around the pillow border. Stitch in the ditch along the seam between the inner border and the flange. Topstitch along the outer flange edge. Insert the pillow form and button up the back.

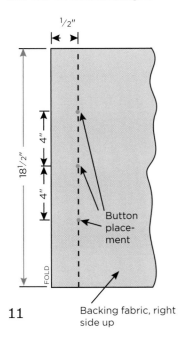

½"

18½"

4"

4"

FOLD

Button placement

11

Backing fabric, right side up

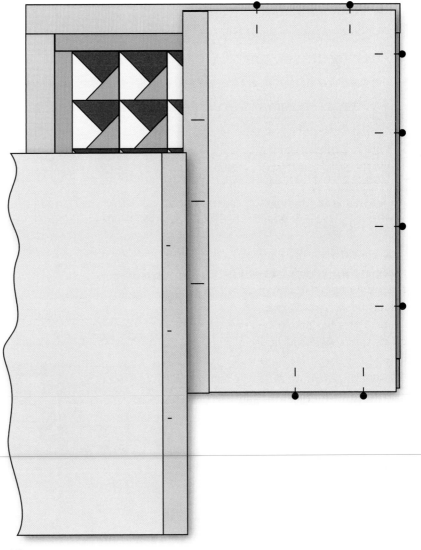

ASSEMBLE THROW PILLOW

Place the pillow top, right side up on a large work surface. Layer the backing panels right side down on top, with the raw edges aligned. First, place the buttonhole panel aligned with the right edge, then the button panel aligned with the left edge. Pin around the entire pillow outer edge. **12**

12

Everything Nice

Everything Nice is just two blocks, one called Sugar and the other, Spice. No border, no background fabrics—nothing but scraps! In fact, this quilt top is made entirely from the scrap bins—and from all three sizes—2 in., 3½ in., and 5 in. Even the binding is made from leftover binding pieces!

You can make any size you want. First, decide the finished quilt size, then select scraps based on the size you've chosen; make the required number of blocks and sew 'em together! The quilt pictured is 60 in. x 77 in., sixty-three blocks—thirty-two Sugar and thirty-one Spice.

When choosing the scrap squares for your quilt, select scraps that fall into two categories—distinctly light value and distinctly dark value. Every fabric square in the light category should be considerably lighter than every scrap in the dark category and vice versa. Don't worry that scrap prints don't match within each block, as long as the lights are light and the darks are dark.

In addition, for my sample, I stuck with an earthy theme as I picked scrap prints to use—no brights allowed.

NOTE: Each Sugar block uses two light-value 5-in. and two dark-value 5-in. scrap squares. Each Spice block uses four dark-value 2-in., two light-value 3½-in., one light-value 5-in., and two dark-value 5-in. scrap squares from your ScrapTherapy boxes.

FINISHED SIZE: varies, 60 in. x 77 in. shown

PATTERN DIFFICULTY: Intermediate

Follow the chart below to select the quilt finished size, then find the number of blocks, scraps, backing, and binding needed to make the quilt in that size.

| | Finished Size* (in.) | BLOCKS | | SCRAPS NEEDED | | | | Backing (yd.) | BINDING** | |
		Sugar	Spice	2 in. Dark	3½ in. Light	5 in. Dark	5 in. Light		Length (in.)/ 2¼-in. Strips Needed	Yd.
Baby	43 x 43 5 rows of 5 blocks	13	12	48	24	50	38	2⅔	180/5	⅜
Toddler	43 x 60 7 rows of 5 blocks	18	17	68	34	70	53	2⅔	214/6	½
Lap	60 x 77 9 rows of 7 blocks	32	31	124	62	126	95	3¾	284/8	⅝
Twin	77 x 94 11 rows of 9 blocks	50	49	196	98	198	149	5½	350/9	⅔
Queen	94 x 94 11 rows of 11 blocks	61	60	240	120	242	182	8½	384/10	⅔
King	111 x 111 13 rows of 13 blocks	85	84	336	168	338	254	9⅔	456/12	⅞

* Add 2 in. to 4 in. to each finished quilt dimension for batting size.
** Binding yardage and number of binding strips needed is based on 40-in. width-of-fabric and 2¼-in.-wide strips.

MAKE SUGAR BLOCKS

Select two light-value 5-in. scrap squares and cut both in half to make two 2½-in. x 5-in. rectangles for block sides. **1**

Select two dark-value 5-in. scrap squares and set one aside uncut for the block center. Cut the other scrap square in half twice to make four 2½-in. squares for the block corner-stones. **2**

Sew the blocks together in rows, and press seams as shown. Sew the rows together to complete the Sugar block. **3, 4**

The block measures 9 in. square. Repeat to make the number of Sugar blocks needed for selected quilt size as indicated in the chart above.

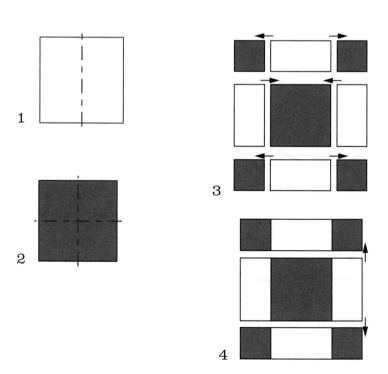

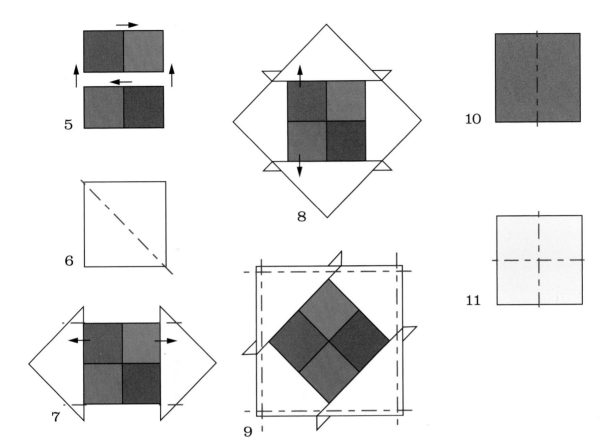

MAKE SPICE BLOCKS

Select four 2-in. dark-value scrap squares. Make two two-patches, press the seams in one direction, then sew the two-patch into one four-patch so the seams nest.

Press the four-patch seam in one direction or furl the seam for an even center (see page 193). **5**

Select two light-value 3½-in. scrap squares and cut both in half once along the diagonal to make four half-square triangles (HST). **6**

Center and sew one HST to opposite sides of each four-patch unit. Press the seams toward the triangles. Trim the points even with four-patch units as shown. **7**

To find the center of the long side of the HST, fold the triangle in half so the points meet and pinch the center with your fingertips. Align the resulting pinch mark with the four-patch seam.

Sew the remaining two HSTs to the last two sides of the four-patch unit to complete the block center. Press the seams toward the triangles. **8**

Trim the resulting center unit to 5 in. square, so the four-patch floats in the block center. Be sure the center of the four-patch seam is aligned with the 2½-in. marks on the ruler. **9**

A square ruler with a bias line is helpful for this step.

Select two dark-value 5-in. scrap squares and cut both in half to make four 2½-in. x 5-in. rectangles for the block sides. **10**

Select one light-value 5-in. scrap square and cut it in half twice to make four 2½-in. squares for the block cornerstones. **11**

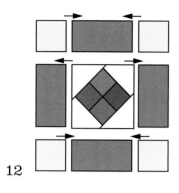

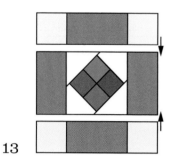

12

13

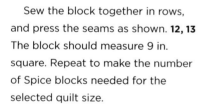

Sew the block together in rows, and press the seams as shown. **12, 13** The block should measure 9 in. square. Repeat to make the number of Spice blocks needed for the selected quilt size.

14

ASSEMBLE QUILT

Arrange the blocks in rows, starting and ending the first and last row with Sugar blocks and alternating Sugar and Spice blocks in each row. Sew the blocks into rows; press the block seams toward the Sugar blocks. Sew the rows; press the row seams in one direction. **14**

QUILT AND BIND

Layer the backing, batting, and quilt top; quilt as desired. Sew 2¼-in. binding strips together end-to-end using a diagonal seam. The number of width-of-fabric binding strips is based on the quilt size indicated in the chart on page 74. Or, connect leftover binding strips to obtain the required length, also indicated in the chart. Press connecting seams open, then press the binding in half lengthwise, wrong sides together. With raw edges aligned, sew the binding to the front of the quilt using a ¼-in. seam. Miter the binding at the corners (see page 46). Turn the folded edge of the binding to the back of the quilt, and hand stitch in place.

Once Upon a Scrap

Once Upon a Scrap originated as a child-size throw using a large-scale directional print for the main focus. It works just as nicely with bold, over-size focus prints in more mature, but still playful, themes. Add some coordinating 2-in. scrap squares and you have the makings of a fairy tale ending!

Start by selecting the large-scale focus print. Choose a few colors from the focus fabric and select scraps in those colors. This project uses one hundred eighty 2-in. novelty print and solid scrap squares for the pieced panels.

FINISHED SIZE: **37 in. x 51 in.**

PATTERN DIFFICULTY: **Easy**

FABRIC REQUIREMENTS

$7/8$ yd. large-scale main focus print (directional print encouraged)

$1/4$ yd. solid coordinate for inner border

$2/3$ yd. for outer border

$3/8$ yd. for binding

$1^1/2$ yd. backing

Batting, 40 in. x 55 in.

ScrapTherapy scraps

ScrapTherapy Small Scrap Grid by Quiltsmart^{SM} (one complete panel with two 5 x 18-square grids) is optional.

PREPARE SCRAPS

Select one hundred eighty 2-in. scrap squares in coordinating prints and colors.

PREPARE LARGE-SCALE MAIN PRINT

Cut the main panel $27^1/2$ in. wide.

Cross-cut main panel into three segments:

Top segment: $5^1/2$ in. x $27^1/2$ in.

Middle segment: $16^1/2$ in. x $27^1/2$ in.

Bottom segment: $5^1/2$ in. x $27^1/2$ in.

Use caution when cutting the directional main fabric. The longest cut dimension runs horizontally across the top and bottom of the print.

PREPARE INNER BORDER

Cut five $1^1/2$-in. width-of-fabric strips.

Sew three strips together end-to-end with a diagonal seam and press the seam allowances open (see page 96). Cut the resulting strip into two segments, each $1^1/2$ in. x $41^1/2$ in. for the side borders.

Trim the remaining two strips to $1^1/2$ in. x $29^1/2$ in. for the top and bottom inner borders.

PREPARE OUTER BORDER

Cut five $4^1/2$-in. width-of-fabric strips.

Sew three strips together end-to-end with a diagonal seam and press the seam allowances open.

Cut the resulting strip into two segments, each $4^1/2$ in. x $43^1/2$ in. for the side borders.

Trim the remaining two strips to $4^1/2$ in. x $37^1/2$ in. for the top and bottom outer borders.

PREPARE BINDING

Cut five $2^1/4$-in. width-of-fabric strips for the binding.

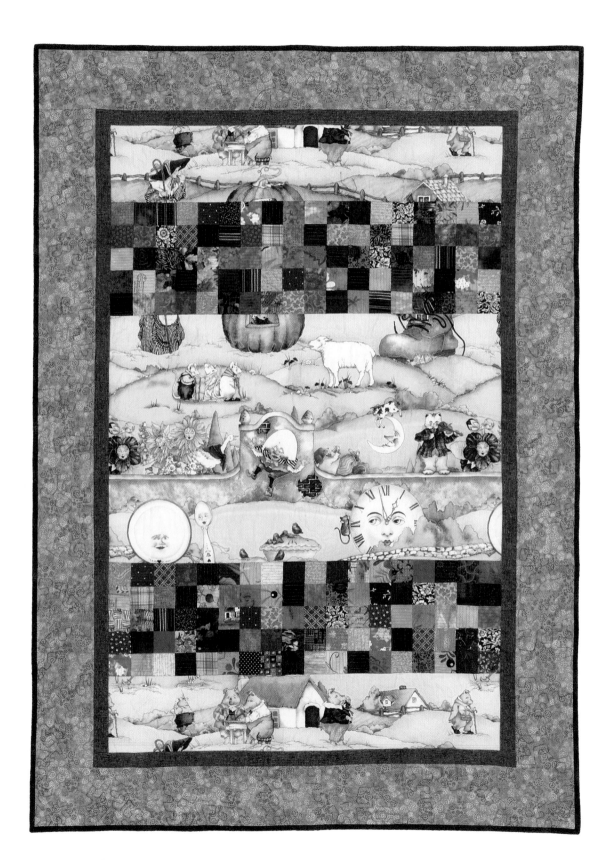

PIECED SCRAP PANELS

Randomly sew 2-in. scrap squares in rows of five. Repeat to make eighteen rows. Press the seam allowances in each row in one direction.

Sew eighteen rows together to create a pieced scrap panel, alternating the seam allowance direction row by row, then press the row seam allowances in one direction. Repeat to make two panels, each measuring 8 in. x 27½ in. **1**

See page 80 for an alternative piecing method.

ASSEMBLE QUILT

Lay out the pieced scrap panels between the main print segments. Sew them together and press the seams away from the pieced panels.

Add the inner borders one at a time—sides first, then top and bottom. Press the seams toward the border after each addition.

Add the outer borders, one at a time—sides first, then top and bottom. Press the seams toward the border after each addition. **2**

QUILT AND BIND

Layer the backing, batting, and quilt top; quilt as desired. Sew five 2¼-in. binding strips together end-to-end using a diagonal seam. Press the connecting seams open, then press the binding in half lengthwise, wrong sides together. With raw edges aligned, sew the binding to the front of the quilt using a ¼-in. seam. Miter the binding at the corners (see page 46). Turn the folded edge of the binding to the back of the quilt, and hand stitch in place.

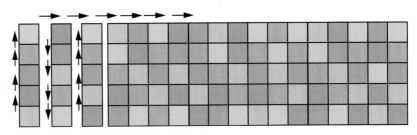

1

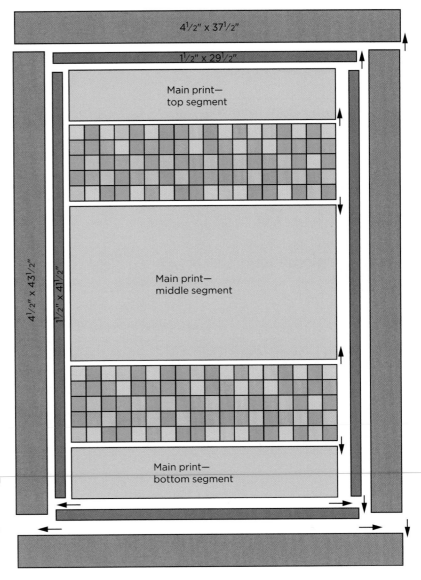

4½" x 37½"

1½" x 29½"

Main print— top segment

4½" x 43½"

½" x 41½"

Main print— middle segment

Main print— bottom segment

2

USING SCRAPTHERAPY SMALL SCRAP GRID BY QUILTSMART

Use the ScrapTherapy Small Scrap Grid to simplify and stabilize the scrappy panel elements. The preprinted interfacing allows you to position your scraps and arrange them randomly with no risk of sloppy seam intersections.

Cut the grid roughly in half to separate the two 5 x 18-square grid segments.

Place one 5 x 18 section on your ironing board with the fusible or "bumpy" side of interfacing up, and place scraps randomly on the grid, right side up, aligned with printed lines. **1**

Partially filled-in grid

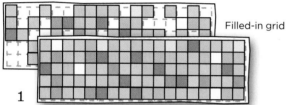

Filled-in grid

1

Fuse the scraps in place using a hot steam iron. Be careful to keep your iron free of the fusible; try not to touch the iron to the interfacing.

Fold the interfacing along one long seamline, so the dotted line is precisely on the fold, even if the scraps don't sit precisely on the fold. Pin and sew a scant $1/4$-in. seam allowance along the folded edge. Repeat for all the long seams. Don't press yet! **2**

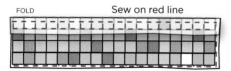

FOLD   Sew on red line

2

With scissors, snip the interfacing on the dotted lines at the seam intersections, cutting through and just beyond stitching. **3**

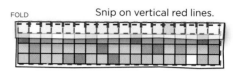

FOLD   Snip on vertical red lines.

3

Repeat until sewn along all seams. Do not press.

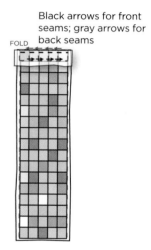

Black arrows for front seams; gray arrows for back seams

FOLD

4

Fold the short seams, as before so the dotted line is directly on the fold, and flip the snipped seams so they nest at the intersections. Pin and sew a scant $1/4$-in. seam allowance on all the short seams. **4**

Trim the excess interfacing on the dotted lines, then press the short seams in one direction. **5**

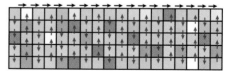

5

Runaway Thread

This quilt is a cheerful study in contrasts. **Runaway Thread** makes a great lap-size throw for anyone who enjoys thread and sewing.

I think that this quilt is nicely framed by a darker border. Working backwards, that means the block backgrounds in the quilt center are light and the scraps in the quilt center are medium or dark value. I chose to work with a white background fabric for the center blocks, so selecting 3½-in. and 5-in. scraps was easy—everything is darker than white! However, rules are made to be broken; I've seen this project made up with holiday fabric scraps and a golden-cream background, and it was simply stunning!

This project uses sixty-four medium-value 5-in. scrap squares and three hundred sixteen medium-value 3½-in. scrap squares.

FINISHED SIZE: **66 in. x 78 in.**

PATTERN DIFFICULTY: **Easy**

FABRIC REQUIREMENTS

4¼ yd. background (white or off-white suggested)

⅝ yd. binding

4½ yd. backing

Batting, 70 in. x 82 in.

ScrapTherapy scraps

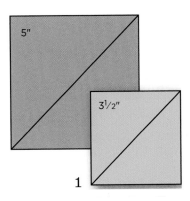

PREPARE SCRAPS

CENTER BLOCKS

Select sixty-four 5-in. squares and sixty-four 3½-in. squares from various novelty scrap prints. With a pencil or fabric-marking tool, draw a diagonal line on the back of all the blocks. **1**

BORDER BLOCKS

Select two hundred fifty-two 3½-in. squares from various bright or novelty scrap prints.

This quilt is a great candidate for a scrappy binding. Instead of cutting strips from binding fabric, pull out a bunch of leftover binding strips in medium values and various lengths. Connect the strips end-to-end as directed below to make the binding.

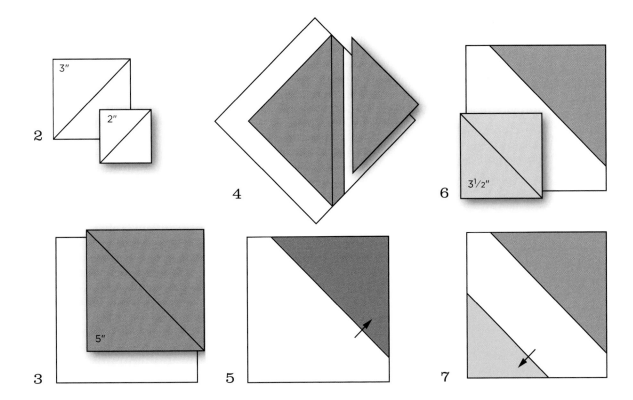

PREPARE BACKGROUND FABRIC

CENTER BLOCKS

Cut fourteen 6½-in. width-of-fabric strips, then cut eighty 6½-in. squares from the strips.

BORDER BLOCKS

Cut thirteen 3-in. width-of-fabric strips, then cut one hundred sixty-eight 3-in. squares from the strips. Cut nine 2-in. width-of-fabric strips, then cut one hundred sixty-eight 2-in. squares from the strips. With a pencil or fabric-marking tool, draw a diagonal line on the back of all the squares. **2**

PREPARE BINDING

Cut eight 2¼-in. width-of-fabric strips for the binding.

ASSEMBLE BLOCKS

For purposes of illustration, scrap colors shown in the pattern identify size and placement. The scraps in your quilt will have much more variety in color and print. Select scraps for blocks randomly!

CENTER BLOCKS

Place a 5-in. scrap square aligned with the corner of a 6½-in. background square, right sides together. Sew on the drawn line. **3**

Trim the middle scrap layer and press the scrap toward the outer corner of the block. **4, 5**

Trimming the middle layer from these blocks is based on personal preference. For the center blocks, I prefer to leave the 6½-in. background whole and trim the outer portion of the scrap to reduce bulk and help compensate for slight inaccuracies in sewing and pressing.

Make sixty-four units and set sixteen completed blocks aside for the quilt center construction. Place a 3½-in. scrap square prepared for the center blocks, right sides together, aligned with the opposite corner of each of the remaining forty-eight partially assembled blocks. Sew on the drawn line. Trim the middle scrap layer; press the scrap toward the outer corner of the block. **6, 7**

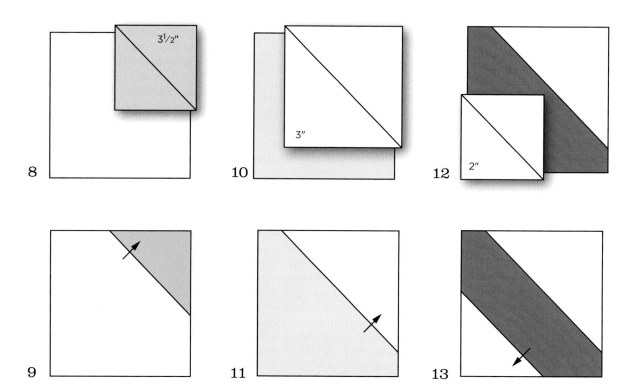

8

9

10

11

12

2"

13

On each of the sixteen remaining unsewn 6¹/₂-in. background squares, place each of the remaining 3¹/₂-in. scrap squares prepared for the center blocks, right sides together, aligned with one corner of the background square. Sew on the drawn line. Trim the middle scrap layer; press the scrap toward the outer corner of the block. **8, 9**

BORDER BLOCKS

Place a 3-in. background square aligned with the corner of a 3¹/₂-in. scrap square, right sides together. Sew on the drawn line. Press the background square toward the outer corner of the block. Make one hundred sixty-eight units and set eighty completed blocks aside for the borders. **10, 11**

For the border blocks, light fabrics are placed over dark scrap squares. To avoid shadowing (dark fabric showing through light fabric), I chose to leave the middle layer untrimmed. The bottom scrap layer remains intact for construction purposes.

Place a 2-in. background square aligned with the opposite corner of each of the eighty-eight partially assembled border blocks, right sides together. Sew on the drawn line.

Press the background square toward the outer corner of the block. **12, 13**

On eighty of the unsewn 3¹/₂-in. scrap squares, place each of the remaining 2-in. background squares

aligned with one corner of a 3¹/₂-in. scrap square, right sides together. Sew on the drawn line. Press the background square toward the outer corner of the block. Four 3¹/₂-in. scrap squares remain unsewn for the border. **14, 15, 16**

ASSEMBLE QUILT

QUILT CENTER

Arrange the 6¹/₂-in. blocks as shown, keeping the scrap placement random. Each block around the outside edge of the quilt center has one scrap corner. Each middle block has two sewn scraps. Sew the blocks into rows. Press the block seams in opposite directions in alternate rows as indicated. Sew the rows; then press the row seams in one direction. **17**

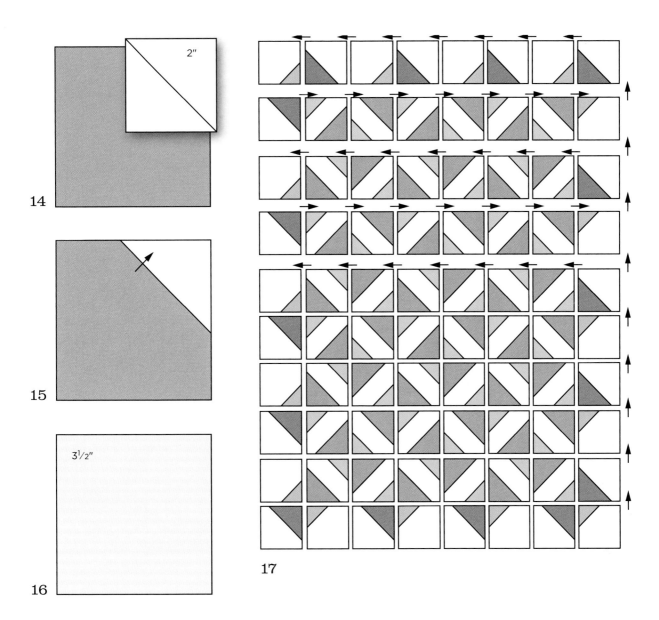

14

15

3½"

16

17

BORDERS

SIDE BORDERS

Arrange the sixty 3½-in. blocks as shown for each border, keeping the scrap placement random. Make two of each side border assembly with identical block placement. Sew the blocks in rows; press the block seams as shown. Sew the rows together. Press the row seams for the left side border as shown in red, and for the right side border as shown in green. **18**

TOP AND BOTTOM BORDERS

Make two borders with identical block placement, pressing the block seams as shown. Press the row seams as shown in red. **19**

Add the borders to the quilt top, sides first, then top and bottom. Notice that the right side border is flipped or inverted from the original layout as shown on page 86. Press the seams as indicated after each border addition. **20**

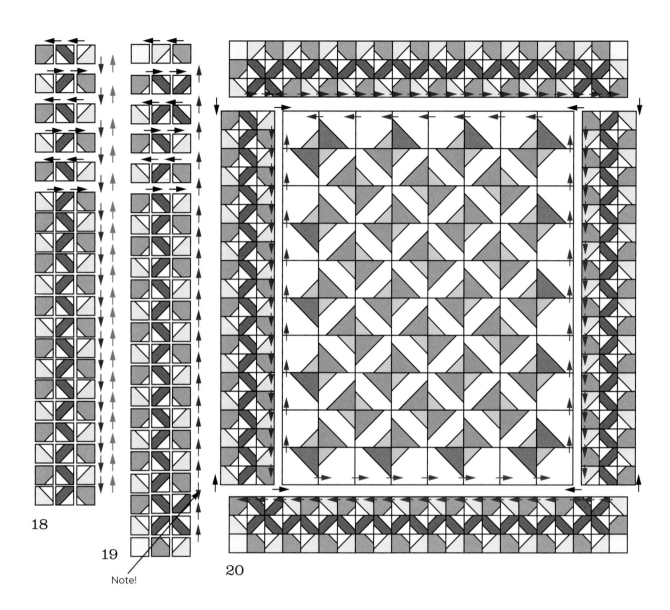

18

19

Note!

20

QUILT AND BIND

Layer the backing, batting, and quilt top; quilt as desired. Sew eight 2¼-in. binding strips together end-to-end using a diagonal seam. Press the connecting seams open, then press the binding in half lengthwise, wrong sides together. With raw edges aligned, sew the binding to the front of the quilt using a ¼-in. seam. Miter the binding at the corners (see page 46). Turn the folded edge of the binding to the back of the quilt and hand stitch in place.

Something Fishy

Each fish block in this toddler-size quilt is unique. Like an I-Spy quilt, no matter where you look, there's something interesting to see. You know you've started going "off the deep end" when you begin naming fish species after the various fabric blocks—Strawberry Fish, Star Fish, Polka-dot Fish, Plaid Fish, and the elusive Sunflower Fish (not to be confused with its more common relative, the Sunfish).

Each fish block is created using a 3½-in. scrap square for the fish body and a 5-in. scrap square for the fins.

Following a sew, cut, press, and trim routine, you'll get eight half square triangle (HST) units from one 5-in. scrap square plus one background square. Each fish block uses five HST units and the remaining three are reserved for the "flying seagull" border. "Flying seagull?" you say. "They look like flying geese!" Perhaps, but the fish in this quilt are most definitely tropical fish, and seagulls are more likely to hang out with tropical fish than geese are!

I used bright novelty prints for the fish blocks, along with watery blue fabric for the block background, setting triangles, and binding.

This quilt uses sixty-five 5-in. squares and fifty-nine 3½-in. squares. The greater the contrast between the fish scraps and the water background, the better!

FINISHED SIZE: **39 in. x 51 in.**

PATTERN DIFFICULTY: **Intermediate**

FABRIC REQUIREMENTS

2¼ yd. blue for background and binding

1½ yd. backing

Batting, 42 in. x 54 in.

ScrapTherapy scraps

PREPARE SCRAPS

BLOCKS AND BORDER

Select fifty-nine 5-in. and fifty-nine 3½-in. squares from various bright prints.

Select six additional 5-in. squares from various bright prints to complete the flying seagull border. Using a pencil or fabric-marking tool, draw two diagonal lines on the back of each 5-in. scrap square, corner-to-corner. **1** (See page 89.)

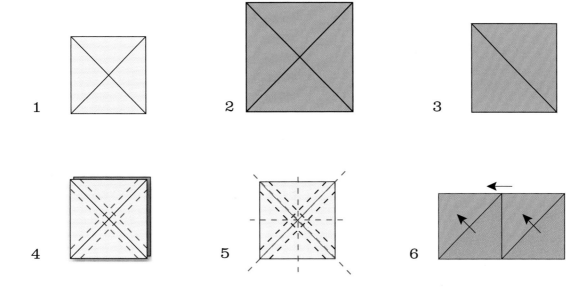

PREPARE BACKGROUND FABRIC

Cut nine 5-in. width-of-fabric strips, then cut sixty-five 5-in. squares. Reserve six squares for the border and use the remaining fifty-nine for the fish. Cut two 10-in. width-of-fabric strips. From the first strip, cut four 10-in. squares. From the second strip, cut one 10-in. square, then trim the remainder of the strip to 7 in. wide and cut two 7-in. squares.

Cut each 10-in. background square in half on the diagonal twice to make twenty side-setting triangles. **2**

Cut each 7-in. square in half on the diagonal once to make four corner-setting triangles. **3**

Cut five 2¼-in. width-of-fabric strips for the binding.

MAKE FISH

Pair one background 5-in. square and one print 5-in. scrap square, right sides together.

Sew ¼ in. away from both sides of the drawn lines to make a total of four stitching lines. **4**

> For faster fish production, chain-sew the blocks together.

Cut through the center four times, being careful not to move the fabric between cuts. First, make a vertical cut 2½ in. from the edge, then a horizontal cut 2½ in. from the bottom, and, lastly, cut diagonally on the drawn lines to make eight half-square triangles. Don't press the seams! **5**

A rotating cutting mat is helpful in cutting these sewn squares. Make the first cut and lift the ruler carefully without moving the fabric beneath it. Turn the mat a quarter turn and make the second cut. Turn the mat again to cut across the squares diagonally. Then turn the mat one more time to make the last cut, all without disturbing the fabric!

Set three of the resulting triangles aside, unpressed, for the border. Press the remaining five HST seams toward the background fabric. Trim each HST unit to 2 in. square.

Sew two HST units together as shown, pressing the seam as indicated. **6**

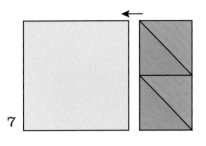

7

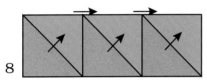

8

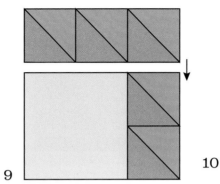

9

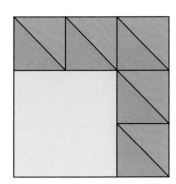

10

Select a coordinating 3½-in. scrap square for the fish body. Sew a two-fin unit on one side as shown. Press the seam toward the body. **7**

> Avoid directional prints for the fish bodies. The blocks will be set on point, and prints may be tilted or turned upside down when sewn into the quilt.

Sew the remaining three fins together in a row and press the seams as shown. Be careful—the three-part unit is sewn differently than the two-part unit. **8**

Sew the three-fin unit to the body, pressing the seam toward the body. **9**

The block should now measure 5 in. square. **10**

Repeat to make fifty-nine fish blocks in a variety of fabric combinations.

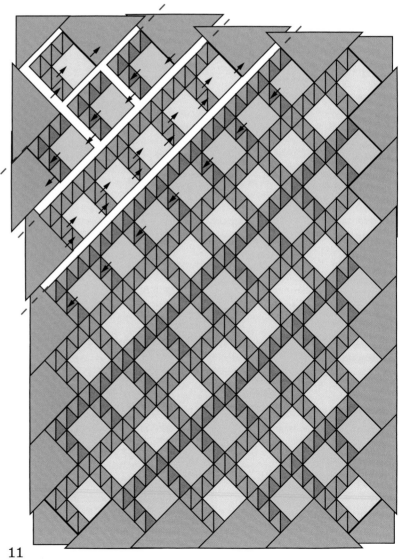

11

These little fish parts can get muddled if you get too far ahead of yourself. To avoid having fish with mismatched fins (unless you like that), create a mini-assembly line to stay organized. Select a fish body and fish fins similar in color and value, but not necessarily matching. Put wild plaids with stripes, flowers with polka-dots! (See "Chain Piecing and Production Sewing" on pages 34–35.)

ASSEMBLE QUILT CENTER

Arrange the fish blocks and setting triangles in rows as shown. For better seam nesting, re-press the 3-in. seam toward the fins in alternating rows. Trim the points from the setting triangles before sewing the rows together. (See "Un-Pressing Basics" on page 34.) **11**

Trim the quilt top to 33½ in. x 45½ in. **12**

Trim the sides of the quilt top first, then the top and bottom. Measure and cut carefully! Trim approximately 1¼ in. from the tip of the fish "nose" on the right side of the quilt and about 1¾ in. from the flat side of the fish "tails" on the left side of the quilt. Trim about ¾ in. from the top and bottom fin tips at the upper and lower quilt edges. Seam allowances may vary; check your quilt's measurements before trimming!

MAKE "FLYING SEAGULL" BORDER

Sew the six remaining 5-in. background squares and six 5-in. scrap squares as before to make forty-eight HSTs. Don't press the seams! Add these HST units to the un-pressed HST units set aside earlier. Randomly press half the triangle seams toward the background and half the triangle seams toward the scrap print and separate into two stacks accordingly.

Randomly sew two HST units together, one from each stack, to make seagulls. Mix them up! Press one-half of the seagull center seams to one side. Reverse the seam pressing direction for the other half of the seagull units. (You'll have one leftover half-square triangle unit.) **13** (See page 92.)

12

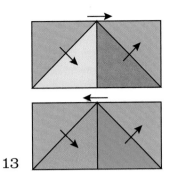

13

Sew thirty flying seagulls together for each of the two side borders. Sew the borders to each side of the quilt, with the seagulls "flying" up on one side and down on the other. Press the seams toward the quilt center.

Sew twenty-six flying seagulls together for the top and bottom borders; turn the last two at a 90-degree angle as shown. Sew the top and bottom borders to the quilt so the seagulls are flying in opposite directions. Press the seams toward the quilt center. **14**

QUILT AND BIND

Layer the backing, batting, and quilt top; quilt as desired. Sew five 2¼-in. binding strips together end-to-end using a diagonal seam. Press the connecting seams open, then press the binding in half lengthwise, wrong sides together. With raw edges aligned, sew the binding to the front of the quilt using a ¼-in. seam. Miter the binding at the corners (see page 46). Turn the folded edge of the binding to the back of the quilt, and hand stitch in place.

14

In the North Woods

Almost any time of the year, scrap fabrics and traditional quilt blocks go hand-in-hand with a blazing fire and a cup of your favorite steamy beverage to take away a north woods chill.

These bear paw blocks, set on point, are a great example of using scraps and background fabrics in high-contrast dark and light values. Nine blocks feature light-value scraps and a dark block background. The remaining four blocks use dark-value scraps and a light block background. Small 2-in. scraps in neutral colors and light and dark values coordinate with the focus print.

Pieced setting triangles, accent sashing, and inner border combine with a woodsy focus border print to complete a rustic Adirondack style. Miter the borders for an impressive finished look—it's easier to do than you might think.

This quilt uses eighteen light-value 5-in. squares, one hundred seventy-seven light-value 2-in. squares, eight dark-value 5-in. squares, and sixty-eight dark-value 2-in. squares.

FINISHED SIZE: **69 in. x 69 in.**

PATTERN DIFFICULTY: **Experienced / Intermediate**

FABRIC REQUIREMENTS

1 yd. dark solid for dark block background
$1/3$ yd. light solid for light block background
1 yd. accent for sashing and inner borders
$1/3$ yd. light coordinate for inner side setting triangles
$1\frac{1}{4}$ yd. dark coordinate for outer setting triangles
$1\frac{1}{2}$ yd. focus print for outer borders
$2/3$ yd. for binding
$4\frac{1}{4}$ yd. backing
Batting, 75 in. x 75 in.
ScrapTherapy scraps

PREPARE SCRAPS

DARK BACKGROUND BLOCKS

Select eighteen light-value 5-in. squares and one hundred fifty-three light-value 2-in. squares for the dark background blocks. Select eight dark-value 5-in. squares and sixty-eight dark-value 2-in. squares for the light background blocks. Using a pencil or fabric-marking tool, draw two diagonal lines corner-to-corner on the back of each 5-in. scrap square. **1** (See page 95.)

Select twenty-four additional light-value 2-in. squares for the cornerstones.

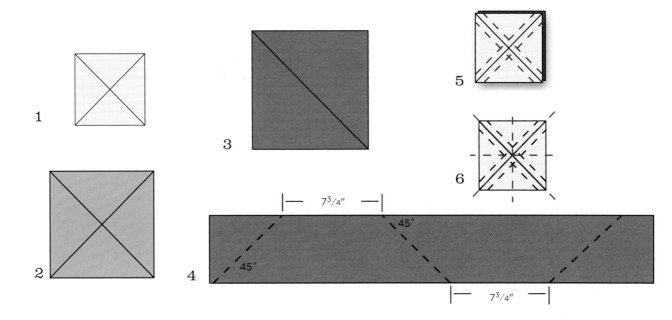

PREPARE BLOCK BACKGROUND FABRIC

DARK BLOCK BACKGROUND

Cut three 5-in. width-of-fabric strips, then cut eighteen 5-in. squares. Next, cut seven 2-in. width-of-fabric strips, then cut thirty-six 5-in. rectangles and thirty-six 2-in. squares.

LIGHT BLOCK BACKGROUND

Cut one 5-in. width-of-fabric strip, then cut eight 5-in. squares. Cut three 2-in. width-of-fabric strips, then cut sixteen 5-in. rectangles and sixteen 2-in. squares.

PREPARE OTHER FABRICS

SASHING AND INNER BORDERS

Cut two 11-in. width-of-fabric strips, then cut thirty-six 2-in. rectangles along the lengthwise grain. Cut six 1½-in. width-of-fabric strips; set aside for the inner borders.

SETTING TRIANGLES

Inner side setting triangle fabric (light value)

Cut one 8¾-in. width-of-fabric strip, then cut two 8¾-in. squares. Cut each square in half on the diagonal twice. Set aside for the setting triangles. **2**

Outer side setting triangle fabric (dark value)

Cut one 12-in. width-of-fabric strip, then cut two 12-in. squares. Cut each square in half on the diagonal. **3**

Cut four 6-in. width-of-fabric strips. Using the 45-degree bias line on your ruler, cut two trapezoid shapes from each strip. Follow the diagram to make sure the shorter parallel line is 7¾ in. Cut a total of eight trapezoids; set aside for the setting triangles. **4**

FOCUS BORDER

Cut seven 6½-in. width-of-fabric strips; set aside for the outer borders.

BINDING

Cut eight 2¼-in. width-of-fabric strips for the binding.

DARK BACKGROUND BLOCKS

Select one 5 in. light-value scrap square. Place one dark block background 5-in. square and the 5-in. scrap square, right sides together. **5**

Sew ¼ in. away from both sides of the drawn lines to make a total of four stitching lines as shown. Cut through the center four times, being careful not to move the fabric between cuts. First, make a vertical cut, 2½ in. from the edge, then a horizontal cut 2½ in. from the bottom, then diagonally on the drawn lines to make eight half-square triangle (HST) units. **6**

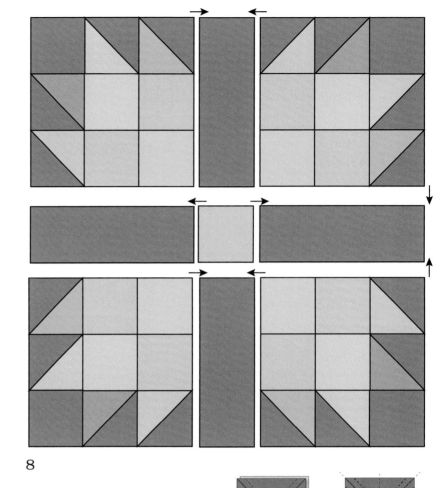

7

8

9   10

Press the HST seams toward the darker fabric. Trim each HST unit to 2 in. square.

Repeat to make a total of one hundred forty-four HST units from eighteen light-value 5-in. scraps and eighteen 5-in. dark background squares.

From the light-value 2-in. scrap squares, randomly select four HST units, four 2-in. light-value scraps, and one 2-in. background square, and arrange the parts into the bear paw subassembly. Sew and press the seams as indicated. **7**

Repeat to make thirty-six bear paw subassemblies, with light-value scraps and dark background.

Randomly select four bear paw subassemblies, one light-value 2-in. scrap square, and four 2-in. x 5-in. background rectangles. Arrange the block, sew, and press the seams as indicated. **8**

The block should measure 11 in. square. Make nine bear paw blocks with a dark background.

LIGHT BACKGROUND BLOCKS

Pair one light block background 5-in. square and a 5-in. scrap square, right sides together.

Sew 1/4 in. away from both sides of the drawn lines to make a total of

four stitching lines as shown. **9**

Cut through the center four times, being careful not to move the fabric between cuts. First, make a vertical cut 2 1/2 in. from the edge, then a horizontal cut 2 1/2 in. from the bottom, then diagonally on the drawn lines to make eight HST units. **10**

Press the HST unit seams toward the darker fabric. Trim each HST unit to 2 in. square. Repeat to make a

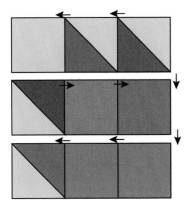

11

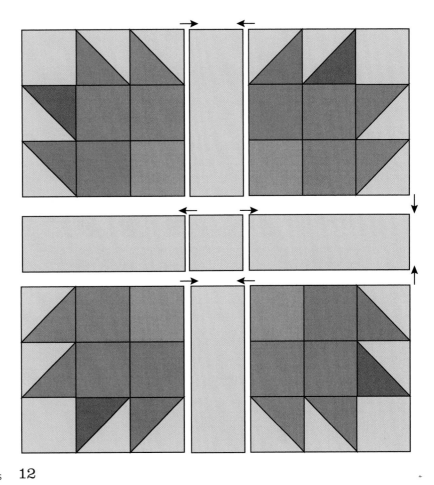

12

total of sixty-four HST units from eight dark-value 5-in. scraps and eight 5-in. light background squares.

From the dark-value 2-in. scrap squares, randomly select four HST units, four 2-in. light-value scraps, and one 2-in. background square. Arrange parts into a bear paw sub-assembly. Sew and press the seams as indicated. **11**

Repeat to make sixteen bear paw subassemblies, with dark-value scraps and a light background. Randomly select four bear paw subassemblies, one light-value 2-in. scrap square, and four 2-in. x 5-in. background rect-angles. Arrange the block, sew, and press the seams as indicated. **12**

The block should measure 11 in. square. Make four bear paw blocks with a light background.

MAKE SIDE-SETTING TRIANGLES

Center and sew the long side of each inner side-setting triangle to the short side of each outer setting triangle trapezoid section. Press the seam toward the trapezoid. Make eight pieced side-setting triangles. **13**

ASSEMBLE QUILT CENTER

Arrange the blocks, sashing strips, cornerstones, and setting triangles in diagonal rows. First, sew the sashing strips and the cornerstones in rows, then sew the sashing and press the seams toward the sashing strips. Sew the blocks and sash-ing strips in rows; press the seams toward the sashing. Sew the sashing rows to the block rows as shown.

13

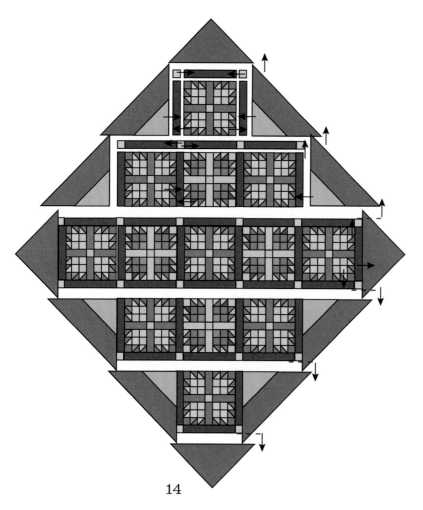

14

Add the setting triangles. Trim the setting triangle points, if desired, as the rows with setting triangles are sewn together. Press the row seams toward the center. **14**

The quilt top should measure approximately 55 in. square. Trim to straighten the sides, if necessary. Blocks, sashing strips, and corner-stones will float.

MITERED BORDER

Sew three 1½-in. inner border strips end-to-end with diagonal seams (see page 194). Press the connecting seams open.

Cut the strip in half to make two inner border strips approximately 60 in. Repeat with the remaining three strips to make a total of four inner borders.

Sew all seven 6½-in. focus border strips end-to-end, with diagonal seams. Press the connecting seams open. Cut the border strip in half

twice to make four focus borders approximately 70 in.

Center and sew each inner border to each focus border. For two border units, press the seams toward the inner border. For the remaining two border units, press the seams toward the focus border.

Mitered borders make a neat, picture-frame finish at the corners. They're especially nice when using striped fabrics. Some quilters are apprehensive about adding mitered borders, but they are easy to do. Once the borders are attached to the quilt, work each corner start to finish, then move on to the next corner. If you prefer, inner and focus borders may be applied with traditional piecing instead of mitering. To make a traditional pieced border, follow the instructions on page 37 to measure the quilt for borders, then add the inner borders to opposite sides, and finish with the top and bottom borders. Follow with the focus borders in the same order.

Center and sew the bottom borders to each side of the quilt, starting and stopping sewing ¼ in. from each edge of the quilt top as shown. Be sure the borders with seams pressed similarly are on opposite sides of the quilt top. **15**

At one corner, fold the quilt top in half diagonally, right sides together. Match the outside edge of the borders in a straight line. Finger-press the seam between the border and quilt top toward the quilt center and lay it flat on the work surface. Place a straight ruler with a 45-degree angle on top of the folded quilt. Place the 45-degree line even with the border outside edges, and the straight edge even with the diagonal fold on the quilt top.

Draw a line with a pencil or fabric-marking tool from the end of the seam to the edge of the border along the 45-degree angle. **16**

Secure with pins along the drawn line, matching the seam intersections between the inner and outer borders. Carefully transfer the quilt to a sewing table and sew directly on the line, starting at the border seam intersection and sewing outward toward the quilt edge.

Return to the work table and trim to a 1/4-in. seam allowance to the outside of the mitered seam. Repeat the above steps for each of the remaining three corners. When all corners are sewn, press from the back, pressing the mitered seam open and the quilt/border seam toward the border. Then press the entire assembly from the front.

QUILT AND BIND

Layer the backing, batting, and quilt top; quilt as desired. Sew eight 2 1/4-in. binding strips together end-to-end using a diagonal seam. Press the connecting seams open, then press the binding in half lengthwise, wrong sides together. With raw edges aligned, sew the binding to the front of the quilt using a 1/4-in. seam. Miter the binding at the corners (see page 46). Turn the folded edge of the binding to the back of the quilt, and hand stitch in place.

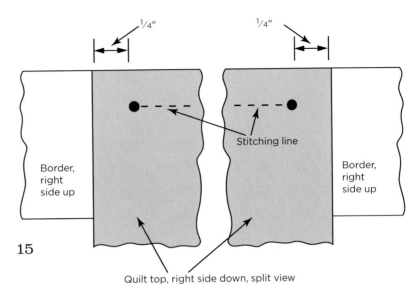

1/4" 1/4"

Stitching line

Border, right side up

Border, right side up

15

Quilt top, right side down, split view

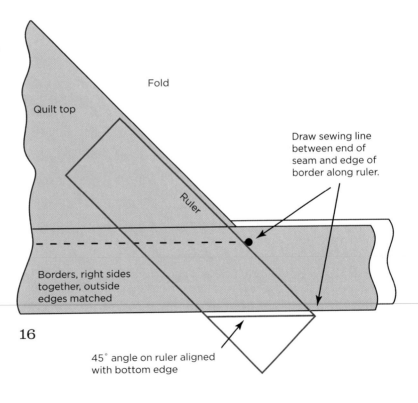

Fold

Quilt top

Draw sewing line between end of seam and edge of border along ruler.

Ruler

Borders, right sides together, outside edges matched

16

45° angle on ruler aligned with bottom edge

Lightning Strikes Twice

The key to this quilt's beauty is to select fabrics with strong color contrast. Choose scraps from three distinct values—dark, medium, and light—to create a primary and secondary lightning strike when the blocks are set in vertical rows.

The quilt blocks may be made using 5-in. or 3½-in. scrap squares; either way, the finished quilt is the same size.

The samples, one made from 5-in. squares in red and black, and one made from 3½-in. squares in orange and gold, each coordinate with the outer border focus print. The neutral sashing strips provide the "calm in the storm." Since the block sections are trued up before they are sewn into the quilt, I recommend the Tucker Trimmer™ tool to make the task a breeze.

To soften the angles and corners predominant in this quilt, use an extra-wide scallop border, made simple using Korner Radial Rules™.

Since this quilt can be made with either 5-in. or 3½-in. squares, the requisite listing is for the larger blocks and the amounts needed for the smaller ones are given in parentheses.

Main zigzag (medium): one hundred eight 5-in. squares (two hundred eighty-eight 3½-in. squares)

Secondary zigzag (dark): fifty-four 5-in. squares (one hundred forty-four 3½-in. squares)

Background (light): fifty-four 5-in. squares (one hundred forty-four 3½-in. squares)

FINISHED SIZE: **77 in. x 76 in.**
PATTERN DIFFICULTY: **Intermediate**

FABRIC AND NOTION REQUIREMENTS

2½ yd. focus fabric for outer borders

2 yd. neutral print for vertical sashing and
   inner borders

⅝ yd. for binding

4¾ yd. for backing

Batting, 80 in. x 84 in.

Ruler with bias lines

Tucker Trimmer (optional)

Radial Rule (optional)

ScrapTherapy scraps

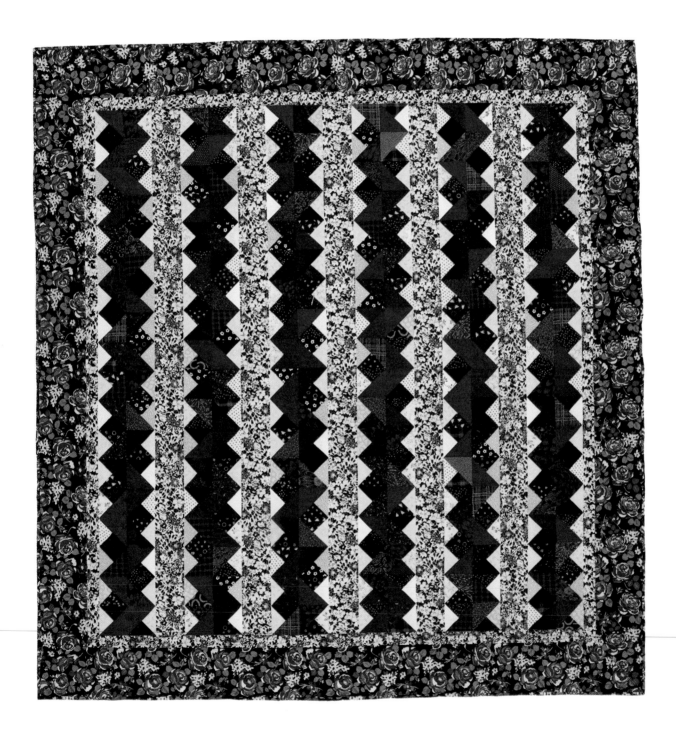

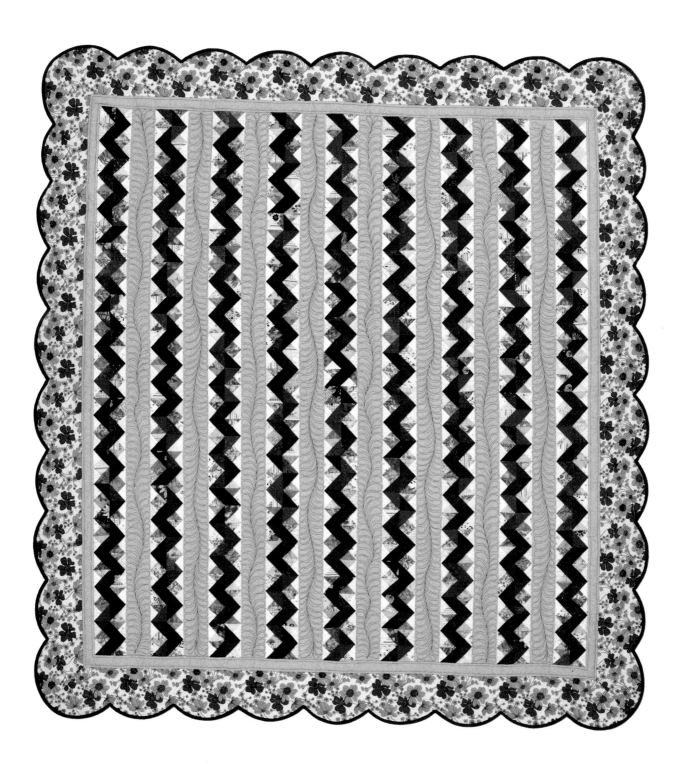

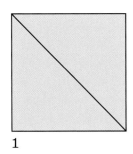

1

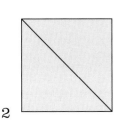

2

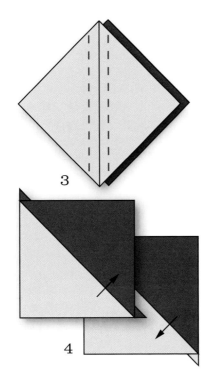

3

4

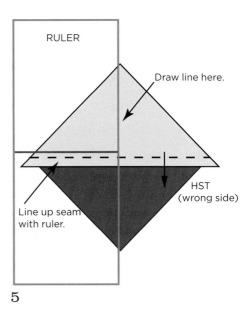

RULER

Draw line here.

Line up seam
with ruler.

HST
(wrong side)

5

PREPARE SCRAPS FOR 5-IN. SQUARES

BLOCKS

Using a pencil or fabric-marking tool, draw a diagonal line corner-to-corner on the back of each light background scrap square. **1**

PREPARE SASHING AND BORDER FABRICS FOR USE WITH 5-IN. SQUARES

VERTICAL SASHING AND INNER BORDERS

Along the lengthwise grain, cut five 4-in. strips for the vertical sashing and four 2-in. strips for the inner border.

OUTER BORDERS

Along the lengthwise grain, cut four 6½-in. strips.

NOTE: You have enough focus fabric to cut four lengthwise 2¼-in. strips for the binding, if desired.

PREPARE SCRAPS FOR 3½-IN. SQUARES

Using a pencil or fabric-marking tool, draw a diagonal line corner-to-corner on the back of each light background scrap square. **2**

PREPARE SASHING AND BORDER FABRICS FOR USE WITH 3½-IN. SQUARES

VERTICAL SASHING AND INNER BORDERS

Along the lengthwise grain, cut eight 3½-in. strips for vertical sashing and four 2-in. strips for the inner borders.

OUTER BORDERS

Along the lengthwise grain, cut four 6½-in. strips.

NOTE: You have enough focus fabric to cut four lengthwise 2¼-in. strips for the binding, if desired.

BINDING

Cut eight 2¼-in. width-of-fabric strips for the binding.

BLOCKS USING 5-IN. SQUARES

MAKE HALF-SQUARE TRIANGLE (HST) UNITS

Pair a 5-in. background square with a 5-in. secondary square, right sides together, and sew ¼ in. on either side of the drawn line. Cut on the drawn line. **3**

Press the seams for one-half of the HST units toward the secondary fabric and the other half toward the light background fabric. **4**

Make a total of one hundred eight HST units. It's not necessary to trim the blocks to size or to trim dog-ears.

MAKE HALF-SQUARE/QUARTER-SQUARE TRIANGLE (HSQS) UNITS

Working on the back of each HST unit, one at a time, use a straight-

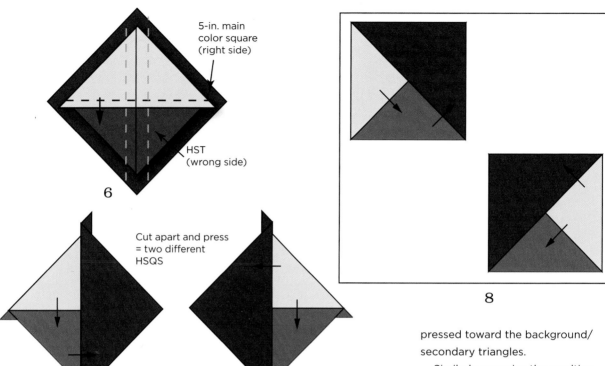

5-in. main
color square
(right side)

HST
(wrong side)

6

Cut apart and press
= two different
HSQS

7

8

edge ruler to align the HST seam with a horizontal line at the center of the ruler. Using a pencil or fabric-marking tool, draw a line corner-to-corner on the back of each pieced square perpendicular to the existing seam. **5**

NOTE: The line may not exactly intersect the HST corners.

Organize the HST units in two separate stacks based on the seam-pressing direction. Starting with the stack of HST units pressed toward the secondary color, pair and center a 5-in. main color square with a HST unit, right sides together with HST facing up. Sew 1/4 in. on either side of the drawn line. (The HST unit will be

smaller than the 5-in. square.) Cut on the drawn line. **6**

Press the seam toward the large main color triangle. Make one hundred eight HSQS units with seams pressed toward the main color triangle. **7**

NOTE: As you press, organize the resulting HSQS units into two stacks as shown. The resulting HSQS units look similar, but the placement of the secondary and background colors will be different. Be careful! **8**

Continue sewing the main color 5-in. squares to the second stack of HSTs with seams pressed toward the background. Make one hundred eight HSQS units with seams

pressed toward the background/secondary triangles.

Similarly, organize the resulting HSQS units into two stacks. The four stacks of HSQS units make up the blocks. **9**

Trim each HSQS unit to 4 in. square. To trim, align a diagonal seam with the 45-degree bias line on the ruler and place the center seam intersection at the 2-in. mark.

The Tucker Trimmer is similar to a square ruler with a bias line, except the Trimmer has only one bias line in one direction and several square-up bias lines in the opposite direction. It's perfectly suited to trim units that incorporate quarter-square triangles. The ruler lines will cross directly over the seam intersection at the center of the scrap unit. Trim all four sides of the block part. Refer to product instructions for additional details.

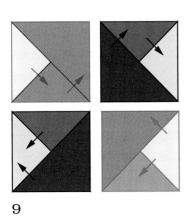

9

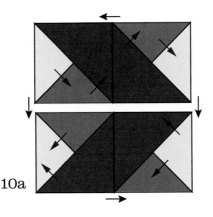

10a

11

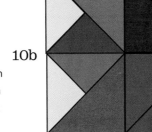

10b

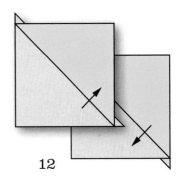

12

Make a total of two hundred sixteen HSQS units, fifty-four of each configuration. Carefully replace each trimmed HSQS unit in the four-stack arrangement as shown. **9**

ASSEMBLE BLOCKS

Following the arranged stacks, sew each block into a four-patch, pressing the seams as shown. **10a** Notice that the block is not symmetrical! Make fifty-four scrappy blocks, each measuring 7½ in. square. **10b**

BLOCKS USING 3½-IN. SQUARES

MAKE HALF-SQUARE TRIANGLE UNITS

Pair a 3½-in. background square with a 3½-in. secondary color scrap square, right sides together, and sew ¼ in. on either side of the drawn line. Cut on the drawn line. **11**

Press the seams for one-half of the HST units toward the secondary color fabric, and press the seams for the other half toward the light background fabric. **12**

Make a total of two hundred eighty-eight HST units, one hundred forty-four pressed toward the secondary color and one hundred forty-four pressed toward the light background. It's not necessary to trim the blocks to size or to trim dog-ears.

MAKE HALF-SQUARE/QUARTER-SQUARE TRIANGLE (HSQS) UNITS

Working on the back of each HST unit, one at a time, use a straight-edge ruler to align the HST seam with a horizontal line in the center of the ruler. Using a pencil or fabric-marking tool, draw a line corner-to-corner on the back of each secondary color/light scrap square perpendicular to the existing seam as shown.

NOTE: The line may not exactly intersect the HST corners. **13**

Organize the HSTs in two separate stacks based on the pressing direction. Starting with the stack of HST units pressed toward the secondary color, pair and center a 3½-in. main color square with a HST unit, right sides together with the HST facing up. Sew ¼ in. on either side of the drawn line. (The HST will be smaller than the 3½-in. square.) Cut on the drawn line. **14**

Press the seam toward the large main color triangle. Make two hundred eighty-eight HSQS units with seams pressed toward the main color triangle. **15**

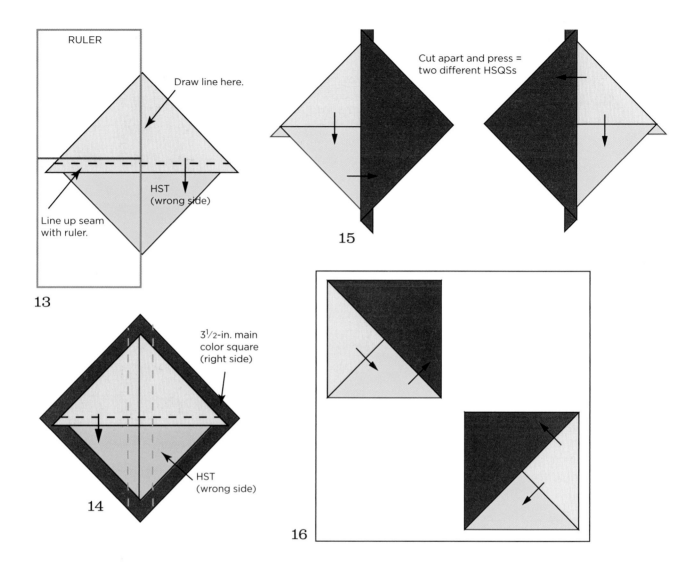

RULER

Draw line here.

HST
(wrong side)

Line up seam
with ruler.

13

Cut apart and press =
two different HSQSs

15

3½-in. main
color square
(right side)

HST
(wrong side)

14

16

Arrange the resulting HSQS units into two stacks as shown. **16**

Continue sewing the main color 3½-in. squares to the second stack of HST units pressed toward the background. Make two hundred eighty-eight HSQS units with seams pressed toward the background/secondary triangles. Similarly, organize the resulting HSQS units into two stacks. Four stacks of HSQS units make up the block.

Trim each HSQS unit to 2½ in. To trim, align a diagonal seam with the 45-degree bias line on the ruler and place the center seam intersection at the 1¼-in. mark.

Refer to the Tucker Trimmer tip box in the 5-in. scrap block instructions (see page 104).

Make a total of five hundred seventy-six HSQS units, one hundred forty-four of each configuration. Carefully place each trimmed HSQS unit in the four-stack arrangement as shown. **17**

ASSEMBLE BLOCKS

Following the arranged stacks, sew each block into a four-patch. Press the seams as shown. Notice that the block is not symmetrical! Make one hundred forty-four scrappy blocks, each measuring 4½ in. square. **18, 19**

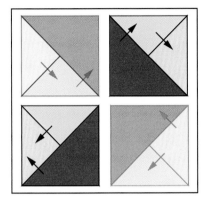

17

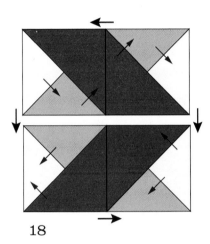

18

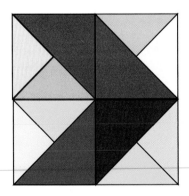

19

ASSEMBLE QUILT TOP MADE FROM 5-IN. SCRAPS

VERTICAL BLOCK ROWS

Randomly arrange and sew nine blocks in a vertical row and make six rows. **20**

VERTICAL SASHING

Measure the block row length. Trim each 4-in. sashing strip to match the length (approximately 63½ in.). If the block rows are different lengths, check the seam allowances and pressing accuracy and adjust as necessary to match the length of the trimmed sashing strips. Sew the sashing strips between the block rows and press the seams toward the sashing.

BORDERS

Trim the inner border strips to 2 in. x 63½ in. for the sides and 2 in. x 63 in. for the top and bottom borders. Trim the outer border strips to 6½ in. x 66½ in. for the sides and 6½ in. x 75 in. for the top and bottom.

ASSEMBLE QUILT TOP MADE FROM 3½-IN. SCRAPS

VERTICAL BLOCK ROWS

Randomly arrange and sew sixteen blocks in a vertical row and make nine rows. **21**

VERTICAL SASHING

Measure the block row length. Trim each 3½-in. sashing strip to match the length (approximately 64½ in.). If the block rows are different lengths, check the seam allowances and pressing accuracy and adjust as necessary to match the length of

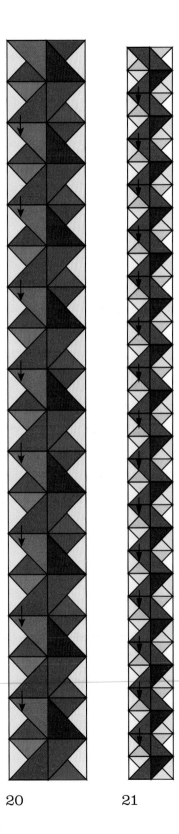

20   21

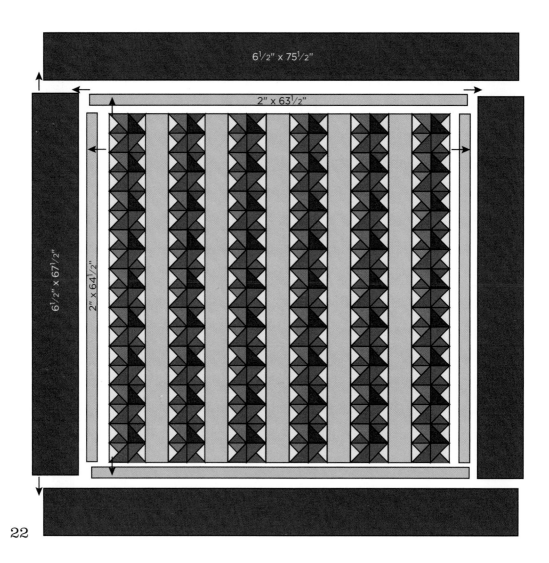

6½" x 75½"

2" x 63½"

6½" x 67½"

2" x 64½"

22

the trimmed sashing strips. Sew the sashing strips between the block rows and press the seams toward the sashing.

BORDERS

Trim the inner border strips to 2 in. x 64½ in. for the sides and 2 in. x 63½ in. for top and bottom borders. Trim the outer border strips to 6½ in. x 67½ in. for the sides and 6½ in. x 75½ in. for the top and bottom.

ATTACH BORDERS

Sew the inner side borders to the quilt top, then add the top and bottom borders. Press the seams toward the border after each addition. Sew the outer side borders to the quilt top, then add the top and bottom borders. Press the seams toward the border after each addition. **22, 23**

OPTIONAL SCALLOPED BORDER

Use your favorite method to shape the scalloped border if desired, or follow the instructions with the Radial Rule. The quilt may also have straight edges, depending on your preference.

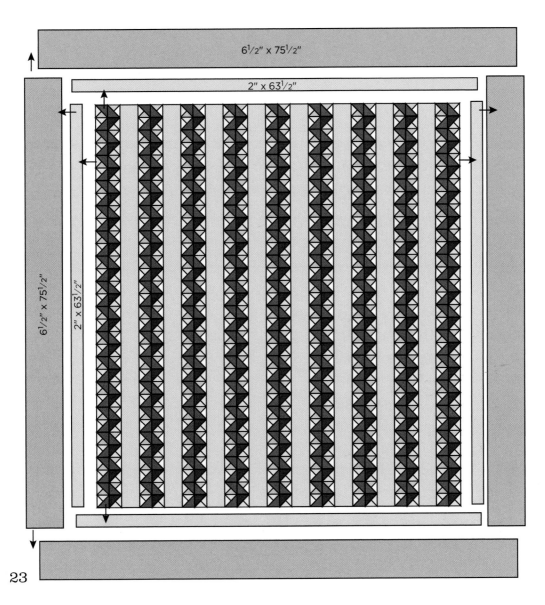

6¹/₂" x 75¹/₂"

2" x 63¹/₂"

6¹/₂" x 75¹/₂"

2" x 63¹/₂"

23

QUILT AND BIND

Layer the backing, batting, and quilt top; quilt as desired. Sew eight 2¹/₄-in. binding strips together end-to-end using a diagonal seam (see page 194). Press the connecting seams open, then press the binding in half length-wise, wrong sides together. With raw edges aligned, sew the binding to the front of the quilt using a ¹/₄-in. seam. Miter the binding at the corners (see page 46). Turn the folded edge of the binding to the back of the quilt, and hand stitch in place.

For a scalloped border, an additional length of bias cut binding will be needed. You may be using the *Katie Lane Radial Scallop Rule* and *Handbook.* If so, please refer to instructions for the binding length calculation.

Scrap Sack

The **Scrap Sack** is a basic oversized tote. It holds up to three ScrapTherapy bins with ample space to slip a 12-in. rotating cutting mat and a few rulers alongside the bins. It's perfect for class or a quilting getaway. The Scrap Sack support, a clear acrylic liner for the bag bottom, keeps the tote looking tidy.

As a bonus, the **Scrap Sack** doubles nicely as a reusable shopping tote! On Saturday mornings, I head to the farmer's market in style, and fresh veggies and treats find their way home in this roomy bag. The bag's also great for travel as it folds flat when not in use.

It seems every time I take this tote out on the town, I receive compliments from the most unlikely sources. No one needs to know it's made from scrappy leftover fabrics!

This project uses seventy-eight dark-value 3½-in. squares and one hundred fifty-six light-value 2-in. squares.

FINISHED SIZE: 15 in. x 18 in. x 9 in.
PATTERN DIFFICULTY: Intermediate

FABRIC REQUIREMENTS

1³/₄ yd. medium-value fabric for sides, lining, and handles
¼ yd. (or fat quarter) coordinate for pocket (directional fabrics not recommended)
Batting, lightweight, 1¼ yd. x 45 in. wide
ScrapTherapy scraps

OPTIONAL NOTION:
Scrap Sack support, 7½-in. x 16¼-in. clear acrylic piece for interior support in bottom

PREPARE SCRAPS
MAIN PANEL
Select seventy-eight dark-value 3½-in. scrap squares. Next, select one hundred fifty-six light-value 2-in. scrap squares.

PREPARE LINING, SIDE PANELS, AND HANDLES
Cut one 20-in. width-of-fabric strip for lining. Next, cut two 10-in. width-of-fabric strips; trim each strip to make two 10-in. x 31-in. rectangles for the side panels. Cut four 5-in. width-of-fabric strips for the handles.

PREPARE POCKET
Cut one 8½-in. width-of-fabric strip, then cut one 8½-in. x 15-in. rectangle.

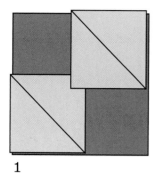

1

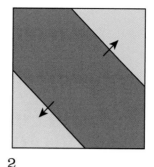

2

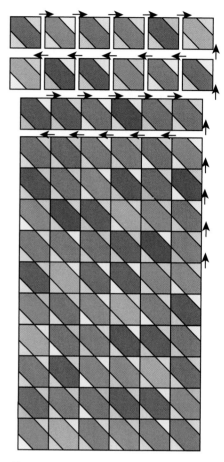

3

PREPARE BATTING

Cut one 21-in. strip, then cut one 21-in. x 42-in. rectangle for the main panel. Cut one 11-in. strip, then cut two 11-in. x 16-in. rectangles for the side panels. Cut four 1¼-in. strips for the handles.

MAIN PANEL

MAKE STRETCHED STAR UNITS

On the back of each 2-in. scrap square, draw a diagonal line corner-to-corner.

Randomly pair each 3½-in. scrap square with two 2-in. scrap squares.

Place 2-in. scrap squares, one at a time, on opposite corners of the 3½-in. scrap square, right sides together, and sew on the drawn line. **1**

Press the small scrap square toward the corners of the 3½-in. square as shown. **2**

Chain-piece to make seventy-eight stretched star units that measure 3½ in. square.

ASSEMBLE MAIN PANEL

Randomly select and arrange stretched star units in rows of six. Sew the rows and press the seams to one side. Make thirteen rows, alternating the seam-pressing direction. Sew the rows to make the pieced top for the main panel. Press the row seams in one direction. **3**

When sewing multiple sack layers together, use a walking foot for even feeding.

LAYER AND QUILT MAIN PANEL

Layer in the following order: 21-in. x 42-in. batting rectangle, 20-in. main panel lining right side up, and pieced main panel right side down. Secure all layers with pins all the way around the edge of the pieced main panel. Sew ¼ in. from the raw edge of the pieced panel all the way around, leaving an 8-in. opening in the center of one long side of the pieced panel for turning. Backstitch at each open end to reinforce the opening.

Trim the lining and batting even with the pieced top and clip corners diagonally to reduce bulk. Remove all pins and turn right side out through the opening. Topstitch the opening closed. Topstitch across each short end of the main panel ¼ in. from the edge. Pin-baste and quilt the main panel as desired.

POCKET

MAKE POCKET

Fold and press the 8½-in. x 15-in. pocket rectangle in half wrong sides together to make a rectangle 8½ in. x 7½ in.

Topstitch across the folded pocket edge ⅛ in. from the fold. **4**

ATTACH POCKET

Place the quilted main panel on a large work surface, pieced side up. Select one five-row section to be the bag front. Center the open raw edge of the pocket about 1 in. from the bottom of the fourth row of piecing. **5**

Sew the pocket onto the main panel ¼ in. from the raw edges, backstitching at each end.

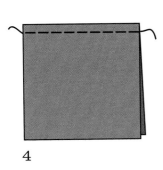

4

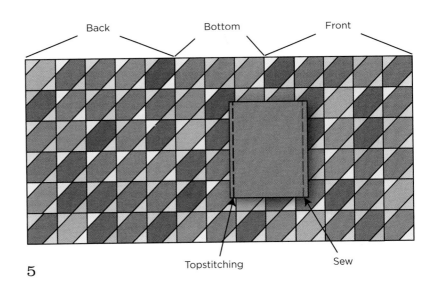

Back   Bottom   Front

Topstitching   Sew

5

NOTE: The main panel consists of three sections. Five pieced rows on each end will be the sack front and back. The center three rows will be the bottom of the sack.

Press the pocket toward the top of the main panel front. Pin the pocket sides in place. **6**

HANDLES

MAKE HANDLES

Sew the four handle strips together end-to-end with diagonal seaming to make one long strip. Press the seam allowances open. **7**

Trim the handle strip to 132 in. long. Connect the ends as shown to make a continuous, untwisted loop. Press the seams open. Press the entire loop in half lengthwise, wrong sides together, then press the edges to the center fold. **8** (See page 114.)

Working with small sections at a time, open the pressed folds and place the 1¼-in. batting strips next to the center fold, then fold the edges of the handle fabric back to the center, encasing the batting strips. **9** (See page 114.)

Fold the handle in half again and pin the edges together. **10, 11** (See page 114.)

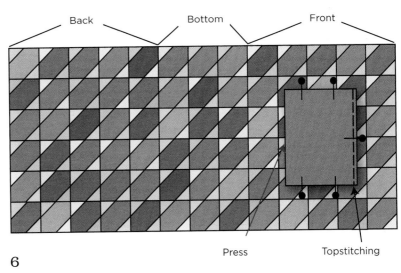

Back   Bottom   Front

Press   Topstitching

6

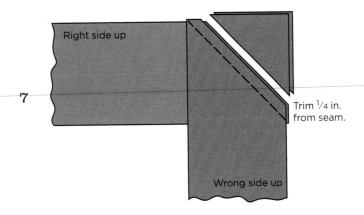

Right side up

Wrong side up

Trim ¼ in. from seam.

7

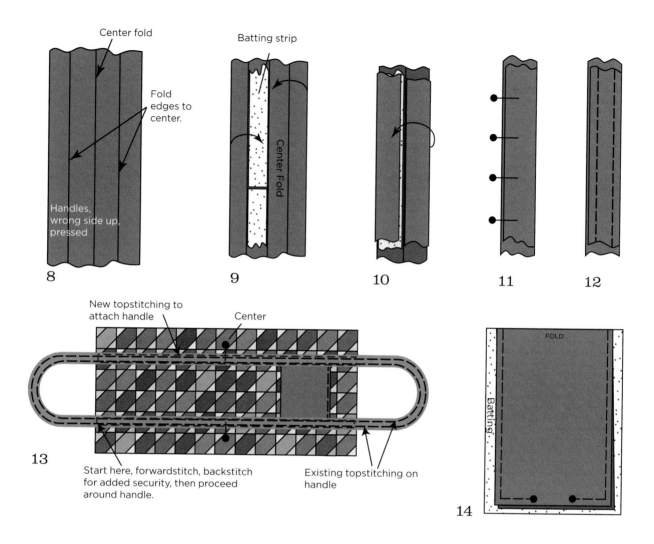

Center fold

Fold edges to center.

Handles, wrong side up, pressed

8

Batting strip

Center Fold

9

10

11

12

New topstitching to attach handle

Center

13

Start here, forwardstitch, backstitch for added security, then proceed around handle.

Existing topstitching on handle

FOLD

Batting

14

Continue in this manner until the entire handle length has batting inside. Topstitch 1/4 in. from both handle edges to hold the batting in place. **12**

ATTACH HANDLES TO MAIN PANEL
Place the main panel on a large work surface, pieced side up. Fold the handle loop in half to find the centers and pin-mark. Place the handle loop on the main panel, centering it along the second pieced row from each . with the handle and pin the handle in place securely. Topstitch the handle

to the main panel 1/8 in. from each long edge and across the handle width at each end, backstitching the ends for reinforcement. **13**

SIDE PANELS
MAKE SIDE PANELS
Fold and press the side panels in half, right sides together to make a folded rectangle approximately 10 in. x 15 1/2 in.

On a flat work surface, layer the batting and a folded side panel, with the short edge of the batting aligned

with the folded edge of the side panel. Pin all edges in place.

Sew the side and lower edges of the side panel, leaving a 4-in. opening for turning. Trim the batting even with the side panel and turn right-side out through the opening. **14**

Pin the opening edges and top-stitch across the entire panel width 1/8 in. from the edge. Topstitch 1/4 in. from the upper fold. Repeat to make two side panels.

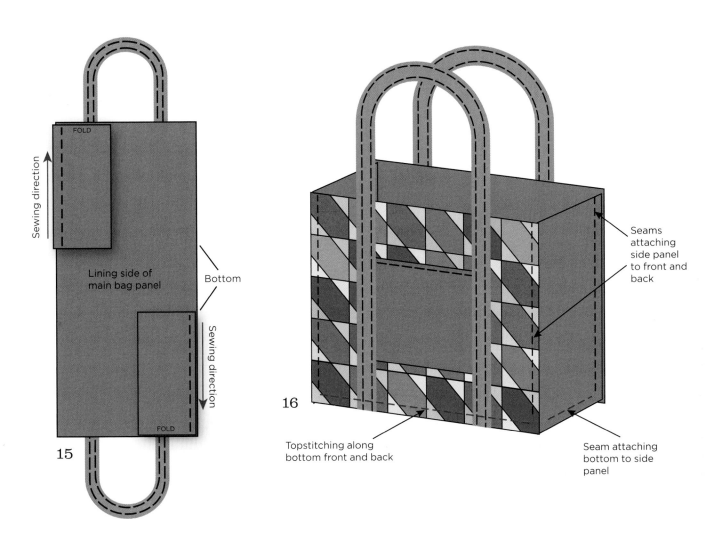

FOLD

Sewing direction

Lining side of
main bag panel

Bottom

Sewing direction

FOLD

15

Seams
attaching
side panel
to front and
back

16

Topstitching along
bottom front and back

Seam attaching
bottom to side
panel

FINAL ASSEMBLY

SIDES

With the main panel lining facing
you, pin one side panel to the main
panel front wrong sides together.
Sew the pieces together ³/₈ in. from
the edge, backstitching at the upper
and lower ends. In a similar manner,
attach the remaining side panel to
the main panel back. **15**

Sew the remaining sides of the
side panels to the main panel in the
same manner.

LOWER EDGE

Sew the side panel lower edges to
the main panel in the same manner,
carefully flattening the seam to fit
under the presser foot. Sew slowly
and start and stop ³/₈ in. from the
corner intersections, backstitching
to secure. Topstitch ³/₈ in. away from
the fold along the main panel front
and back to box the bag. Carefully
flatten the seam, then start and stop
sewing ³/₈ in. from the corner intersections, backstitching to secure. **16**

NOTE: The seams attaching the
side panels to the main panel and
lower edge topstitching will not
intersect.

OPTIONAL: Insert the acrylic support
into the bag bottom.

Table Stripes Runner

Fast and easy, **Table Stripes Runner** is a perfect use for small scrap fabrics as well as leftover border stripe fabric. Consider holiday or seasonal prints for a festive table setting.

Since the backing is not pieced, the border stripe width determines how many scraps are needed for the runner center. Choose small scraps in light and medium/dark values to coordinate with the border stripe fabric.

With a runner this pretty, does anyone really need to know you're serving up leftover fabrics to dress up your centerpiece? This project uses up to eighty 2-in. light scrap squares and eighty 2-in. medium/dark scrap squares.

FINISHED SIZE: **15 in. x 42 in.**

PATTERN DIFFICULTY: **Easy**

FABRIC REQUIREMENTS

1 fat quarter border stripe fabric with at least two complete repeating stripes

1/8 yd. solid for side borders

1/4 yd. binding

1/2 yd. backing

Batting, 16 in. x 44 in.

ScrapTherapy scraps

PREPARE BORDER STRIPE AND BACKING

From the border stripe fabric, carefully cut two matching, equal-width stripes at least 6½ in. wide. Remember to add ¼-in. seam allowance above and below the chosen stripe design. Press the backing and lay it flat on a work surface, right side up or down, it does not matter.

> Border stripe prints come in a variety of sizes and repeating patterns. This table runner can accommodate almost any border stripe size.

Align the cut border stripes on top of each end of the backing fabric. Measure the backing fabric between the border stripes and divide by 3. Round down to determine the number of scrappy rows. **1**

Multiply the number of scrappy rows by 8 (the runner has eight squares across) to determine the number of light and dark coordinating colors needed (an equal number of each). Set the border stripes and backing aside for final assembly and quilt completion.

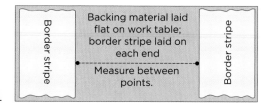

1

To avoid piecing the backing and to determine how many rows of scraps to sew together, do some easy math. The number of scrappy rows is determined by the selvage-to-selvage width of the backing material and the width of the cut border stripe.

Example: If the distance between the border stripes is 29 in., divide 29 by 3. The result is 9.7, or 9 rounded down. The table runner will have nine rows. Now, multiply 9 by 8. The result is 72. So, 72 dark and 72 light 2-in. squares are needed.

PREPARE SCRAPS

SCRAPPY ROWS

Select the number of 2-in. squares needed from various light prints and an equal number of 2-in. squares from various medium/dark prints.

PREPARE BORDERS AND BINDING

SIDE BORDERS

Cut two 2-in. width-of-fabric strips.

BINDING

Cut three 2¼-in. width-of-fabric strips for the binding.

MAKE SCRAPPY CENTER

Sew each light-value 2-in. scrap square to each medium/dark 2-in. scrap square. Press seams toward the darker fabric. Sew the resulting two-patch units in pairs, right sides together, with dark fabric facing light fabric, to make four-patches. Each four-patch measures 3½ in. square. **2**

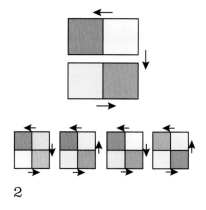

2

Sew the four-patch units into four rows, keeping the dark square in the upper left corner. Flip the adjoining four-patches so the horizontal center seams interlock. Remember, the number of rows assembled is based on your earlier calculation. To complete the scrappy center, sew the rows together. Press the seams in one direction.

ASSEMBLE RUNNER TOP

SIDE BORDERS AND BORDER STRIPE

Sew one side border to each long side of the scrappy center; trim the excess length and press the seams toward the side borders.

Add border stripes on each runner end; trim excess length and press the seams toward the border stripe.

NOTE: If your border stripe is a directional print, the lower edge should face outward on both ends. **3**

QUILT AND BIND

Layer the backing, batting, and quilt top; quilt as desired. Sew three 2¼-in. binding strips together end-to-end using a diagonal seam

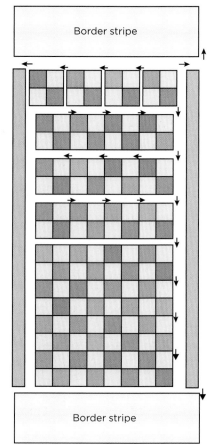

3

(see page 194). Press the connecting seams open, then press the binding in half lengthwise, wrong sides together. With raw edges aligned, sew the binding to the front of the runner using a ¼-in. seam. Miter the binding at the corners (see page 46). Turn the folded edge of the binding to the back of the runner, and hand stitch in place.

Fly Away

If you've never used Paintstiks® before and you've been intrigued by them, this quilt offers a terrific opportunity to test the waters. Paintstiks are oil paints packaged like a crayon.

Peeling away the hardened coating that forms on the end of the stick exposes a soft center of oil paint that can be applied directly to fabric. The paint can also be applied to a palette and brushed or painted onto the fabric. For this project, paint your block background fabric or simply select two yards of a print fabric instead.

You can make a significant dent in your 2-in. scrap collection or work with your 5-in. scrap stacks. Either way, this quilt creates an impressive statement with four big bold blocks.

I decided to dig into my 2-in. scraps in colors that coordinate with the Paintstik combination set of iridescent yellow, spring green, and copper. I also used a stencil set to apply the color because paints brushed onto the fabric take less time to dry than applying the paint directly with the stick.

This quilt uses eighty medium-value 5-in. squares or seven hundred twenty medium-value 2-in. squares, plus thirty-six medium-value 2-in. squares for the small cornerstones.

FINISHED SIZE: **76 in. x 76 in.**

PATTERN DIFFICULTY: Intermediate

FABRIC AND NOTION REQUIREMENTS

1³/₄ yd. for block background, either a dark-value solid to paint or a focus print to use unpainted

1 yd. dark-value solid for sashing (may be same fabric as block background fabric)

¹/₃ yd. for inner borders

1³/₄ yd. for outer borders (cut lengthwise)

²/₃ yd. for binding

4¹/₂ yd. for backing

Batting, 80 in. x 80 in.

ScrapTherapy scraps

OPTIONAL NOTIONS:

Flying geese trimming tool, such as the Wing Clipper™

ScrapTherapy Paintstik and Stencil set

¹/₄-in. stencil brush

PREPARE SCRAPS

Select seven hundred fifty-six 2-in. scrap squares for the block and cornerstone piecing, or select eighty 5-in. scrap squares for the blocks and large cornerstone piecing and thirty-six 2-in. scrap squares for the small cornerstone piecing.

> If you're using Paintstiks, pre-wash the fabrics and consider cutting the pieces about ½ in. larger than needed in both directions. After the paint is dry, trim the fabric to the sizes needed.

PREPARE BLOCK BACKGROUND FABRIC

FOCUS OR SOLID FABRIC FOR BLOCKS

If you're using a flying geese trimming tool, such as the Wing Clipper, cut the first strip 9½ in. instead of 9¼ in.—the extra will be trimmed after sewing the flying geese units.

Cut two 9¼-in. width-of-fabric strips, then cut eight 9¼-in. squares for flying geese in blocks.

Cut one 6¼-in. width-of-fabric strip, then cut four 6¼-in. squares for the block centers.

Cut six 5-in. width-of-fabric strips, then cut forty 5-in. squares for the block and large cornerstone piecing.

SASHING

Cut one 24½-in. width-of-fabric strip, then cut ten 3½-in. x 24½-in. strips along the lengthwise grain. Next, cut two 3½-in. width-of-fabric strips, then cut two 24½-in. strips, for a total of twelve 3½-in. x 24½-in. strips.

INNER BORDER

Cut six 1½-in. width-of-fabric strips.

OUTER BORDER PRINT

Along the lengthwise grain, cut four 8½-in. x 59½-in. strips.

BINDING

Cut eight 2¼-in. width-of-fabric strips for the binding.

MAKE NINE-PATCHES

> You may use 2-in. scrap squares or 5-in. scrap squares for the pieced block elements. If you are using 2-in. scraps, make nine-patches.

Sew seven hundred twenty 2-in. scraps randomly into eighty nine-patches. Nine-patch blocks may be monochromatic or multicolor as shown. **1**

Seam-pressing direction at the outside of the block is not critical. Nine-patch blocks should measure 5 in. square.

Using a square ruler, trim thirty-two 5-in. scrap squares or 5-in. nine-patch blocks to 4⅞-in. square. For nine-patches, center the middle square when you trim to size. If you're using a trimming tool, do not trim the nine-patches. Set these thirty-two scrap blocks aside for the flying geese units.

Using a pencil or fabric-marking tool, draw a diagonal line corner-to-corner on the back of each of the thirty-two trimmed scrap squares or nine-patch blocks. Using a pencil or fabric-marking tool, draw a diagonal line corner-to-corner on the back of

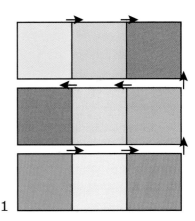

1

forty untrimmed 5-in. scrap squares or nine-patch blocks. Draw directly through the seam intersections and over the seam allowances. Set these forty untrimmed scrap blocks aside for half-square triangle units (HST).

PAINT FABRICS (OPTIONAL)

Using Paintstiks, stencils, and brushes, paint each of the 9¼-in., 6¼-in., and 5-in. squares set aside earlier. Get creative and have fun—use one or more paint colors.

(For more information on colorizing, refer to the book *Paintstiks on Fabric* by Shelly Stokes.)

> Let the paint dry 24 hours, or until dry to the touch. Heat-set the paint by placing a piece of parchment paper on the ironing board. Lay the fabric on the parchment paper, paint side down, then place a hot iron on the back of the fabric, holding it in place at least 10 seconds. Pick up and move the iron until all the painted sections are set.
>
> If you cut your square sizes larger than needed, trim each shape to its appropriate size after setting the paint.

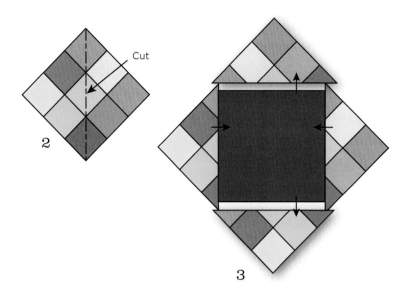
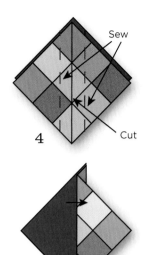

MAKE BLOCK CENTERS

Choose one 6¼-in. painted focus square and two nine-patches or 5-in. scraps, without drawn lines on the back.

Cut each nine-patch or 5-in. scrap in half along the diagonal as shown to make a total of four HSTs. **2**

Sew two HSTs to opposite sides of the 6¼-in. focus squares. Press the seams toward the focus fabric. Next, sew two HSTs to the remaining sides of the 6¼-in. focus squares. Press the seams toward the HSTs. **3**

Trim the block center to 8½ in. square. Repeat the steps above to make four block centers. Set aside.

MAKE HALF-SQUARE TRIANGLE UNITS

Choose one 5-in. painted focus square and one nine-patch or 5-in. square.

Place the focus fabric square and the scrap square right sides together.

Sew ¼ in. away from each side of the drawn line. Cut on the drawn

line and press the seam toward the focus fabric. Trim to 4½ in. square. Repeat to make eighty HST units. Set aside. **4, 5**

MAKE FLYING GEESE UNITS

Choose one 9¼-in. painted focus square and four trimmed 4⅞-in. scrap squares or nine-patches. Place one 4⅞-in. scrap square or nine-patch on opposite corners of the 9¼-in. focus square, right sides together. The raw edges of the 4⅞-in. squares should be aligned with the corner of the 9¼-in. focus square. The drawn lines on the 4⅞-in. squares should be lined up. **6**

Sew ¼ in. away from both sides of the drawn line. Cut on the drawn line and press the smaller triangles away from the larger triangle. You'll have two units that look like those shown. **7**

Align one 4⅞-in. scrap square or nine-patch, right sides together, with the remaining corner of each cut-apart unit. The raw edges of the

4⅞-in. square should be aligned with the 90-degree corner of the original 9¼-in. focus square. **8**

> If you're using a trimming tool like the Wing Clipper, be sure to check the package instructions. You may need to align the smaller square just one or two thread widths inside the larger square 90-degree corner edges.

Sew ¼ in. away from both sides of the drawn line. Cut on the drawn line and press the smaller triangle seams away from the larger triangle. Make four flying geese from the original 9¼-in. focus square and four 4⅞-in. scrap squares or nine-patches. **9**

NOTE: Repeat seven more times to make a total of thirty-two 4½-in. x 8½-in. flying geese units.

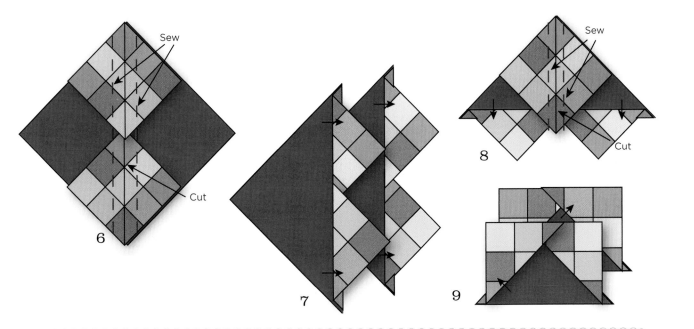

6 · Sew · Cut

7

8 · Sew · Cut

9

THE WING CLIPPER

A trimming tool allows you to sew 5-in. scrap squares or nine-patches and 9½-in. focus squares without trimming each one before sewing. Once the units are sewn, cut apart, and pressed, the tool is an easy way to trim each flying geese unit to the perfect size for piecing.

When using the Wing Clipper trimming tool, find the 8½-in. x 4½-in. "square up" rectangle. Place one flying geese unit on your cutting mat with the point down. Place the Wing Clipper tool on top of the flying geese unit and align the flying geese unit seams with the two crossed bias lines within the 8½-in. x 4½-in.

rectangle on the ruler. The point will align perfectly where the bias lines cross.

Trim along the right side and top of the geese unit. Use care when cutting across the top of the tool. **1**

Lift the Wing Clipper and turn the flying geese unit upside down. Now align the 8½-in. x 4½-in. rectangle on the ruler with the trimmed edge of the flying geese unit. Double-check that the geese unit point is aligned with the crossmark on the ruler's top edge.

Trim along the side and top. Use care when cutting across the top of the tool. **2**

Repeat to make thirty-two flying geese units.

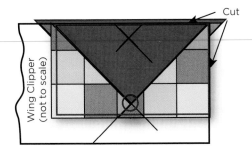

Cut

Wing Clipper (not to scale)

1

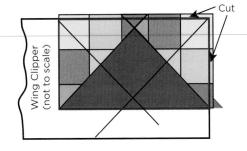

Cut

Wing Clipper (not to scale)

2

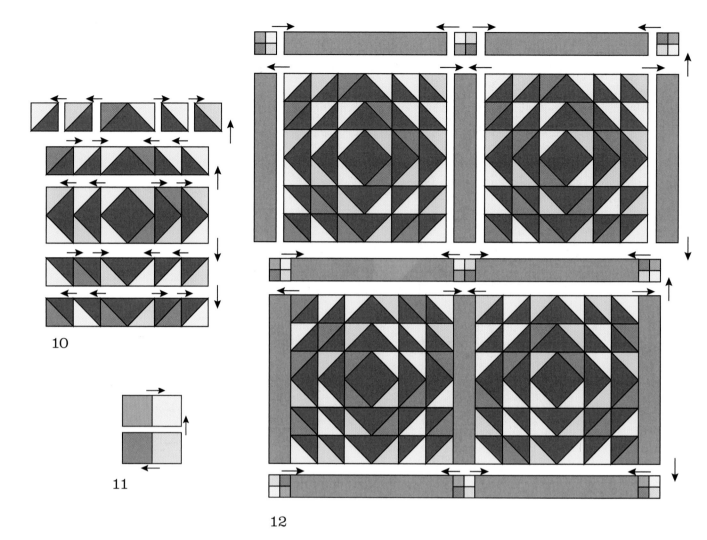

10

11

12

ASSEMBLE BLOCKS

Select one block center unit, eight flying geese units, and sixteen HST units. Arrange the blocks in rows as shown.

Sew units into rows and press the seams as indicated.

Sew the rows and press the seams as indicated. Make four 24½-in. square blocks. **10**

SASHING

Select four random 2-in. scrap squares and sew a four-patch unit as shown. Repeat to make nine four-patch units for the small cornerstones. **11**

Arrange the blocks and sew the small cornerstones, sashing, and blocks as shown, pressing the seams as indicated. **12**

ASSEMBLE QUILT

INNER BORDER

Sew six 1½-in. width-of-fabric strips together end-to-end using diagonal seaming (see page 194).

Cut the long strip into two 57½-in. strips for the side borders and two 59½-in. strips for the top and bottom borders. Sew the side borders to the quilt top, then the top and bottom borders, pressing the seams toward the border after each addition. **13**

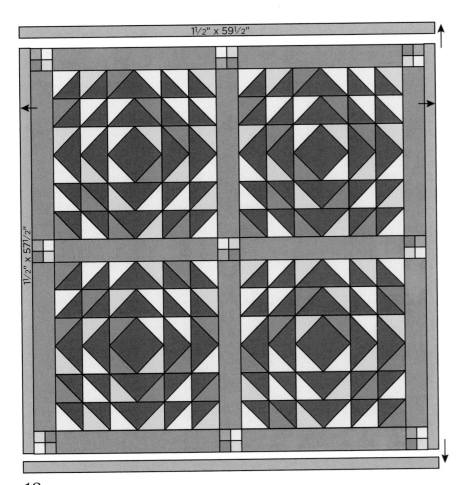

11/2" x 591/2"

11/2" x 571/2"

13

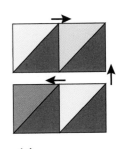

14

LARGE CORNERSTONES

Sew four HST units together as shown for the large cornerstones, which are 8½ in. square. **14**

OUTER BORDER

Sew two outer border strips to the sides of the quilt top, pressing the seams toward the border.

Sew the cornerstones on each end of the remaining border strips, then sew the strips to the top and bottom of the quilt.

CAUTION: Watch the orientation of the large cornerstones when attaching them to the border fabric.

Press seams as shown. **15** (See page 126.)

QUILT AND BIND

Layer the backing, batting, and quilt top; quilt as desired. Sew eight 2¼-in. binding strips together end-to-end using a diagonal seam (see page 194). Press the connecting

seams open, then press the binding in half lengthwise, wrong sides together. With raw edges aligned, sew the binding to the front of the quilt using a ¼-in. seam. Miter the binding at the corners (see page 46). Turn the folded edge of the binding to the back of the quilt, and hand stitch in place.

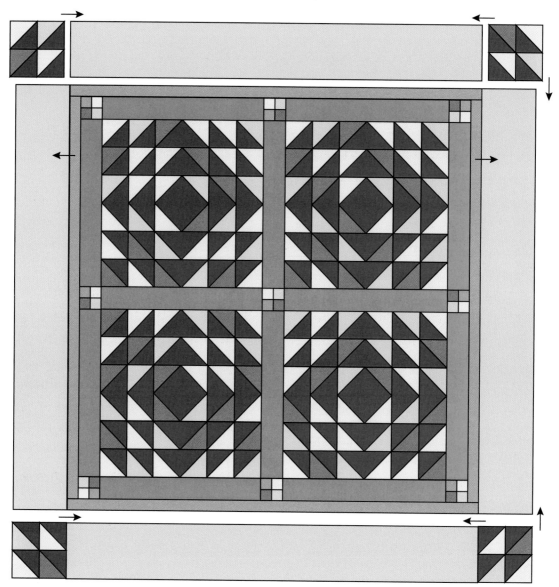

15

Bloomin' Steps

"What am I going to do with all these 2-in. scrap squares?!" Once scrap fabrics get organized, ScrapTherapy enthusiasts discover that the 2-in. scrap squares can accumulate more quickly than other scrap sizes. Making a **Bloomin' Steps** quilt solves this 2-in. scrap square overload. Blocks include both 2-in. and 3½-in. scrap squares, but the real kicker is the super-scrappy border made from nearly one thousand 2-in. scrap squares.

Because there are so many scraps involved in this quilt, I chose to work with a pure white background fabric—any scraps selected, even those with just a little print, are darker than white. Following similar logic for an alternate version made with black background fabric (see page 2), most every scrap is lighter than black.

In selecting scraps for the lighter version I picked anything that blooms—scrap prints with flowers and leaves exclusively. The darker version of the quilt has a semi-scrappy border, so a handful of colors from the focus fabric provided the theme for the scrap selection.

This project uses one hundred sixty 3½-in. squares and three hundred twenty 2-in. squares for the blocks *and* for the border, nine hundred eighty 2-in. squares (for the Scrappy-Scrappy border version) or three hundred sixty-eight 2-in. squares (for the Semi-Scrappy border).

FINISHED SIZE: **75 in. x 87 in.**
PATTERN DIFFICULTY: **Intermediate**

FABRIC REQUIREMENTS
3½ yd. background (white, off-white, or black)
1 yd. contrasting solid for flange (or piping) and binding
5 yd. backing
For Semi-Scrappy border option: 1½ yd. focus fabric
For Not-So-Scrappy border option: 2½ yd. focus fabric
Batting, 80 in. x 90 in.
ScrapTherapy scraps

OPTIONAL NOTIONS
Half-Square Triangle ruler
For Scrappy-Scrappy border option: ScrapTherapy Small Scrap Grid by Quiltsmart, six panels, each with two 5 x 18 2-in. grids
Piping Hot Binding by Susan K. Cleveland
8 yd. ¹⁄₁₆-in.-diameter cord for piping

NOTE: This quilt has three border variations. One is the Scrappy-Scrappy border, with five rows of scraps surrounding the entire quilt. This version is the best choice to use an out-of-control 2-in. scrap stash. **1** (See page 129.)

1

Scrappy-Scrappy Border

5" x 75¹/₂"

5" x 78¹/₂"

2

Semi-Scrappy Border

8" x 75$\frac{1}{2}$"

8" x 72$\frac{1}{2}$"

3

Not-So-Scrappy Border

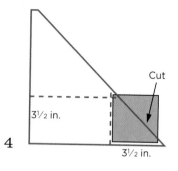

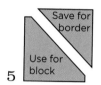

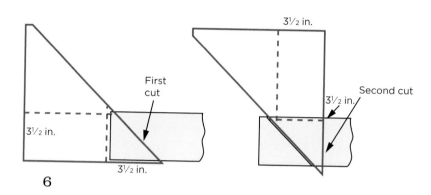

4

5
Save for border
Use for block

6

A second version, the Semi-Scrappy border, sports a black solid background fabric and has two rows of scraps, plus a focus fabric. **2** (See page 130.)

A third border option, Not-So-Scrappy, uses only focus fabric, no square scraps. **3** (See page 131.)

PREPARE SCRAPS
BLOCKS

Select one hundred sixty 3½-in. squares and three hundred twenty 2-in. squares from various scrap prints. Position the Half-Square Triangle ruler so the bottom edge of the ruler and the vertical 3½-in. mark are aligned with two adjacent edges of the 3½-in. scrap square. Cut along the ruler diagonal. Repeat for all the squares. Be aware that half-square triangle rulers may vary from brand to brand, so refer to the instructions that came with your ruler as needed. **4**

NOTE: Reserve the cut-away triangle for the inner border. **5**

BORDER

Select from three border treatment options:

Option 1. Scrappy-Scrappy border (five rows of scraps) (See page 129.)
Select nine hundred eighty 2-in. scrap squares.

Option 2. Semi-Scrappy border (two rows of scraps, plus a focus fabric border) (See page 130.)
Select three hundred sixty-eight 2-in. scrap squares.

Option 3. Not-So-Scrappy border (focus fabric border, no scraps) (See page 131.)
No additional scrap selection needed.

PREPARE BACKGROUND FABRIC

Cut sixteen 2-in. width-of-fabric strips for the blocks. Set aside. Cut twenty-four 3½-in. width-of-fabric strips for the blocks and inner border.

From nine 3½-in. strips, using the Half-Square Triangle ruler, cut one hundred sixty half-square triangles (HSTs) for blocks. Trim points, if desired. **6**

NOTE: Each 3½-in. strip should yield eighteen HSTs using the HST specialty ruler.

From fifteen 3½-in. strips, cut one hundred sixty 3½-in. squares for the inner diamond border.

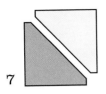

7

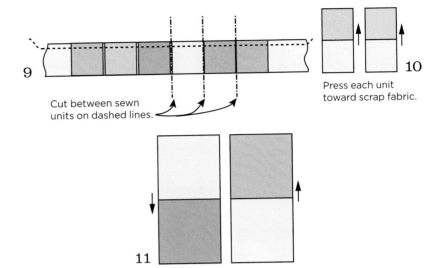

9

Cut between sewn units on dashed lines.

Press each unit toward scrap fabric.

10

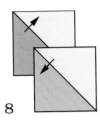

8

11

PREPARE FLANGE AND BINDING

Cut nine 2¼-in. width-of-fabric strips for the binding. If using a flange, cut seven 1-in. width-of-fabric strips. If using piping, the strips will be cut on the bias, following the instructions in the *Piping Hot Binding* book.

A flange is a simple but elegant quilt detail—it's a narrow, flat, folded strip of fabric inserted into the seam around the quilt center. Select a bold coordinating fabric to transition from the quilt top to the borders.

For a different effect, replace the flange with tiny covered piping. The piping or flange can be applied either at the binding or around the pieced center (see the photo on p. 137).

PREPARE OUTER BORDER FOCUS FABRIC

SEMI-SCRAPPY BORDER

Cut nine 5-in. strips from the focus fabric.

NOT-SO-SCRAPPY BORDER

Cut four 8-in. strips along the length-wise grain from the focus fabric.

Trim two strips to 8 in. x 75½ in. for the side borders, and trim two strips to 8 in. x 75½ in. for the top and bottom borders.

MAKE BLOCKS

MAKE HALF-SQUARE TRIANGLE UNITS

Pair each background 3½-in. HST right sides together with each scrap 3½-in. HST. Sew with a ¼-in. seam allowance along the long side of the triangle. Chain-piece to make one hundred sixty HST units. **7**

Press the seams on half of the units toward the scrap fabric and half of the units toward the background fabric. Each HST unit should measure 3½ in. square. **8**

MAKE FOUR-PATCHES

Randomly select and align a 2-in. scrap square on a 2-in. background strip, right sides together. Sew each scrap square to the background strip with a ¼-in. seam allowance. Without breaking the thread, sew a second scrap square to the background strip, leaving minimal space in between the sewn scrap squares. Continue adding scrap squares to the background strips until all three hundred twenty 2-in. scrap squares are sewn to all sixteen 2-in. background strips. **9**

Cut the two-patch units apart, even with the scrap squares, and press seams toward the scrap fabric to make three hundred twenty two-patch units that measure 2 in. x 3½ in. **10**

Pair two-patch units randomly and sew together to make one hundred sixty four-patch units.

IMPORTANT: Sew the pairs of two-patches so each feeds into the sewing machine the same way—either scrap first or background first. **11**

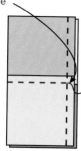

Four-patch before pressing. Last 2 or 3 stitches from two-patch seam pulled out on each side.

12

Press from the back (shown), then from the front so each seam rotates around a center miniblock.

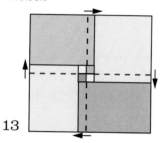

13

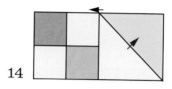

14

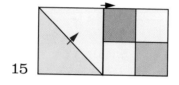

15

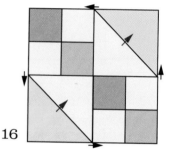

16

Furl the block seams.

Furling the seam intersection is a technique borrowed from hand piecing. All four-patch units in this pattern are pressed with this method to simplify final assembly.

Chain-piece to make one hundred sixty four-patch units that measure $3\frac{1}{2}$ in. square. Press each four-patch the same way. **12, 13**

ASSEMBLE BLOCKS
Randomly select two HST units, one with the seams pressed toward the background and one with the seams pressed toward the scrap, and two four-patch units. Sew each four-patch unit to each HST unit. Press the seams toward the four-patch unit. **14, 15**

NOTE: Each block has one HST unit with seam pressed toward the scrap and one HST unit with seam pressed toward the background fabric.

Rotate the resulting parts into place to complete the block. Follow the pressing instructions for four-patch blocks to furl the center seam intersection. Press the block from the wrong side to rotate the seams, then press from the front. Repeat with all remaining block units to make eighty blocks. The block should measure $6\frac{1}{2}$ in. square. **16**

ASSEMBLE QUILT CENTER
Lay out blocks randomly, alternating the direction of the pressed HST units within the blocks. Sew the rows together, alternating the pressing direction in each row. In other words, press the block seams in the first row to the right, then press the block

seams in the second row to the left, and so on. Then sew the rows; press the row seams in one direction. **17**

ATTACH FLANGE
Sew two flange strips together, end-to-end with a diagonal seam. Make two, one for each side of the quilt top. Next, sew three flange strips together, end-to-end with a diagonal seam. Cut in half to make two strips approximately 60 in. long for the top and bottom.

Press the connection seams open, then press each flange strip lengthwise, wrong sides together. Working one side at a time, pin the flange carefully to the side of the quilt top with raw edges aligned. Trim the ends even with the top. Baste the flange to the quilt by machine using less than a $\frac{1}{4}$-in. seam allowance. Repeat to attach the flanges to all four sides of the quilt top.

17

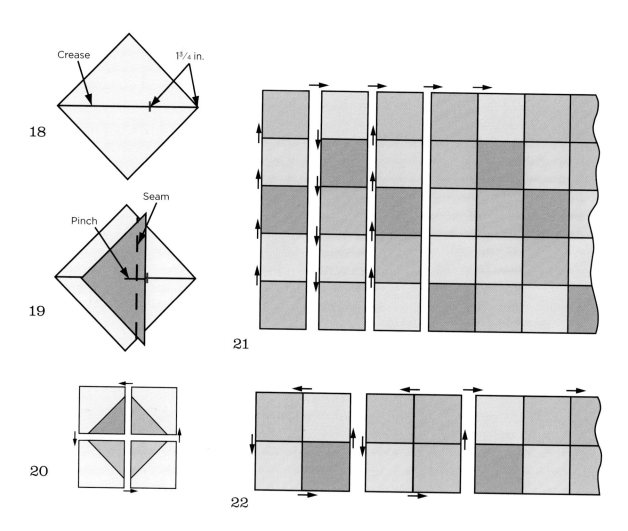

18

19

20

21

22

ADD INNER PIECED BORDER

Finger-press a diagonal crease, right sides together, on a 3½-in. background square.

Measure 1¾ in. from the corner along the crease and make a small mark with a pencil or fabric-marking tool. **18**

Randomly select a leftover triangle reserved earlier for border assembly. Align the corners, wrong sides together, as if to fold, but only pinch the center of the bias edge to locate the middle. Align the crease on the leftover triangle with the mark on the background 3½-in. square. Pin in place and sew a ¼-in. seam allowance. Do not trim the excess background fabric. Press the scrap toward the corner. **19**

Repeat the previous four steps to make one hundred sixty 3½-in. border units. Randomly select four border units and sew together as four-patches, furling the center seam intersection as described on page 134. Make forty border four-patch units. **20**

Randomly sew ten border four-patches together in a row. Press the block seams in the same direction.

Make four borders of ten four-patch units—two for the side borders, one each for the top and bottom borders. Sew the side borders to the quilt, right sides together, with the basted flange sandwiched between the border and the quilt top. Attach the remaining side, top, and bottom borders in the same fashion. Press the seam toward the border and the flange toward the quilt top after each addition. The quilt top should measure 60½ in. x 72½ in.

MAKE OUTER BORDER
SCRAPPY-SCRAPPY BORDER

Randomly select and sew 2-in. scrap squares in rows of five. Make one hundred ninety-six rows of five 2-in. squares. Press the seam in one direction. Sew forty-eight rows together for the side border, alternating seam direction row by row, then press the row seams in one direction. Make two forty-eight row borders for the sides. **21**

In similar fashion, sew fifty rows together to make the top border. Make a second border exactly the same for the bottom. **20**

Attach the borders, one at a time, first to the sides, then to the top and bottom. Press the seams toward the middle border after each addition. **1**

SEMI-SCRAPPY BORDER

Randomly select and sew one hundred eighty-four pairs of 2-in. scrap squares (three hundred sixty-eight 2-in. squares). Next, randomly sew two-patches to make ninety-two four-patches each 3½ in. square. **22**

Make two borders of twenty-four four-patch units for the sides and two borders of twenty-two four-patch units for the top and bottom. Attach the scrap border, one side at a time, first to the sides, then to the top and bottom. Press the seams toward the middle border after each addition. Sew two 5-in. focus fabric strips together end-to-end with a diagonal seam. Make four.

Trim two to 5 in. x 75½ in. for the side borders and trim two to 5 in. x 75½ in. for the top and bottom borders. Attach the side borders to the quilt, then the top and bottom.

SEWING LOTS OF SMALL SCRAPS TOGETHER CAN BE DIFFICULT

So many seams concentrated in one area of the quilt, as in a border, can be inconsistent and unstable. The Small Scrap Grid by Quiltsmart is recommended for the Scrappy-Scrappy border on this quilt to add stability (see page 80). To complete the border on **Bloomin' Steps**, you'll need six panels of the grid interfacing.

To make each side border, you need forty-eight rows of five scraps. Since each grid has eighteen rows of five scraps, you'll need two full grids plus one partial grid with twelve rows filled in with scraps to make up the forty-eight scrap rows.

Similarly, the top and bottom borders require fifty scrap rows of five. So two full grids of eighteen plus one partial grid, 5 x 14, are needed for the top and bottom borders.

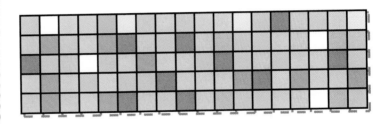

Press the seams toward the focus border after each addition. **2**

NOT-SO-SCRAPPY BORDER

Sew the side borders to each side of the quilt top. Press the seams toward the focus border. Next, sew the top and bottom borders to the quilt top. Press the seams toward the focus border. **3**

QUILT AND BIND

Layer the backing, batting, and quilt top; quilt as desired. Sew nine 2¼-in. binding strips together end-to-end using a diagonal seam (see page 194). Press the connecting seams open, then press the binding in half lengthwise, wrong sides together. With raw edges aligned, sew the folded binding to the front of the quilt using a ¼-in. seam. Miter the binding at the corners (see page 46). Turn the folded edge of the binding to the back of the quilt and hand stitch in place.

Lucky Chain

If you want to make an easy, scrappy throw that uses all three sizes of the ScrapTherapy scraps from your bins, look no further! **Lucky Chain** sews up in a hurry and helps you concentrate on using novelty scrap prints in medium-dark values. For the featured quilt, I chose a fairly intense lime green solid for the block piecing and border. The bright green holds its own among wildly varied neighboring scraps. A small accent border in electric blue frames the scrappy activity of the quilt center. The scraps are dark-value novelty prints and solids that create lots of interest, encouraging closer inspection.

This quilt uses forty-nine dark-value 5-in. novelty print squares for the blocks, sixty-six dark-value 3½-in. novelty print squares for the pieced border, and two hundred dark-value 2-in. novelty print squares for the nine-patch blocks.

FINISHED SIZE: **51 in. x 60 in.**
PATTERN DIFFICULTY: **Easy**

FABRIC REQUIREMENTS
1¼ yd. accent for blocks and borders
¼ yd. solid for inner borders
½ yd. for binding
3 yd. backing (pieced with a horizontal seam)
Batting, 53 in. x 62 in.
ScrapTherapy scraps

PREPARE ACCENT FABRIC

Cut nineteen 2-in. width-of-fabric strips. Set eight strips aside for the blocks, uncut.

Cut five strips into one hundred 2-in. squares for block piecing. Set six strips aside for the borders.

PREPARE INNER BORDERS

Cut six 1¼-in. width-of-fabric strips; set aside for the inner borders.

PREPARE BINDING

Cut six 2¼-in. width-of-fabric strips for the binding.

MAKE NINE-PATCHES

Randomly select and align a 2-in. scrap square on a 2-in. accent strip, right sides together. Sew the 2-in. scrap square to the accent strip.

Without breaking the thread, sew a second scrap square to the accent strip, leaving minimal space between the scrap squares. Continue adding scrap squares to accent strips until one hundred-fifty 2-in. scrap squares are sewn to the eight strips. **1** (See page 140.)

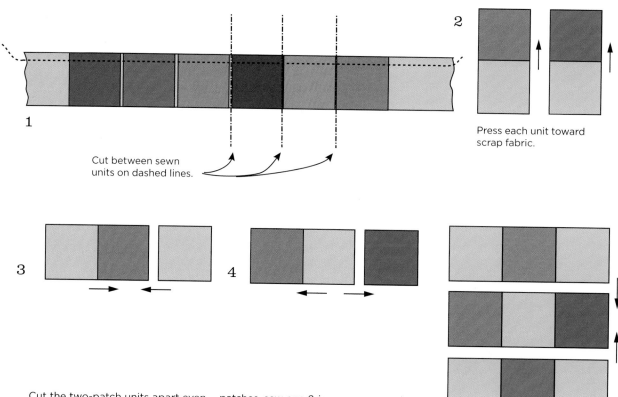

1

2

Cut between sewn
units on dashed lines.

Press each unit toward
scrap fabric.

3

4

5

Cut the two-patch units apart even with the scrap squares, and press seams toward the scrap fabric to make one hundred fifty two-patch units, each 2 in. x 3½ in. **2**

Set fifty two-patch units aside.

To each of the remaining two-patches, sew one 2-in. accent square to the scrap fabric to form a row. Press the seam toward the scrap fabric. **3**

Even though it may seem tedious to cut and press each two-patch before sewing and pressing it again into a three-patch, use the opportunity to test the accuracy of your seam allowance and to mix up the sewn units so scrap fabrics are scrambled up.

Retrieve the fifty two-patch units set aside earlier. To each of the two-

patches, sew one 2-in. scrap square to the accent square to form a row. Press the seam toward the scrap fabric. **4**

You should have one hundred fifty accent-scrap-accent three-patch rows and fifty scrap-accent-scrap three-patch rows that each measure 2 in. x 5 in. Sew two accent-scrap-accent and one scrap-accent-scrap rows together to make a nine-patch block. Press the row seams in one direction. **5**

ASSEMBLE QUILT CENTER

Arrange blocks in eleven rows of nine, alternating nine-patch blocks and 5-in. scrap squares randomly, starting and ending the first and last row with a nine-patch block. Press the block seams toward 5-in. scrap squares. Press the row seams in one direction. **6**

BORDERS
INNER BORDERS

Connect three 1¼-in. strips, end-to-end, using a diagonal seam (see page 194) to make one long strip; press the connecting seams open. Make two. From each long strip, cut one 50-in. side border and one 42½-in. top and bottom border. Sew the inner borders to the quilt center, sides first, then top and bottom. Press the seams toward the accent border after each addition.

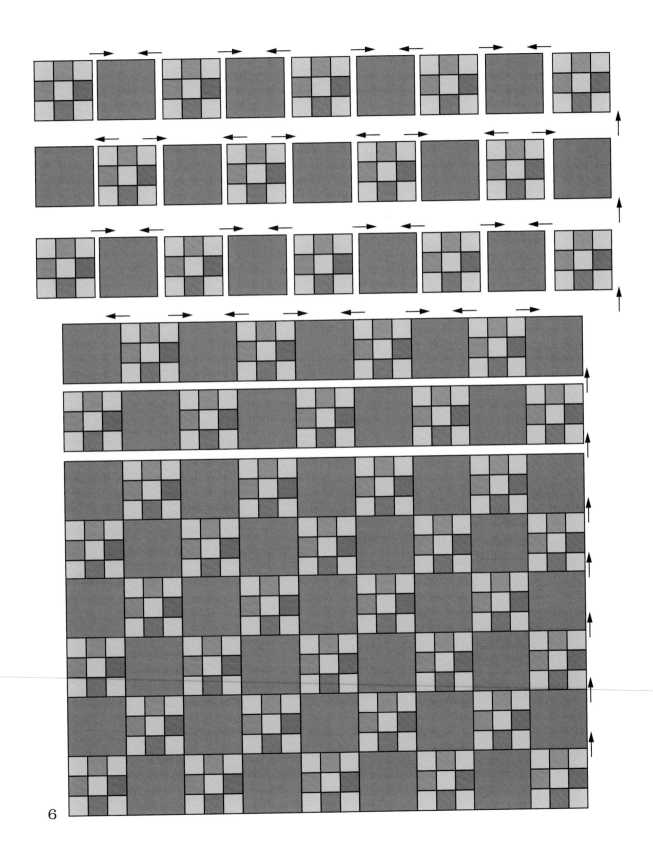

6

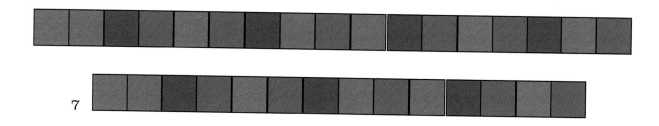

7

ACCENT BORDER

Sew three 2-in. strips end-to-end using a diagonal seam to make one long strip. Press the connecting seams open. Make two. From each long strip, cut two $51\frac{1}{2}$-in. strips, for a total of four long border strips. From the remainder of the border strips, cut four $3\frac{1}{2}$-in. short border strips. Set the borders aside.

OUTER PIECED BORDER

Sew seventeen $3\frac{1}{2}$-in. dark-value scrap squares randomly in a row. Press the seams in one direction. Make two. Next, sew fourteen $3\frac{1}{2}$-in. dark-value scrap squares randomly in a row. Press the seams in one direction. Make two. **7**

ASSEMBLE QUILT

Sew a pieced border made from seventeen $3\frac{1}{2}$-in. scraps to one long accent border. Press the seam toward the accent border. Make two. Sew the side border assemblies to the quilt. Press the seam in either direction. Sew in sequence, one $3\frac{1}{2}$-in. scrap square, one 2-in. x $3\frac{1}{2}$-in. short accent border, one pieced border made from fourteen $3\frac{1}{2}$-in. scrap squares, one 2-in. x $3\frac{1}{2}$-in. short accent border, and a scrap square. Press the seams toward the borders. Make two.

Sew a long accent border to one side of each pieced border assembly as shown.

Attach the top and bottom border assemblies. Press the seam toward the accent border. **8**

QUILT AND BIND

Layer the backing, batting, and quilt top; quilt as desired. Sew six $2\frac{1}{4}$-in. binding strips together end-to-end using a diagonal seam (see page 194). Press the connecting seams open, then press the binding in half lengthwise, wrong sides together. With raw edges aligned, sew the binding to the front of the quilt using a $\frac{1}{4}$-in. seam. Miter the binding at the corners (see page 194). Turn the folded edge of the binding to the back of the quilt, and hand stitch in place.

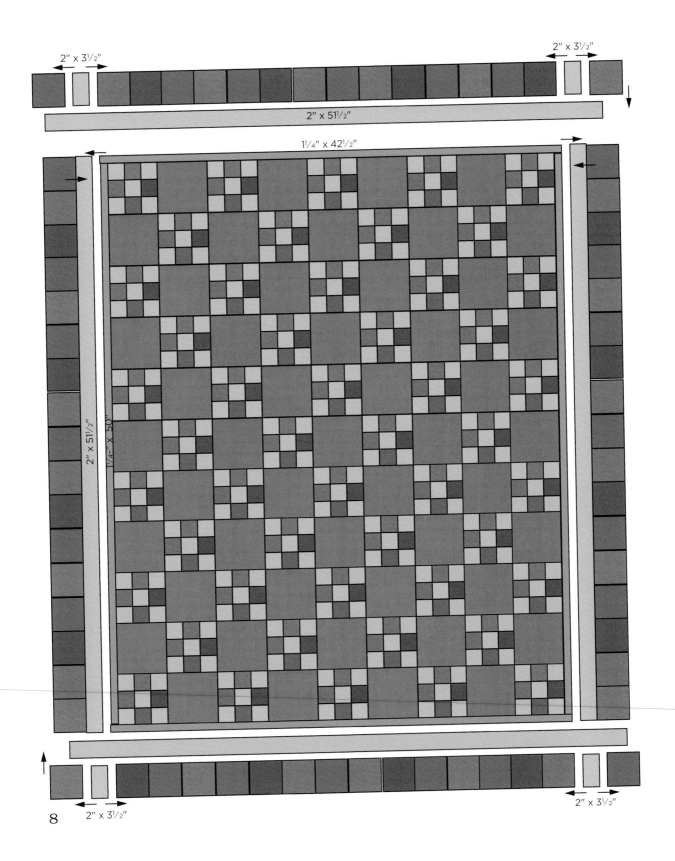

2" × 3½"

2" × 3½"

2" × 51½"

1¼" × 42½"

2" × 51½"

¼" × 50"

2" × 3½"

2" × 3½"

8

Cheap Frills Pouch

Got a pile of extra binding ends? You know, those last little pieces that remain after the quilt is done . . . the lengthwise fold dutifully steamed in permanently. They're too good to throw away, so put them into action in this practical, sporty shoulder bag.

Pick out a few binding pieces that play well together, then pair them with some scraps. Add some stash fabric for the lining, and make this quick and easy tote in no time. Can you believe this frilly little tote uses about 7 yd. of leftover binding strips? That's enough binding to go around an entire quilt! You'll also need four 3½-in. squares for the bag and covered button, and seventy-eight 2-in. squares for the bag.

FINISHED SIZE: **9 in. x 10 in.**
PATTERN DIFFICULTY: **Easy**

FABRIC AND NOTION REQUIREMENTS
⅓ yd. for lining, directional fabric not recommended
7 yd. leftover binding strips (originally cut 2¼ in. wide
　and pressed in half lengthwise) for ruffles
Batting, 14 in. x 26 in.
1½-in. covered button kit
ScrapTherapy scraps

PREPARE BINDING LEFTOVERS
Dig into your leftover binding strips and color coordinate them if you like. You'll need twelve 16-in. folded binding strips set aside for the ruffles.

Select additional leftover binding strips and sew them together with a diagonal seam (see page 194) to make a 60-in. length for the strap and button loop. Press the connecting seams open, and press the strip in half lengthwise, wrong sides together. Open the fold and press the lengthwise edges toward the center twice, as if you are making double-fold bias tape. 1

Topstitch the center of the folded binding strip. Move the needle position left or right as needed so the narrow folded strip will engage the feed dogs. From the stitched strip, cut a 48-in. section for the strap and a 6½-in. section for the button loop. Make a square knot 2 in. from each end of the long strap.

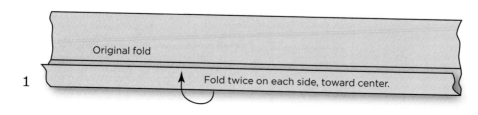

Original fold

1　Fold twice on each side, toward center.

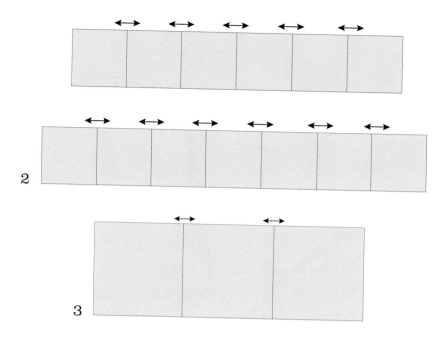

2

3

If you don't have leftover binding strips, cut seven 2¼-in. width-of-fabric strips. Connect the strips end-to-end with a diagonal seam, then cut the pieces needed to make the Cheap Frills project according to the binding preparation section on page 144.

PIECED BAG STRIPS

Sew six 2-in. scraps together in a row. Press the seams open. Make six strips 2 in. x 9½ in. Set aside. Sew seven 2-in. scraps together in a row. Press the seams open. Make six strips 2 in. x 11 in. Set aside. **2**

Sew three 3½-in. scraps together in a row. Press the seams open. Make one strip 3½ in. x 9½ in. Set aside. **3**

MAKE BAG EXTERIOR

RUFFLES

I like to pick up a needle and thread sometimes as a break from machine work, so I make the ruffles by hand. If you prefer, use a gathering stitch on your machine or even your serger.

To make the ruffles, knot a 20-in. length of heavy thread at one end— a good coated hand-quilting thread or 40-weight thread will work fine. Sew a running stitch ⅛ in. away from the raw edges of the 16-in. folded binding strips. The stitches should be about ⅛ in. apart. Don't worry about making the stitches perfect; "close enough" is what you're shooting for! Place the ruffle on a ruler, pull up the thread to adjust the fullness, and tie off when the ruffle is 9½ in. long. Make twelve ruffles.

ASSEMBLE

Using a Hera marker or other fabric-marking tool, draw a line 2 in. from one long batting edge. **4**

Place the 3½-in.-wide pieced strip in the center of the batting with one short end aligned with the marking. This strip becomes the bag bottom. **5**

Select one ruffle and pin to one side of the 3½-in. scrap strip, with raw edges aligned. Evenly distribute the ruffle fullness and pin in place. **6**

Place one pieced strip made from six 2-in. scraps over the ruffle, right sides together, raw edges aligned. Pin in place. Sew a ¼-in. seam, sandwiching the ruffle raw edges between the pieced strips. **7** (See page 148.)

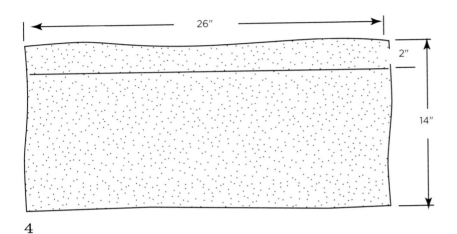

4

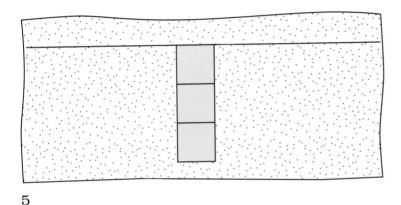

5

If your machine resists the extra
layers, increase your needle size
to a 90/14 or use a denim needle.
A walking foot helps feed the
multiple layers of batting and
fabric.

Finger-press the pieced strip
toward the upper part of the bag. **8**
(See page 148.)

Repeat on the opposite side of the
3½-in. scrap strip. Continue adding ruffles and 2-in. pieced strips to
each side of the bag exterior until all
ruffles and scrap rows are sewn (six
ruffles and strips on each side of the
3½-in. bag bottom). Alternate
7-scrap strips and 6-scrap strips,
ending with a 7-scrap strip at the top
edge of the bag—this staggers the
scrap seaming. Trim the bag exterior
panel to measure 9½ in. wide. Trim
the batting on the short ends even

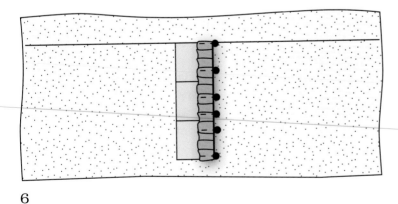

6

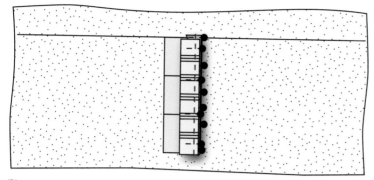

7

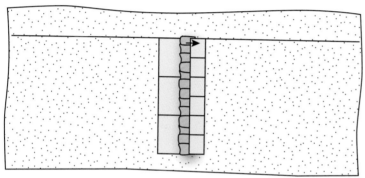

8

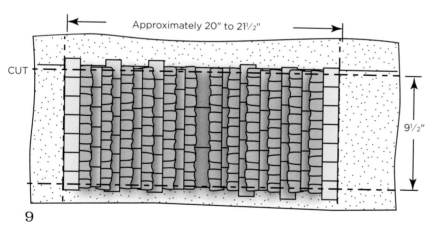

Approximately 20" to 21½"

CUT

9½"

9

with the last scrap strip row. The exterior bag panel should measure 9½ in. x 20-21½ in. **9**

MAKE BAG LINING

From the lining fabric, cut one 9½-in. width-of-fabric strip, then cut one 9½-in. x 12½-in. rectangle for the inside pocket. Fold the pocket in half, wrong sides together, and press the fold firmly. Edgestitch the fold.

Since seam allowances may vary from person to person, calculate the length of the lining panels by dividing the length of your exterior panel in half and adding ¼ in. For the purposes of this example, let's assume that the bag exterior is 20½ in. long. One half of 20½ in. is 10 ¼ in. Add ¼ in. for a final cutting measurement of 10½ in.

From the remainder of the 9½-in. lining fabric strip, cut two 9½-in. x 10½-in. (or your calculated measurement) rectangles for the bag lining. Make a line 2¼ in. from one short lining rectangle edge on the right side. Place the pocket on the lining fabric with the bottom raw edges of the pocket aligned with the drawn line. Sew a ¼-in. seam at the bottom pocket edge. **10**

Press the pocket toward the bag top. Draw and stitch a divider line on the pocket. Baste the raw edges to the bag, if desired. **11**

With the exterior bag panel right side up, fold the button loop in half and center on one short side. Pin the loop in place matching raw edges; baste if desired. Place a lining rectangle on each end of the exterior panel, right sides together and raw edges aligned. Double-check that the pocket is placed so it opens toward the top of the bag! Sew the lining to each bag end using a 1/4-in. seam. **12**

Open the entire assembly and center the strap ends along the sides of one upper pieced row, raw edges aligned. Be careful that the strap isn't twisted, and pin it in place on both sides of the bag. Baste if desired.

Fold the bag in half, right sides together, so the bag bottom (the 3 1/2-in. scrap strip) is centered on the fold. Pin the bag side seams, aligning the pieced rows and ruffles. Sew the bag side seams, being careful not to catch the strap as you stitch. Leave the lining ends open. **13**

Turn the bag right side out through the lining opening. Turn under the lining raw edges and sew the opening closed. Tuck the lining inside the bag, press the upper edge, and edge-stitch the upper bag opening using a straight or decorative stitch. Use the remaining 3 1/2-in. scrap square to cover a 1 1/2-in. button. Sew the button to the bag front through all layers.

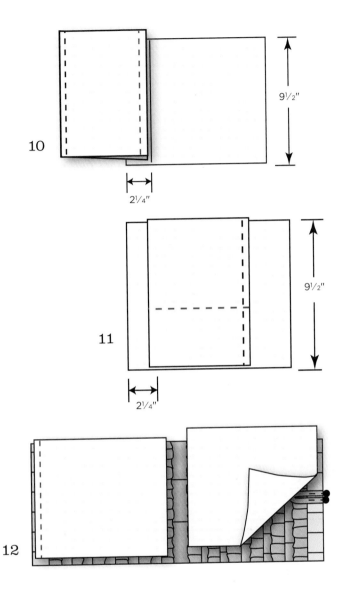

10

9 1/2"

2 1/4"

11

9 1/2"

2 1/4"

12

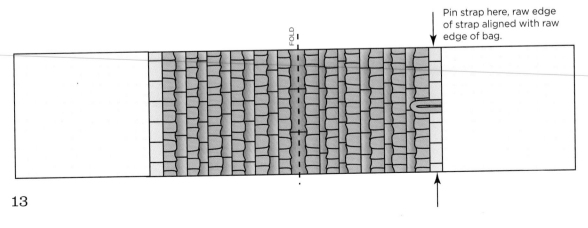

Pin strap here, raw edge of strap aligned with raw edge of bag.

FOLD

13

Tulip Patches

A little bit of spring is welcome any time of year! Use your scrap fabrics to create a tulip garden full of prints or soft-color solids. To keep the scrappy pieced border and sashing on track, the quilt is constructed with a series of smaller sections. You might be surprised by how the blocks and rows are assembled.

The fabric choices for **Tulip Patches** were inspired by the outer border focus print, with coordinating fabrics purchased for the block and accent borders and the binding. The featured quilt has solid brown appliqué block backgrounds. The colors listed are keyed to the featured quilt, but feel free to personalize it with colors in reversed values.

This quilt uses ten dark-value 5-in. squares, twenty light-value 5-in. squares, forty dark-value 2-in. squares for the pieced blocks, one hundred seventy-seven light-value 2-in. squares, one hundred ninety-six dark-value 2-in. squares for the sashing and borders, and twenty green 5-in. squares, thirty blue and pink 3½-in. squares, and twenty blue and pink 2-in. squares for the appliqué blocks.

FINISHED SIZE: **65 in. x 77 in.**
PATTERN DIFFICULTY: Intermediate

FABRIC AND NOTION REQUIREMENTS

1½ yd. dark brown solid for appliqué block background and inner border
1¼ yd. bright blue for block borders
⅓ yd. light brown solid for accent borders
1¼ yd. focus print for outer borders
⅔ yd. for binding
4½ yd. backing
Batting, approximately 70 in. x 82 in.
Optional:
½ yd. fusible web or fusible interfacing, depending on appliqué method
ScrapTherapy scraps

PREPARE SCRAPS
PIECED BLOCKS

Cut each 5-in. light-value scrap square into two 2-in. x 5-in. rectangles. Discard the remainder. Make a total of forty rectangles.

PREPARE OTHER FABRICS
APPLIQUÉ BACKGROUNDS AND INNER BORDERS

Cut three 8½-in. width-of-fabric strips, then cut ten 8½-in. squares for the appliqué backgrounds. Cut seven 2½-in. width-of-fabric strips for the inner borders.

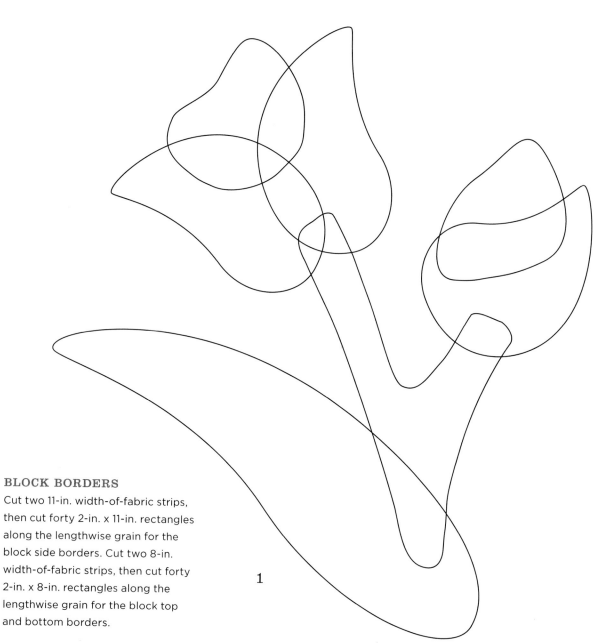

BLOCK BORDERS

Cut two 11-in. width-of-fabric strips, then cut forty 2-in. x 11-in. rectangles along the lengthwise grain for the block side borders. Cut two 8-in. width-of-fabric strips, then cut forty 2-in. x 8-in. rectangles along the lengthwise grain for the block top and bottom borders.

ACCENT BORDER

Cut seven 1½-in. width-of-fabric strips for the accent borders.

OUTER BORDER

Cut eight 5-in. width-of-fabric strips for the outer borders.

BINDING

Cut eight 2¼-in. width-of-fabric strips for the binding.

APPLIQUÉ BLOCKS

Refer to the appliqué details on page 194. Using your favorite hand or machine appliqué method, make ten blocks using the blue, pink, and green scraps for the various appliqué pieces. Trim each block to 8 in. square, centering the motif.

NOTE: Appliqué pattern shapes are reversed. **1**

PIECED BLOCKS

Select one dark-value 5-in. scrap square, four light-value 2-in. x 5-in. scrap rectangles, and four dark-value 2-in. scrap squares. Sew a nine-patch as shown, pressing seams as indicated. Make ten pieced blocks that are 8 in. square from various light and dark scrap prints. **2**

1

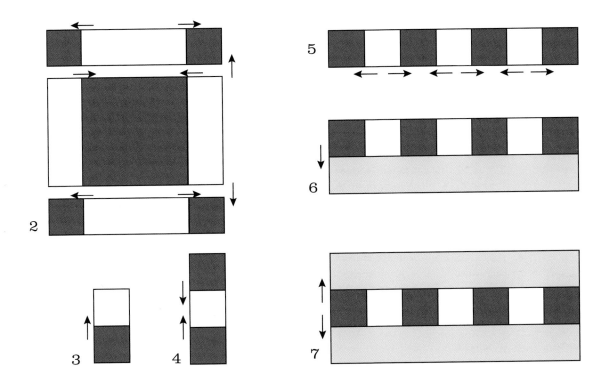

SASHING

To make the sashing strips, sewing lots and lots of 2-in. scrap squares together in a row can create disappointing results if seam allowances are off even a little bit. All those pieced squares have a good chance of going astray when final measurements are made. For more accuracy, the sashing and block borders have been broken down into more manageable sizes. If a seam allowance or two is a tiny bit off, you'll discover it early on. Check the measurements for each sashing element and eliminate any fudging headaches in the final quilt construction.

Select ten dark-value 2-in. scraps and ten light-value 2-in. scrap squares. Sew each dark-value 2-in. square to a light-value 2-in. square to make ten two-patch units. Press the seams toward the light squares. Each two-patch unit should measure 2 in. x 3½ in. **3**

Select forty dark-value 2-in. scraps and twenty light-value 2-in. scrap squares. Sew a dark 2-in. square to each side of a light 2-in. square to make twenty three-patch units. Press the seams toward the center light square. Each three-patch unit should measure 2 in. x 5 in. **4**

Select ninety-six dark-value 2-in. scraps and seventy-two light-value 2-in. scrap squares.

Sew four dark-value 2-in. squares and three light-value 2-in. squares in a row, starting and ending with a dark square. Make twenty-four seven-patch units. Press seams toward the dark squares. Each seven-patch should measure 2 in. x 11 in. **5**

Sew a blue 2-in. x 11-in. strip to one side of each seven-patch unit. Press the seam toward the blue fabric. Each unit should measure 3½ in. x 11 in. Make twenty-four seven-patch assemblies; set eight aside. **6**

Sew a second blue 2-in. x 11-in. strip to the opposite side of the sixteen remaining seven-patch units. Press the seam toward the blue fabric. Each unit should measure 5 in. x 11 in. **7**

Select fifty dark-value 2-in. scraps and seventy-five light-value 2-in. scrap squares. Sew two dark 2-in. squares and three light 2-in. squares in a row, starting and ending with a light square. Make twenty-five five-patch units. Press the seams toward

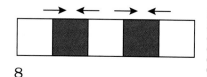

8

9

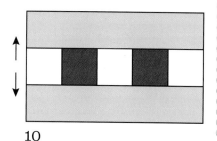

10

MITERED BORDER

When adding multiple borders, it's nice to sew them together first, then add them to the quilt top. The corners are then mitered for a tidy finish.

If you decide to miter the borders for Tulip Patches, you'll need strips in the following lengths.

Inner Border (dark brown): two strips $2\frac{1}{2}$ in. x approximately 60 in. for top and bottom, and two strips $2\frac{1}{2}$ in. x approximately 70 in. for sides.

Accent Border (light brown): two strips $1\frac{1}{2}$ in. x approximately 60 in. for top and bottom, and two strips $1\frac{1}{2}$ in. x approximately 72 in. for sides.

Outer Border (focus print): two strips 5 in. x approximately 72 in. for top and bottom, and two strips 5 in. x approximately 80 in. for sides.

Follow the step-by-step mitering instructions on page 40.

the dark squares. Each five-patch unit should measure 2 in. x 8 in. **8**

Sew a blue 2-in. x 8-in. strip to one side of each five-patch. Press the seam toward the blue fabric. Make twenty-five units; set ten aside. Each unit should measure $3\frac{1}{2}$ in. x 8 in. **9**

Sew a second blue 2-in. x 8-in. strip to the opposite side of the fifteen units. Press the seam toward the blue fabric. Each unit should measure 5 in. x 8 in. **10**

Arrange the blocks and sashing units as shown. Sew the units into rows, pressing seams as indicated. Sew the rows together, pressing the row seams as indicated. **11** (See page 155.)

BORDERS

Make the borders by connecting the strips end-to-end using a diagonal seam (see page 194). Be sure to measure your pieced quilt before cutting the borders. Sew four dark-brown $2\frac{1}{2}$-in. strips together, then cut two 62-in. side inner borders. Sew three dark-brown $2\frac{1}{2}$-in. strips together, then cut two 54-in. inner borders for the top and bottom. Next, sew two sets of two light-brown $1\frac{1}{2}$-in. strips together, then cut two 66-in. side accent borders. Sew three light-brown $1\frac{1}{2}$-in. strips together, then cut two 56-in. accent borders for the top and bottom. Sew four 5-in. focus

strips together, then cut two 68-in. side outer borders. Sew four 5-in. strips together, then cut two 65-in. borders for the top and bottom. Add the borders in order (inner, accent, outer), sides first, then top and bottom as shown. Press the seams toward the border fabric after each addition. **12** (See page 156.)

11

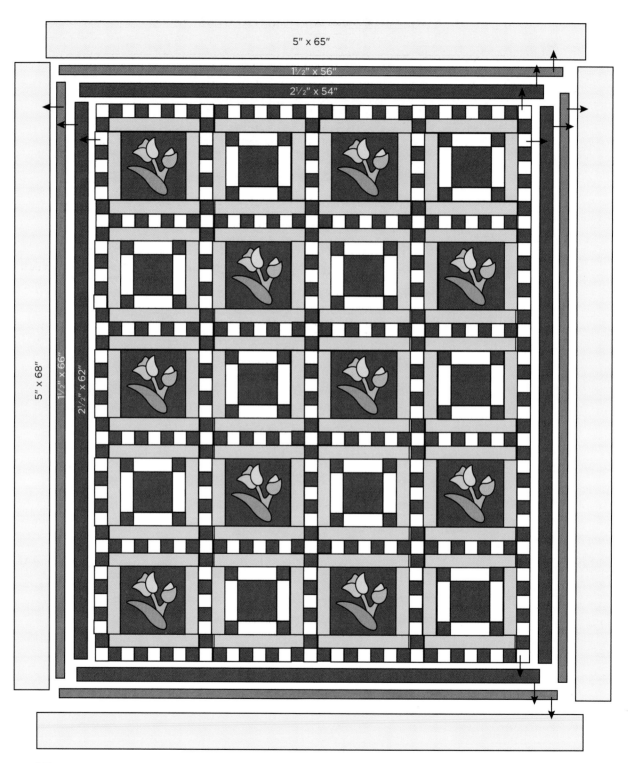

5" x 65"

1½" x 56"

2½" x 54"

5" x 68"

1½" x 66"

2½" x 62"

12

An easy straight-line border quilting pattern is something I call "three times around." With a walking foot attached, start just off any side edge of the quilt with the needle down in the batting. Turn the quilt at an angle and sew a straight line until you reach the border. With the needle down, lift the presser foot and turn the quilt at a random angle and sew another straight line until the stitching reaches the edge. Proceed in this fashion, making random angles at the quilt edge and at the border edge, until you have stitched around the quilt border three times. This quilt pattern works especially well with contemporary quilts.

QUILT AND BIND

Layer the backing, batting, and quilt top; quilt as desired. Sew eight 2¼-in. binding strips together end-to-end using a diagonal seam. Press the connecting seams open, then press the binding in half lengthwise, wrong sides together. With raw edges aligned, sew the binding to the front of the quilt using a ¼-in. seam. Miter the binding at the corners (see page 46). Turn the folded edge of the binding to the back of the quilt, and hand stitch in place.

SEW ODD

I'd rather be odd! The next time you border your quilt, consider adding three! And make the inner accent border the smallest width. Odd quantities create interest and unpredictability; even numbers of items can be balanced and predictable, and sometimes not as interesting.

It's all in the numbers. **Tulip Patches** has:

10 appliqué blocks and 10 pieced blocks (even)

5 rows of blocks (odd)

Appliqué block with 2 flowers (even) but a total of 5 flower petals (odd) and 1 leaf (odd), so each block has 3 focal points—2 flowers plus 1 leaf (odd)

Pieced blocks that are 9-patches (odd)

5 appliqué blocks (odd) in the entire quilt that have a splash of pink

3 borders (odd)

Next time you wander through an art museum, take a look at the paintings and sculptures. Count the items that you notice immediately. Are they odd, too?

Star Gazing

The key to this quilt project is selecting scraps in two very distinct colors. One of the colors selected will be represented in both light and dark values. Add a consistent neutral background fabric and a whole lot of time to piece and sew!

Before getting too deeply immersed in planning the blocks and inner border, I highly recommend making a sample block to make sure your scrappy color and value selections work well together. Without strong variation in tone, these blocks can easily become muddy and flat.

Since you need two colors and a neutral background to make this quilt work, it's perfect for a dorm throw dedicated to the home team; or choose a bold patriotic spin. Since I use red a lot, and I always seem to have a lot of blue fabrics, it was easy to come up with enough red scraps and dark- and light-value blue scraps for the featured version.

This quilt uses two hundred thirty-eight dark-value 3½-in. squares (dark blue in the featured quilt), one hundred eighty-six medium-value 3½-in. squares (red in the featured quilt), and three hundred eighty light-value 2-in. squares.

FINISHED SIZE: 67 in. x 82 in.

PATTERN DIFFICULTY: Intermediate

FABRIC REQUIREMENTS

1²/₃ yd. focus print for border cut crosswise or 2 yd. focus print border cut lengthwise

2 yd. cream or solid neutral for block background

²/₃ yd. for binding

5 yd. backing

Batting, approximately 72 in. x 88 in.

ScrapTherapy scraps

PREPARE SCRAPS

STAR BLOCKS

Select one hundred forty-four dark-value 3½-in. squares; ninety-six medium-value 3½-in. squares; and one hundred ninety-two light-value 2-in. squares. Draw a diagonal line corner-to-corner on the back of each 2-in. square. **1**

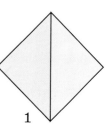

1

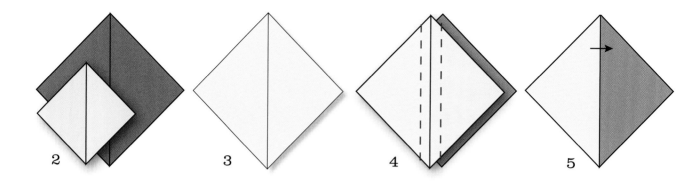

2   3   4   5

BORDER BLOCKS

Select ninety-four dark-value $3\frac{1}{2}$-in. squares and ninety medium-value $3\frac{1}{2}$-in. squares. Draw a diagonal line from corner-to-corner on the back of each medium-value $3\frac{1}{2}$-in. square. Select one hundred eighty-eight light-value 2-in. squares. Draw a diagonal line from corner-to-corner on the back of each 2-in. square. **2**

PREPARE ADDITIONAL FABRICS

NEUTRAL BACKGROUND USED IN STAR BLOCKS

Cut eighteen $3\frac{1}{2}$-in. width-of-fabric strips, then cut one hundred ninety-two $3\frac{1}{2}$-in. squares from those strips. Draw a diagonal line corner-to-corner on the back of each $3\frac{1}{2}$-in. background square as shown. **3**

FOCUS PRINT OUTER BORDERS

Double-check the quilt top measurements once the pieced border is added before you cut the outer focus borders. Remember, you can cut these pieces either lengthwise or crosswise grain, depending on the print.

Crosswise-grain border strips

Cut eight $6\frac{1}{2}$-in. width-of-fabric strips. Sew two $6\frac{1}{2}$-in. border strips together end-to-end using a diagonal seam (see page 194). Make four. From these strips, cut two $70\frac{1}{2}$-in. side borders and two $67\frac{1}{2}$-in. borders for the top and bottom.

Lengthwise-grain border strips

Cut four $6\frac{1}{2}$-in.-wide strips along the lengthwise grain of the fabric. From the strips, cut two $70\frac{1}{2}$-in. side borders and two $67\frac{1}{2}$-in. top and bottom borders.

BINDING

Cut eight $2\frac{1}{4}$-in. width-of-fabric strips for binding.

STAR BLOCKS

Select forty-eight dark-value $3\frac{1}{2}$-in. scraps. Trim each scrap to 3 in. square for the star block center. Set aside. Select ninety-six dark-value $3\frac{1}{2}$-in. scraps and ninety-six $3\frac{1}{2}$-in. background squares for the star point units. Pair one $3\frac{1}{2}$-in. background square with one dark-value $3\frac{1}{2}$-in. scrap square, right sides together with the background fabric

on top. Sew $\frac{1}{4}$ in. away from both sides of the drawn line. **4**

Cut on the drawn line, and press the seam toward the dark-value scrap. **5**

Trim each resulting half-square triangle (HST) unit to 3 in. square. Each pair of $3\frac{1}{2}$-in. squares will yield two 3-in. star point units. Make a total of one hundred ninety-two star point units from the dark-value scraps and background squares. Set aside.

Select ninety-six medium-value $3\frac{1}{2}$-in. scraps, ninety-six $3\frac{1}{2}$-in. background squares, and one hundred ninety-two light-value 2-in. scraps for the block corner units. Pair one $3\frac{1}{2}$-in. background square with one medium-value $3\frac{1}{2}$-in. scrap square, right sides together with the background fabric on top. Sew $\frac{1}{4}$ in. away from both sides of the drawn line. Cut on the drawn line, and press the seams toward the medium-value scrap. Trim each HST unit to 3 in. square.

Pair one light-value 2-in. scrap square right sides together with a medium background HST. Align the 2-in. square on the corner of the medium triangle with the drawn

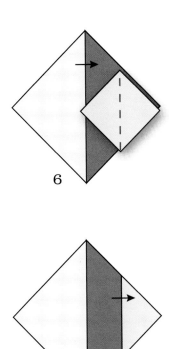

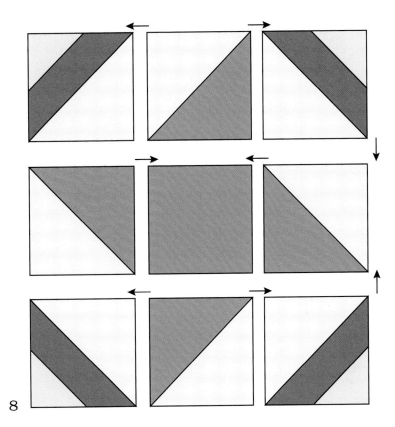

line parallel to the existing seam as shown. **6**

Sew directly on the line of the 2-in. square. Press the light fabric as shown. Trim the extra layers, if desired. **7**

Make a total of ninety-six block corner units from medium- and light-value scraps and background squares.

ASSEMBLE STAR BLOCK

Arrange the block parts as shown— one center, four star point units, and four block corner units. Sew the block parts in rows, then sew the rows together, pressing the seams as indicated. The block should measure 8 in. square. Make forty-eight star blocks. **8**

ASSEMBLE QUILT CENTER

Arrange blocks in eight rows of six blocks each, rotating alternate blocks 90 degrees so the seams nest. Sew the blocks into rows. Press the seams in one direction, alternating every other row. Sew the rows together. Press the row seams in one direction. **9** (See page 162.)

BORDER BLOCKS
"A" UNITS

Select forty-two dark-value 3½-in. scraps, forty-two medium-value 3½-in. scraps, and eighty-four light-value 2-in. squares. Pair one dark-value 3½-in. scrap with one medium-value 3½-in. scrap, right sides together with the medium scrap on top. Sew ¼ in. away from

both sides of the drawn line. Cut on the drawn line to make two HST units. Press the seam toward the dark-value scrap. Trim each HST unit to 3 in. square. Repeat to make eighty-four HST units, pressed toward the dark-value fabric. **10** (See page 163.)

Place one light-value 2-in. scrap square right sides together on a medium/dark HST unit. Align the 2-in. square on the HST unit with the drawn line perpendicular to the existing seam. *Be careful; it's easy to get this step upside down!* Sew directly on the line on the 2-in. square. Press the light fabric as indicated. Trim the extra layers, if desired. Make eighty-four identical medium/dark HST border units, labeled with an "A" in next few diagrams. **11** (See page 163.)

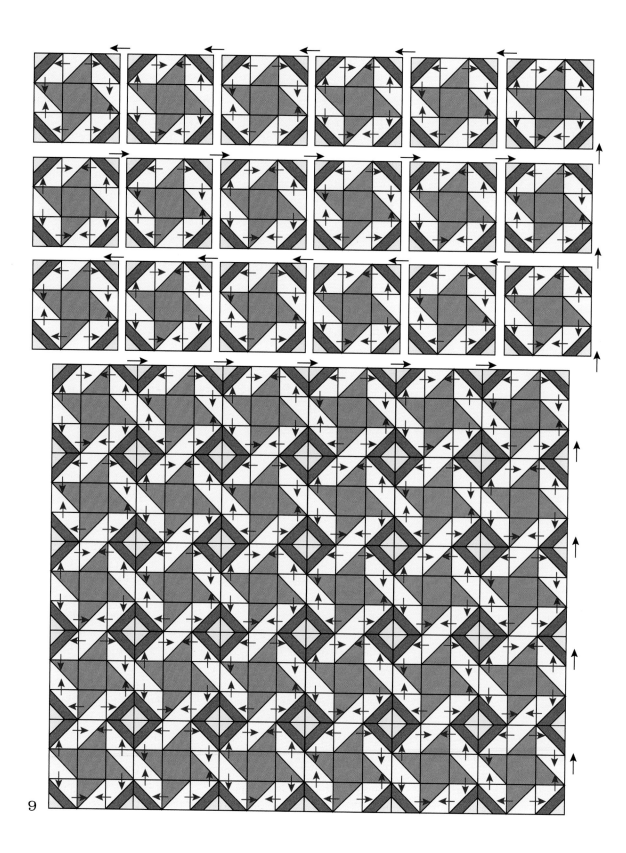

9

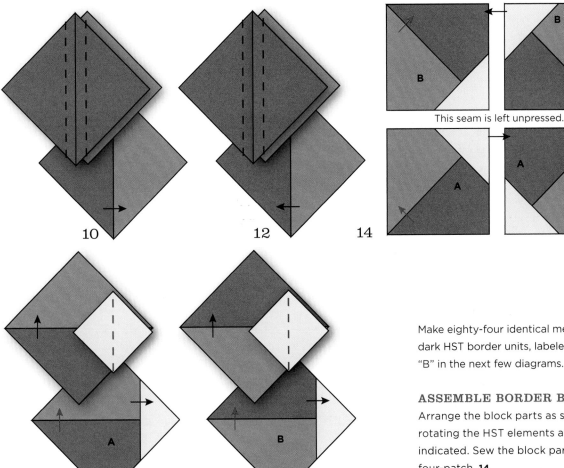

This seam is left unpressed.

"B" UNITS

From the remaining scrap fabrics selected for the border, choose forty-two dark-value 3¹/₂-in. scraps, forty-two medium-value 3¹/₂-in. scraps, and eighty-four light-value 2-in. squares.

Pair one dark-value 3¹/₂-in. scrap with one medium-value 3¹/₂-in. scrap, right sides together with the medium scrap on top. Sew ¹/₄ in. away from both sides of the drawn line. Cut on the drawn line to make two HST

units. Press the seam toward the medium-value scrap. **12**

Trim each HST unit to 3 in. square.

Place one light-value 2-in. scrap square right sides together with a medium/dark HST. Align the 2-in. square on the medium triangle with the drawn line perpendicular to the existing seam. *Be careful; It's easy to get them reversed!*

Sew directly on the line on the 2-in. square. Press the light fabric as shown. Trim the extra layers if desired.

Make eighty-four identical medium/dark HST border units, labeled with "B" in the next few diagrams. **13**

ASSEMBLE BORDER BLOCK

Arrange the block parts as shown, rotating the HST elements as indicated. Sew the block parts into a four-patch. **14**

Press the two-patch seams as indicated; leave the longer four-patch seam unpressed for now. Be careful to arrange the block units the same for each border block, watching the seam direction on the HST units. The border block should measure 5¹/₂ in. square. Make forty-two border blocks.

CORNER BLOCKS

Select ten dark-value 3¹/₂-in. scraps, six medium-value 3¹/₂-in. scraps, and twenty light-value 2-in. scraps. Select four dark-value 3¹/₂-in. squares and trim each to 3 in. square. Place one light-value 2-in. scrap square right sides together on a trimmed

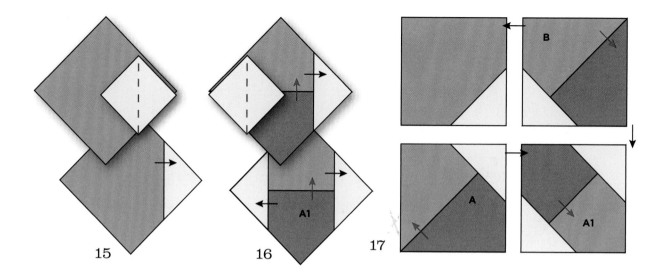

15   16   17

dark-value 3-in. square, with corners aligned and with the drawn line running from edge to edge as shown. **15**

Sew directly on the line on the 2-in. square. Press the light fabric as shown. Trim the extra layers, if desired. Make four and set aside.

Select four dark-value 3½-in. scraps, four medium-value 3½-in. scraps and twelve light-value 2-in. squares. Follow the instructions on p. 161 to make eight border A units.

Set four A units aside. On each of the remaining four A units, place an additional light-value 2-in. scrap square right sides together on the opposite corner of the medium/dark HST as shown. Align the 2-in. square with the drawn line perpendicular to the existing seam.

Sew directly on the line on the 2-in. square. Press the light fabric as indicated. Trim the extra layers, if desired. Make four identical medium/dark HST corner units, labeled "A1." **16**

Select two dark-value 3½-in. scraps, two medium-value 3½-in. scraps, and four light-value 2-in.

squares. Follow the instructions on page 163 to make four border B units. Arrange the block parts, rotating the HST elements as shown. Sew the block parts into a four-patch. **17**

Press the seams as indicated. Be careful to arrange the block units the same for each corner block, watching the seam direction on the HSTs. The block should measure 5½ in. square.

Make four corner blocks.

COMPLETE BORDERS

Sew twelve border blocks together for each side border. Follow the diagram carefully to position and sew the blocks and press the seams in the proper direction. Notice the left and right side borders are sewn the same, though the right border is reversed.

Sew nine border blocks and two corner blocks for the top and bottom borders. Follow the diagram carefully to position and sew the blocks. Notice the top and bottom borders are sewn the same, though the bottom border is reversed.

Follow the diagram to press the seams before attaching the borders to the quilt top. Some seams may not nest, especially at the corners; use extra pins as needed. Add the pieced borders to the sides, then the top and bottom. Add the side focus borders, then the top and bottom focus borders, pressing as indicated after each addition. **18**

QUILT AND BIND

Layer the backing, batting, and quilt top; quilt as desired. Sew eight 2¼-in. binding strips together end-to-end using a diagonal seam (see page 194). Press the connecting seams open, then press the binding in half lengthwise, wrong sides together. With raw edges aligned, sew the binding to the front of the quilt using a ¼-in. seam. Miter the binding at the corners (see page 46). Turn the folded edge of the binding to the back of the quilt, and hand stitch in place.

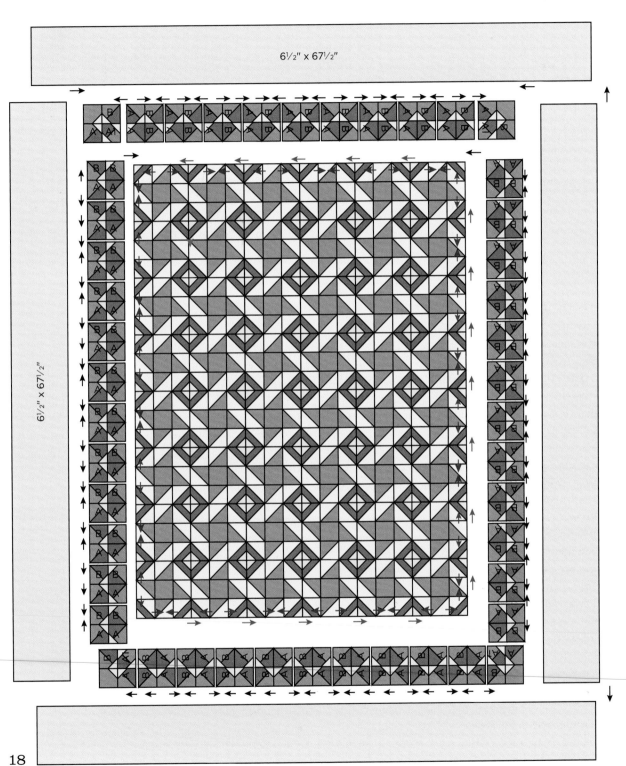

6½" x 67½"

6½" x 67½"

Town Tote

This stylish carry-along showcases your scrap fabrics with a luxurious textured surface made simple with a product called Texture Magic. The roomy interior pockets and secure button closure make it great for a shopping spree on the town.

The featured bag was made with batiks because the colors tend to blend well without being too "matchy-matchy." However any prints that scream, "Make me into a bag!" will do. These scraps were selected in dark-value, low-contrast colors that coordinate with the colors of the focus fabric used for the accents and lining.

This tote uses eighteen 5-in. squares for the main bag panel, fifty-four 3½-in. squares for main bag panel, and eighty-one 2-in. squares for the main bag panel and covered button.

FINISHED SIZE: **10 in. x 9 in. x 4 in.**
PATTERN DIFFICULTY: **Intermediate**

FABRIC AND NOTION REQUIREMENTS
1 yd. for lining, directional fabric not recommended
³/₄ yd. plain fusible interfacing
Batting, 8 in. x 42 in. and 4 in. x 42 in.
Texture Magic, 18 in. x 47 in.
One ³/₄-in. magnetic purse closure
2½-in. covered button kit
ScrapTherapy scraps

PREPARE FOCUS/LINING FABRIC
Cut one 14½-in. width-of-fabric strip, then cut one 23-in. rectangle for the bag lining, and two 7½-in. rectangles for the inside pockets. To add stability, fuse interfacing to the back of each pocket rectangle, and fuse a 4-in. interfacing square to the wrong side of one end of the lining rectangle, centered about 3-in. from the edge. **1**

Cut one 6-in. width-of-fabric strip. Layer it with the 8-in. x 42-in. batting section. Baste and quilt as desired. Cut the quilted strip into two 2½-in. width-of-fabric strips for the bag side panels. Set aside.

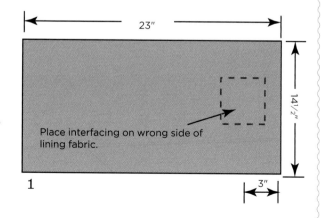

Place interfacing on wrong side of lining fabric.

1

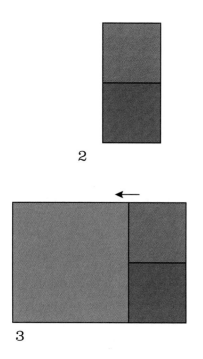

2

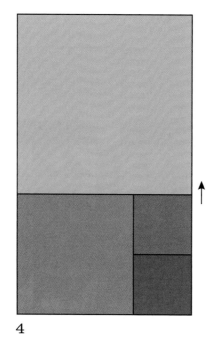

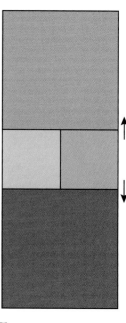

3   4   5

Next, cut one 3-in. width-of-fabric strip. Layer it with the 4-in. x 42-in. batting section. Baste and quilt as desired. Cut the quilted strip into two 14½-in. strips for the bag trim band.

> Consider quilting the trim band with a straight stitch, about ½ in. away from each long edge. Then quilt between the straight stitching lines with a random free-motion pattern.

Cut two 3-in. width-of-fabric strips for straps. Then cut one 2-in. width-of-fabric strip, then cut one 12-in. strip for the button loop. Set aside.

MAIN TEXTURED PANEL
Randomly select and sew seventy-two 2-in. scraps into thirty-six two-patch units. Press the seam to either side. **2**

Sew a two-patch to one side of a 3½-in. scrap square as shown. Press the seam toward the 3½-in. square. Make eighteen three-patch units. **3**

Sew a 5-in. scrap square to each three-patch unit to make eighteen large block subassembly units. Press the seam toward the 5-in. square. **4**

Sew one 3½-in. square to both sides of the remaining eighteen two-patches to make eighteen small block subassembly units. Press the seams toward the 3½-in. squares. **5**

Sew two block subassemblies together as shown. Furl the center seam intersection (see "Furling" in Quiltmaking Basics on page 193). **6**

Sew the blocks in six rows of three blocks each. Press the block seams in alternate directions; press row seams in one direction. **7**

Place the Texture Magic under the pieced main panel, centering the

panel. Avoid the temptation to press the wrinkles out of the Texture Magic!

NOTE: About ½ in. of the pieced panel will extend beyond the width of the Texture Magic—don't worry about this.

Pin-baste the layers together. Use a walking foot or darning foot to quilt liberally over entire the panel, removing pins as you sew.

Place the quilted panel on the ironing board, right side down. With a hot iron, steam the Texture Magic evenly using several passes of the iron. Watch as it curls, then reshapes itself to lie flat! The pieced fabric panel on the reverse will be permanently texturized.

The main panel should now measure approximately 14 in. x 36 in. (size may vary slightly depending on the shrinkage).

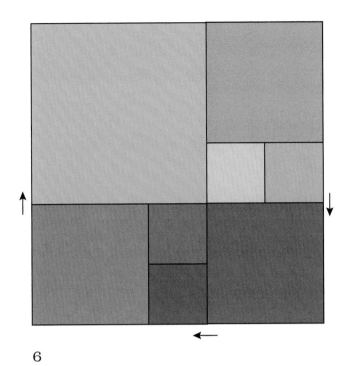

6

True up one long side, then cut
two 1½-in. x 36-in. strips for straps.
True up one short side, then cut one
1-in. x 11-in. strip for button loop. **8**

> When cutting the textured panel,
> think about it as a new piece
> of fabric. Don't worry about
> aligning the cuts with the block
> piecing seam intersections.

Using a walking foot and ¼-in.
seam allowance, sew a quilted 2½-in.
width-of-fabric focus fabric strip to
each side of the textured panel. Press
the seam toward quilted fabric strip.
From the right side of the panel,
topstitch about ⅛-in. away from the
seam to flatten. Repeat for both sides
of the panel.

Cut the panel into three segments:
one 14½ in. x 16½ in. for the bag
outer panel, and two 14½-in. x 6-in.
interior pockets. Set pockets aside. **9**

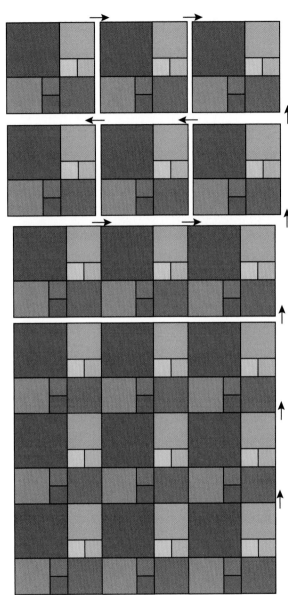

7

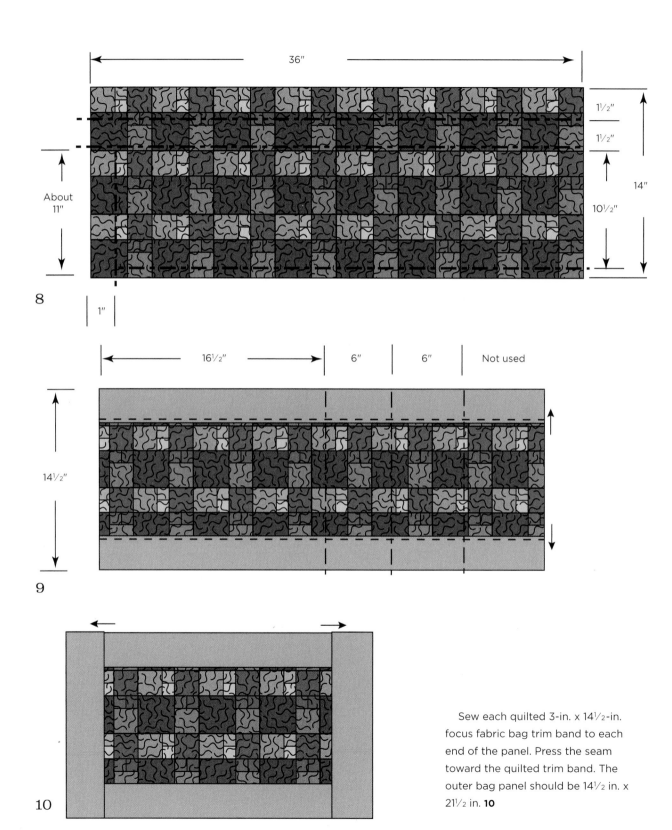

36"

1½"

1½"

14"

10½"

About
11"

8

1"

16½"   6"   6"   Not used

14½"

9

10

Sew each quilted 3-in. x 14½-in. focus fabric bag trim band to each end of the panel. Press the seam toward the quilted trim band. The outer bag panel should be 14½ in. x 21½ in. **10**

Fold

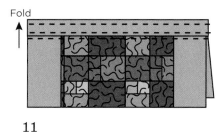

11

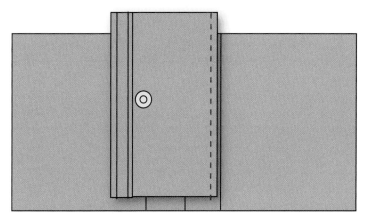

12

Basting stitch

Place magnet on lining here

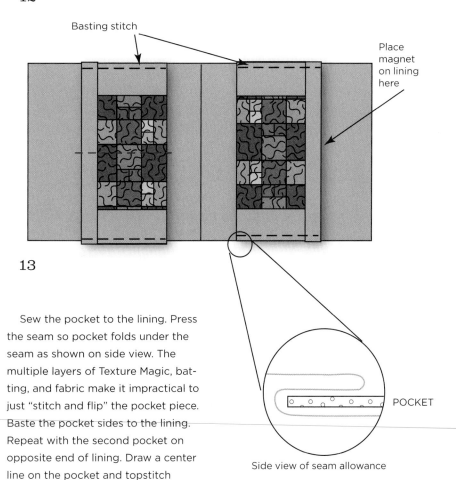

13

POCKET

Side view of seam allowance

MAKE POCKETS

Place the 6-in. x 14½-in. pocket panel and 7½-in. x 14½-in. pocket lining right sides together with one long side aligned. Stitch and press the seam toward the lining. Fold the pocket wrong sides together, creating a ¾-in. focus fabric cuff. Stitch in the ditch, as well as ⅛ in. away from the seam, and ⅛ in. away from fold. Repeat for both pockets. **11**

Insert the magnetic closure on the lining side of one pocket. Center the closure ½ in. below the in-the-ditch stitching.

PREPARE LINING

Make a center crease in the 14½-in. x 23-in. lining fabric. Then draw a line 2¾ in. away on both sides of the line. Right sides together, place the pocket with the magnetic closure on the 2¾-in. line located on the same side as the 4-in. interfacing scrap, aligning the bottom pocket edge with the line. **12**

Sew the pocket to the lining. Press the seam so pocket folds under the seam as shown on side view. The multiple layers of Texture Magic, batting, and fabric make it impractical to just "stitch and flip" the pocket piece. Baste the pocket sides to the lining. Repeat with the second pocket on opposite end of lining. Draw a center line on the pocket and topstitch creating a divider. Attach the other half of the magnetic closure under the pocket magnet. **13**

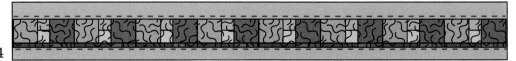

14

MAKE STRAPS AND BUTTON LOOP

Sew the long sides of each textured strap to a 3-in. focus strip, right sides together, leaving the short ends unsewn. Note that the focus fabric is wider than the strap. Turn the straps right side out through the opening on one end. Press so that the focus fabric forms an even border on each side of the textured fabric and stitch in the ditch on each seam. The strap should measure 1³/₄ in. wide. Trim each strap to 28 in. long. **14**

To make the button loop, sew both sides of the textured loop strip to the 2-in. x 12-in. focus fabric strip, leaving both ends unsewn. Turn the loop right side out through one open end. Press and stitch in the ditch on each seam. The finished loop should be 1-in. wide. Mark the loop center and fold each side to form a "V." Pin the folds and sew horizontally across the layers. **15**

> To turn the loop right side out, pin a large safety pin to one open end of the loop and ease the pin though the middle of the sewn loop. If you prefer, use a loop-turning tool. Whichever method you choose, the fabric gets quite wrinkled in the process of turning, so be sure to press the edges after turning.

ASSEMBLE TOTE

Place the outer bag panel on your worktable right side up and pin one strap on each end, 3 in. from each long edge. Make sure the straps aren't twisted and that the textured sides are facing down.

Center and pin the button loop on one end with the textured side facing down. **16**

Fold the bag panel right sides together with the top edges aligned; pin in place matching the trim band seams, and sew the side seams.

To box the tote corners, open the bag at the bottom corner, then re-fold with right sides together to form a triangle shape. Align the side seam with the center of the bag bottom. Pin and sew across 2 in. from the point. Don't turn bag right side out yet. **17**

Fold the lining right sides together with top edges aligned, and sew one side seam. On the opposite side, sew about 2 in. at the top edge and about 3 in. at the bottom fold of the bag, leaving about 6 in. open on one side for turning. **18**

Box the lining corners following the same process as for the bag. Turn the lining right side out. Right sides together, insert the bag lining into the bag and pin the upper edges. Sew around the upper bag, encasing the strap ends and button loop. **19**

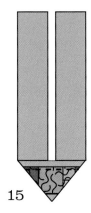

15

Turn the bag right side out through the lining opening. Turn under the raw edges and sew the lining opening closed. Topstitch ¹/₄ in. from the bag upper edge.

BUTTON

Make a nine-patch block from the remaining 2-in. scrap squares. Cover the button.

Sew the button to the outer bag under the button loop point.

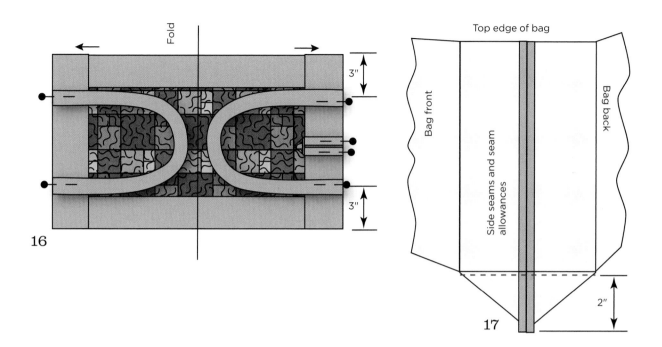

16

Fold

3"

3"

Top edge of bag

Bag front

Bag back

Side seams and seam
allowances

2"

17

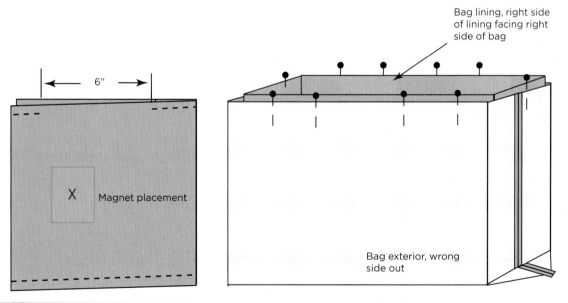

6"

X   Magnet placement

18

Bag lining, right side
of lining facing right
side of bag

Bag exterior, wrong
side out

19

Duck, Duck, Goose Place Mats and Table Runner

You'll be digging deep into your scrap bin for leftovers when you make one or both of these flying geese projects. When selecting the main focus print at the center of the place mat or runner, choose a small-scale print fabric that is somewhat quiet. Save the bold statement for the busy-ness in the scrappy flying geese.

Four flying geese units can be made at a time from one 3½-in. scrap square and four 2-in. scrap squares, but you'll have to do some trimming first. I recommend using a trimming tool that allows you to make the flying geese units without trimming the squares first. Then, each unit is trimmed to perfection after sewing!

The place mats are turned and stitched, so no binding is needed.

The place mats use twenty-four medium-value 3½-in. squares and ninety-six dark-value 2-in. squares. The table runner uses thirty-one medium-value 3½-in. squares and one hundred twenty-four dark-value 2-in. squares. Choose medium prints that coordinate with your light focus print center. Choose 2-in. scraps in dark values and a color that accents your light focus center. Then, it's up, up, and away!

FINISHED SIZE: **14 in. x 18 in. (place mats); 16 in. x 52 in. (table runner)**
PATTERN DIFFICULTY: **Intermediate**

FABRIC AND NOTION REQUIREMENTS

	TWO PLACE MATS	TABLE RUNNER
Light-value focus print	⅓ yd.	¾ yd.
Dark-value solid coordinate	⅔ yd. (includes backing)	---
Binding	---	⅓ yd.
Backing	---	1 yd.
Batting	16 in. x 20 in. (two)	18 in. x 55 in.

ScrapTherapy scraps
Optional notion: Flying geese trimming tool, such as the Wing Clipper

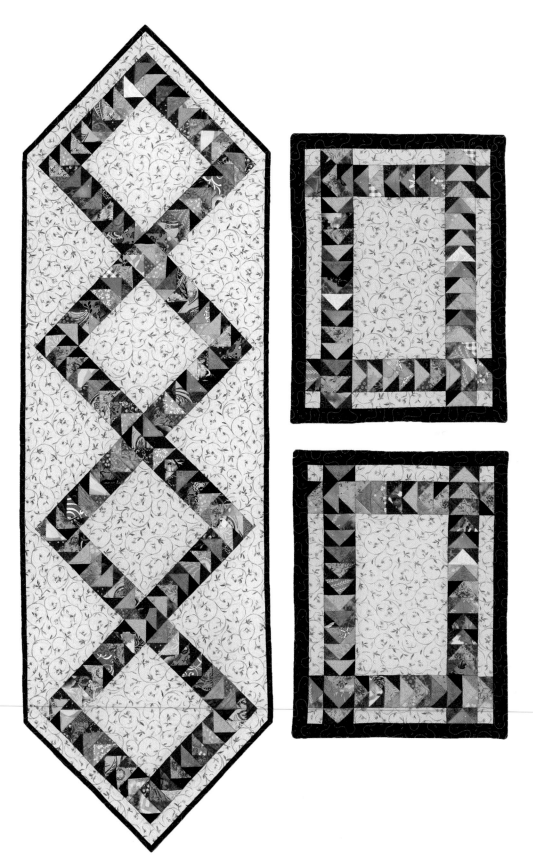

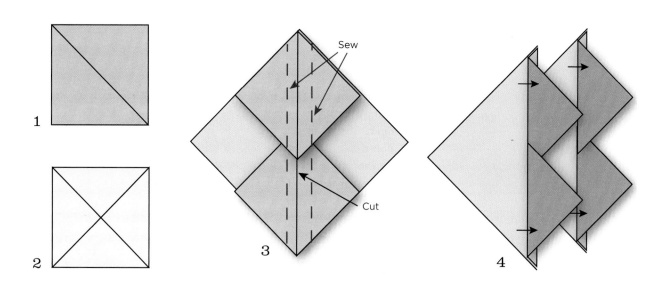

Pay close attention to the illustrations as you sew flying geese units together. These silly geese can change their flight direction at a moment's notice.

PREPARE SCRAPS

PLACE MATS

Select twenty-four medium-value 3½-in. scrap squares for the geese. Then select ninety-six dark-value 2-in. scrap squares for the geese background. Using a pencil or fabric-marking tool, draw a diagonal line corner-to-corner on the back of each 2-in. scrap square. **1**

TABLE RUNNER

Select thirty-one medium-value 3½-in. scrap squares for the geese. Next, select one hundred twenty-four dark-value 2-in. scrap squares for the geese background. Using a pencil or fabric-marking tool, draw a diagonal line corner-to-corner on the back of each 2-in. square.

PREPARE ADDITIONAL FABRICS, PLACE MATS

LIGHT-VALUE FOCUS PRINT

Cut one 6½-in. width-of-fabric strip, then cut two 6½-in. x 10½-in. rectangles for the place mat center. Cut two 1½-in. width-of-fabric strips, then cut four 1½-in. x 10½-in. rectangles, four 1½-in. x 6½-in. rectangles, and eight 1½-in. squares.

DARK-VALUE SOLID COORDINATE

Cut four 1½-in. width-of-fabric strips, then cut four 1½-in. x 12½-in. rectangles for the side borders and four 18½-in. rectangles for the top and bottom borders. You need two of each size for each place mat. Cut one 16-in. width-of-fabric strip, then cut in half to make two rectangles approximately 16 in. x 20 in. for the place mat backing.

PREPARE ADDITIONAL FABRICS, TABLE RUNNER

LIGHT-VALUE FOCUS PRINT

Cut one 14-in. width-of-fabric strip, then cut two 14-in. squares. Cut each square in half twice on the diagonal, to make eight quarter-square setting triangles. Two triangles will be unused. **2**

Cut one 6½-in. width-of-fabric strip, then cut four 6½-in. squares. Cut two 1½-in. width-of-fabric strips, then cut two 1½-in. x 10½-in. rectangles, one 1½-in. x 11½-in. rectangle, and one 1½-in. x 13-in. rectangle.

BINDING

Cut four 2¼-in. width-of-fabric strips for the binding.

No doubt about it, there are tons of flying geese in these two projects. The flying geese units are made with five scrap squares, each trimmed slightly to accommodate the traditional piecing method and create four flying geese at once. If you'd rather not start out with all that trimming, use a geese trimming tool such as the Wing Clipper by Studio 180 Design. Follow the pattern illustrations and the instructions that come with the trimming tool to trim the geese after they've been sewn, cut apart, and pressed. You may have to make a few adjustments to how the fabric squares are aligned before you sew, so follow the tool instructions carefully.

MAKE FLYING GEESE UNITS

Choose one medium-value 3½-in. scrap square; trim to 3¼ in. Next, choose four dark-value 2-in. scrap squares; trim each to 1⅞ in. Place one 1⅞-in. scrap square on opposite corners of the 3¼-in. scrap square, right sides together. The raw edges of the 1⅞-in. squares should be aligned with the corner of the 3¼-in. scrap square. The drawn lines on the 1⅞-in. squares should be lined up. **3**

Sew ¼ in. away from both sides of the drawn line. Cut on the line and press the smaller triangles away from the larger triangle. You'll have two units that look like those shown. **4**

Align one 1⅞-in. scrap square, right sides together, with the remaining corner of each cut-apart unit. The raw edges of the 1⅞-in. square should be aligned with the 90-degree corner of the original 3¼-in. scrap square. **5** (see page 178.)

THE WING CLIPPER TRIMMING TOOL

A trimming tool allows you to sew 2-in. and 3½-in. scrap squares without trimming each one first. Once the units are sewn, cut apart, and pressed, the tool is an easy way to trim each flying geese unit to the perfect size for piecing.

When using the Wing Clipper trimming tool, find the 2½-in. x 1½-in. square up rectangle. Place one flying geese unit on your cutting mat with the point down.

Place the Wing Clipper tool on top of the flying geese unit (the numbers on the clipper are now along the top and the right side), and align the flying geese unit seams with the two crossed bias lines within the 2½-in. x 1½-in. rectangle on the ruler. The point will align perfectly where the bias lines cross.

Trim along the right side and top of the geese unit. Use care when cutting across the top of the tool. 1

Lift the Wing Clipper and turn the flying geese unit upside-down. Now align the 2½-in. x 1½-in. rectangle on the ruler with the trimmed edge of the flying geese unit. Double-check that the geese unit point is aligned with the X-marking on the top edge of the ruler.

Trim along the side and top. Use care when cutting across the top of the tool. 2

Left-handed quilters should refer to the instructions with the Wing Clipper for additional details. Repeat to make ninety-six flying geese for the place mats and one hundred twenty-two flying geese for the table runner.

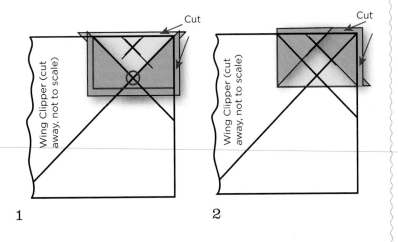

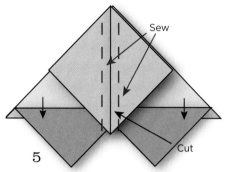

5

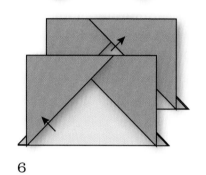

6

If you're using a trimming tool like the Wing Clipper, be sure to check the instructions that come with the tool. Depending on the tool, you may need to align the smaller square just one or two thread widths inside the larger square's 90-degree corner edges.

Sew $1/4$ in. away from both sides of the drawn line. Cut on the drawn line and press the smaller triangle seams away from the larger triangle. Make four geese from the original $3^{1}/_{4}$-in. scrap square and four $1^{7}/_{8}$-in. scrap squares. **6**

Make a total of ninety-six $1^{1}/_{2}$-in. x $2^{1}/_{2}$-in. flying geese units for the place mats and one hundred twenty-two $1^{1}/_{2}$-in. x $2^{1}/_{2}$-in. flying geese

units for the table runner. Proceed to "Make Place Mats" below and/or "Make Table Runner" on page 180 to complete the projects.

MAKE PLACE MATS

Sew six flying geese units together in a row. Press the seams in one direction as shown. Make four six-geese strips, two for each place mat. **7**

Sew one six-geese strip unit to each side of a $6^{1}/_{2}$-in. x $10^{1}/_{2}$-in. light-value focus rectangle. Press the seams toward the focus fabric. Make two, one for each place mat.

Sew one $1^{1}/_{2}$-in. x $6^{1}/_{2}$-in. light-value focus strip to each side of the center assembly as shown. Press the seams toward $1^{1}/_{2}$-in. x $6^{1}/_{2}$-in. strips. Make two, one for each place mat. **8**

Sew sixteen flying geese units together in a row as shown. Be careful, two flying geese units are sewn at a 90-degree angle—watch the pressing! Make four flying geese strips, two for each place mat. **9**

Sew two flying geese units, two $1^{1}/_{2}$-in. squares, and one $1^{1}/_{2}$-in. x $10^{1}/_{2}$-in. light-value focus fabric strip as shown. Press the seams as indicated. Make four, two for each place mat. **10**

Assemble and sew the place mat parts as shown. Press the seams as indicated. Make two. **11**

Add the dark-value coordinate strips to the sides, then to the top and bottom. Press the seams as indicated. Make two. **12** (See page 180.)

Layer the batting and backing right side up, and the place mat top right side down.

Secure the edges with pins. With a walking foot, sew $1/4$ in. away from

the raw edge of the place mat top, leaving an opening about 6 in. long. Trim the batting and backing even with the place mat edge and trim the corners to reduce bulk. Turn the place mat right side out through the opening and hand or machine stitch the opening closed. Quilt place mats as desired.

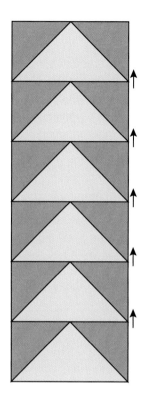

7

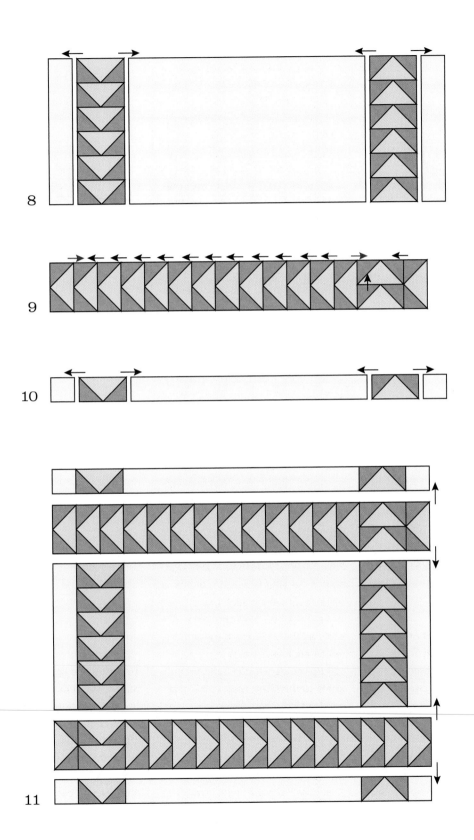

8

9

10

11

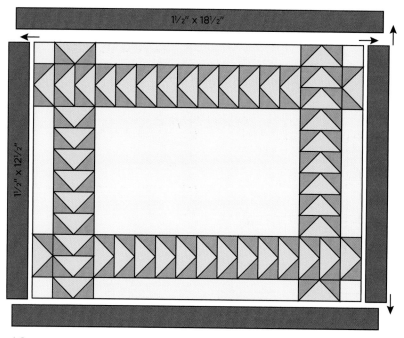

1½" x 18½"

1½" x 12½"

12

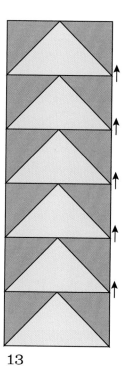

13

MAKE TABLE RUNNER

Sew six flying geese units together in a row as shown. Press the seams as indicated. Make eight six-geese strips. **13**

Sew each six-geese strip unit to opposite sides of each 6½-in. light-value focus square as shown. Press the seam toward the focus fabric.

NOTE: Notice that there are two different combinations (A & B) that seem similar but are different.

Make two of each configuration. **14**

Sew ten flying geese units together in a row as shown. Press the seams as indicated. Make two ten-geese strips. Sew a ten-geese strip to the top of unit A as shown. Repeat for both A units. Set aside. **15, 16**

Sew ten flying geese units together in a row as shown. Press the seams as indicated. Make two ten-geese strips. **17**

Sew the ten-geese strip to the top of unit B as shown. Repeat for both B units. Sew one 1½-in. x 10½-in. light-value focus strip to the top of one of the units. Set aside. **18**

Sew ten flying geese units together in a row as shown. Press the seams as indicated. Sew the 1½-in. x 10½-in. light-value focus strip to the side of the ten-geese strip as shown. Press the seam as indicated. **19**

Sew the ten-geese strip to the bottom of one A unit as shown. Press the seam as indicated. Then sew a 1½-in. x 11½-in. light-value focus strip to the side of the subassembly as shown. Set aside. **20**

Sew eight flying geese units together in a row as shown. Press the seams as indicated. Make two eight-geese strips. **21**

Sew an eight-geese strip to one short side of a light-value focus quarter-square setting triangle as shown. Trim the point. Make two. **22**

Sew eight flying geese units together in a row as shown. Press seams as indicated. **23** (See page 182.)

Sew the eight-geese strip to one short side of a light-value focus quarter-square setting triangle. Trim the point. **24** (See page 182.)

Assemble all the remaining parts and sew the seams, working from left to right in the numbered sewing order. Press the seams toward the focus fabric after each addition. Some seam intersections will not

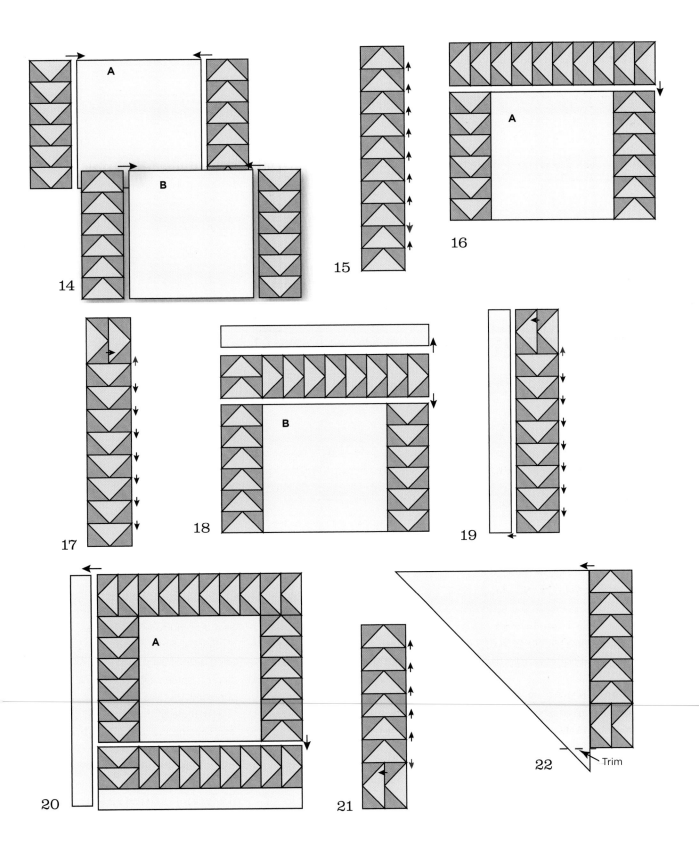

14

15

16

17

18

19

20

21

22

Trim

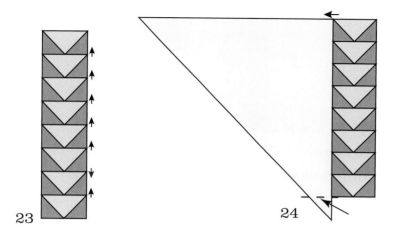

23

24

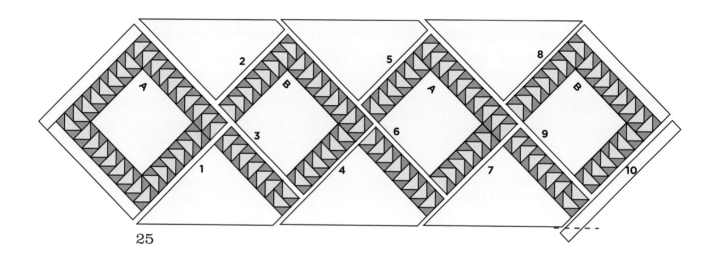

25

nest; use extra pins as needed. Once the runner is sewn, trim the 1½-in. x 13-in. rectangle even with the side setting triangle. **25**

QUILT AND BIND

Layer the backing, batting, and runner top; quilt as desired. Sew four 2¼-in. binding strips together end-to-end using a diagonal seam (see page 194). Press the connecting seams open, then press the binding in half lengthwise, wrong sides together. With raw edges aligned, sew the binding to the front of the runner using a ¼-in. seam. Miter the binding at the corners (see page 46). Turn the folded edge of the binding to the back of the runner, and hand stitch in place.

Wild Salmon Run

Dig into your scrap bins and find a wild collection of bright or medium-value squares. Slice 'em up, and start sewing! From a distance, the eclectic wild colors blend together for a striking design. When you take a closer look, you'll see there's a traditional log cabin block variation at the heart of this quilt.

Select a color family of scraps in bright or medium tones—the featured quilt uses salmon pink—but consider the color family only loosely when pulling scrap fabrics.

This quilt uses sixty-eight medium-value 2-in. squares, sixty-eight medium-value 3½-in. squares, and one hundred ninety medium-value 5-in. squares.

FINISHED SIZE: **70 in. x 70 in.**

PATTERN DIFFICULTY: **Intermediate**

FABRIC REQUIREMENTS

1¼ yd. solid black for blocks and narrow borders

⅔ yd. solid black for binding

¾ yd. solid for wide borders

4½ yd. backing

Batting, 74 in. square

ScrapTherapy scraps

PREPARE SCRAPS

PIECED BLOCKS AND BORDERS

Select sixty-eight medium-value 2-in. squares.

Select two 3½-in. squares. From each 3½-in. square, cut one 2-in. x 3½-in. rectangle. **1**

Select sixty-six 3½-in. squares. From each 3½-in. square, cut one 2-in. x 3½-in. rectangle and one 1½-in. x 3-in. rectangle. **2**

Select twenty-five 5-in. squares. From each 5-in. square, cut two 2-in. x 5-in. rectangles. **3**

(See page 185.)

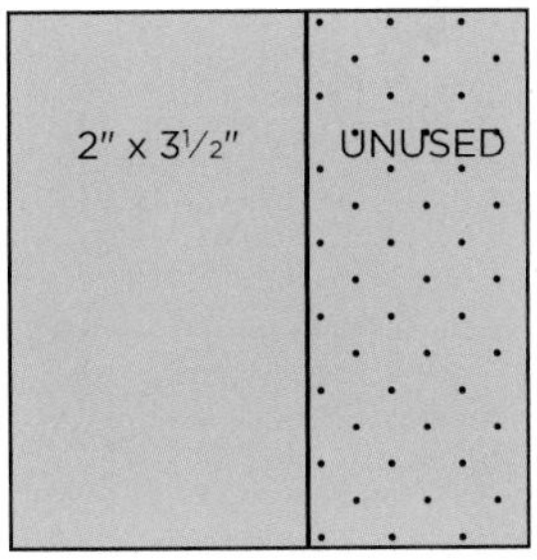

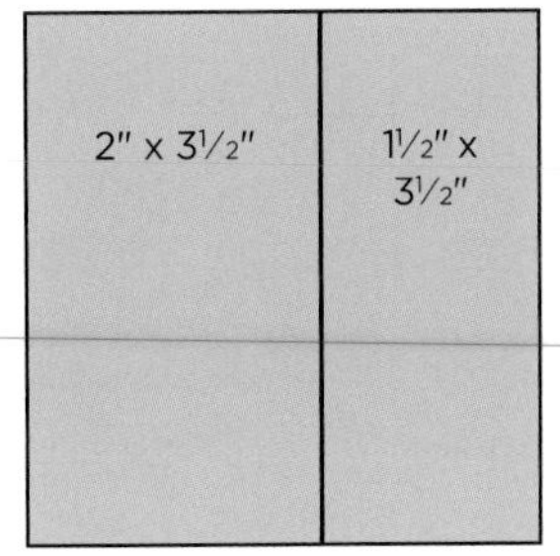

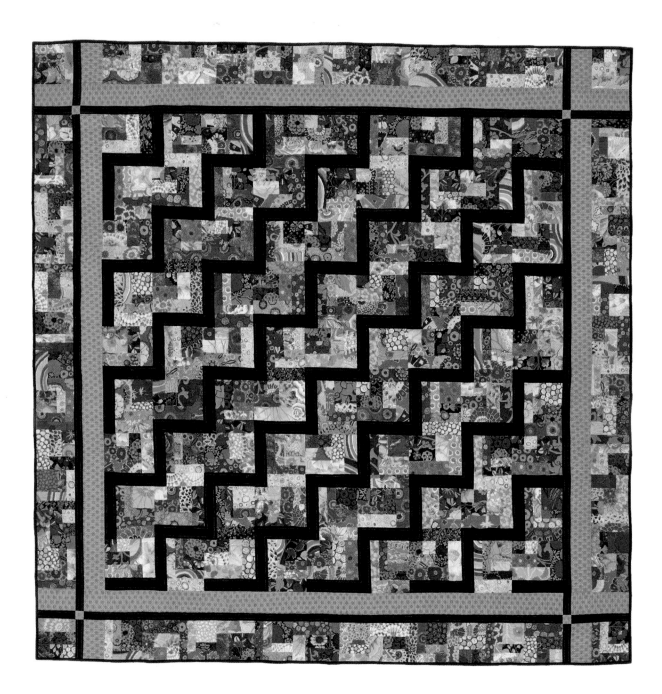

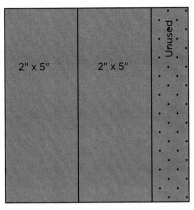

3

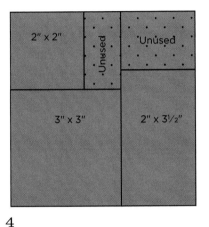

4

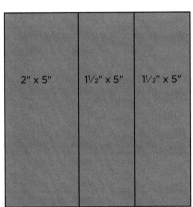

5

6

PREPARE BLACK FABRIC

BLOCKS

Cut fourteen 2-in. width-of-fabric strips, then cut eighty-one 2-in. x 6½-in. rectangles for blocks.

NARROW BORDERS

Cut eight 1½-in. width-of-fabric strips.

BINDING

Cut eight 2¼-in. width-of-fabric strips for the binding.

PREPARE ACCENT FABRIC

WIDE BORDERS

Cut eight 3-in. width-of-fabric strips; set aside for the inner accent border.

MAKE "A" BLOCKS

Arrange stacks of block parts on your sewing table according to the finished block layout. Sew the scraps in sequence, mixing them up and pressing seams after each addition.

Sew each 2-in. scrap to a second 2-in. scrap square; chain-piece until all 2-in. scraps have been sewn to make a total of sixty-seven units 2-in. x 3½-in.; press.

Select sixty-six 5-in. squares. From each 5-in. square, cut one 3-in. square, one 2-in. square, and one 2-in. x 3½-in. rectangle. **4**

Select sixty-six 5-in. squares. From each 5-in. square, cut one 2-in. x 5-in. rectangle, and two 1½-in. x 4-in. rectangles. **5**

Select thirty-three 5-in. squares. From each 5-in. square, cut one 2-in. x 5-in. rectangle and two 1½-in. x 5-in. rectangles. **6**

THE DAY'S CATCH

You should have the following numbers of scraps, cut in these sizes:

134	2-in. squares
134	2-in. x 3½-in. rectangles
149	2-in. x 5-in. rectangles (one will be unused)
66	3-in. squares
66	1½-in. x 3-in. rectangles
132	1½-in. x 4-in. rectangles
66	1½-in. x 5-in. rectangles

Chain piecing can keep your in-process blocks organized.

Sew the first two squares for each A block without breaking the thread between. Snip the threads, then press the seams for the entire stack of two-patch pieced units. Sew in sequence the next fabric rectangle piece to each A block. To keep the blocks really scrappy, mix up the prints as you sew them together. As you press, you can also shuffle the various prints to scramble the fabrics randomly. See page 34 for more information on chain piecing.

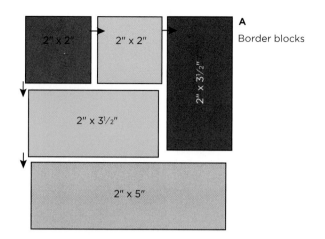

A
Border blocks

Add a 2-in. x 3½-in. rectangle to the lower edge of each two-patch unit until all sixty-seven units are sewn, then snip apart and press. Sew a second 2-in. x 3½-in. rectangle to the side of each unit. Chain-piece until all sixty-seven units have been sewn, snip apart, and press. Add a 2-in. x 5-in. rectangle to the lower edge of each unit; chain-piece until all sixty-seven units have been sewn, snip apart, and press. Before proceeding, set twenty-six 5-in. A blocks aside for the pieced border (A border blocks).

Add a 2-in. x 5-in. scrap rectangle to the side of each remaining block. Chain-piece until all forty-one units have been sewn; snip apart and press. Add a 2-in. x 6½-in. black rectangle on the lower edge of the blocks; chain-piece, snip apart, and press to make forty-one 6½-in. blocks. **7**

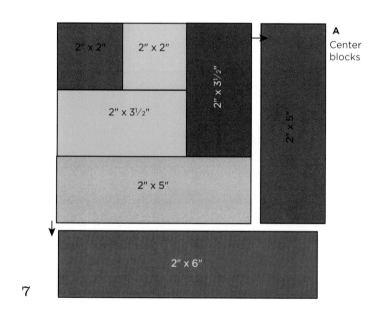

A
Center blocks

7

MAKE "B" BLOCKS

Arrange stacks of block parts on your sewing machine table according to the finished block layout. Sew the scraps in sequence, mixing them up. Press the seams after each addition.

Sew each 3-in. square to a 1½-in. x 3-in. rectangle; chain-piece, snip apart, and press to make a total of sixty-six 3-in. x 4-in. units. Add a 1½-in. x 4-in. rectangle to the lower edge of the two-patch unit; chain-piece until all sixty-six units are sewn; snip apart and press. Sew a second 1½-in. x 4-in. rectangle to the side of each unit. Chain-piece until all units have been sewn; snip apart and press. Add a 1½-in. x 5-in. rectangle to the lower edge of

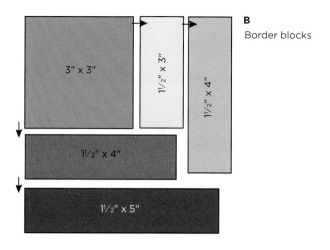

B
Border blocks

3" x 3"

1½" x 3"

1½" x 4"

1½" x 4"

1½" x 5"

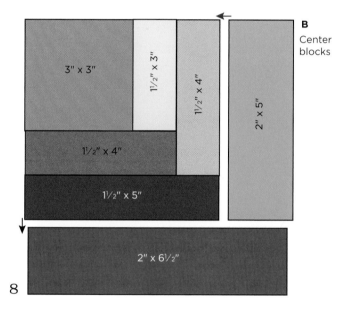

B
Center
blocks

3" x 3"

1½" x 3"

1½" x 4"

2" x 5"

1½" x 4"

1½" x 5"

2" x 6½"

8

ASSEMBLE THE QUILT CENTER

Arrange the 6½-in. A and B blocks in nine rows of nine blocks. Alternate A blocks and B blocks and rotate the B blocks 90 degrees as illustrated. Sew the blocks into rows and press the seams as indicated. Sew the rows together and press the row seams in one direction.

Look for the prominent diagonal lines staggered across the quilt center to double-check your block placement. The quilt center should measure 54 in. square. **9** (See page 188.)

> Before proceeding to the borders, measure the quilt top carefully and adjust the border lengths as needed. Be careful! This can be tricky, because the top and bottom borders are sewn together first before adding them to the quilt top.

BORDERS
ACCENT AND BLACK BORDERS

Connect three 3-in. strips end-to-end, using a diagonal seam (see page 194) to make two 3-in.- by approximately 120-in.-long strips; press the connecting seams open.

From one strip, cut two 54½-in. side borders. From the second strip, cut two 57-in. top and bottom borders. From the remainder of the 3-in. strips, cut six 5-in. rectangles, two 7½-in. rectangles, and four 1½-in. squares. Connect three 1½-in. black strips end-to-end, using a diagonal seam to make two approximately 120-in.-long strips; press the connecting seams open. From one long black strip, cut two 54½-in. side borders.

each unit; chain-piece, snip apart, and press. Before proceeding, set twenty-six 5-in. B blocks aside for the pieced border (B border blocks).

Add a 2-in. x 5-in. scrap rectangle to the side of each remaining block; chain-piece, snip apart, and press the forty B blocks.

NOTE: The seam connecting the 2-in. x 5-in. rectangle is pressed toward the block center, unlike all other seams that are pressed toward the outer edge of the block.

Add a 2-in. x 6½-in. black rectangle to the lower edge of each block; chain piece, snip apart, and press to make forty 6½-in. blocks. **8**

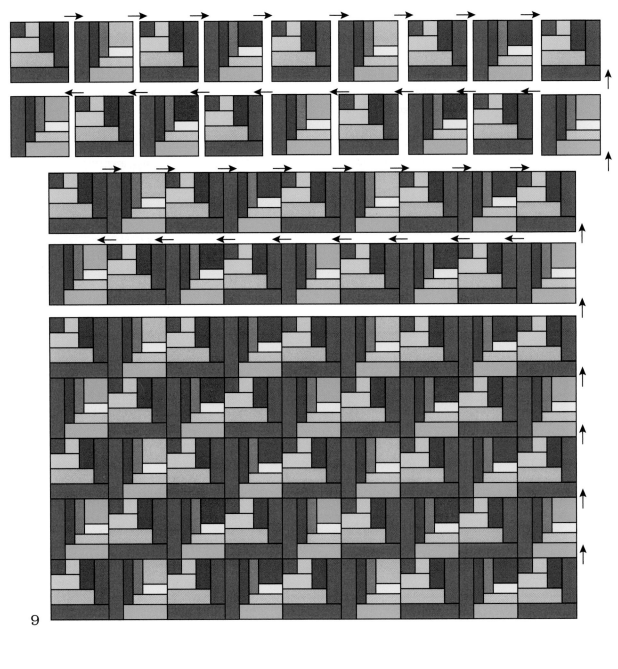

9

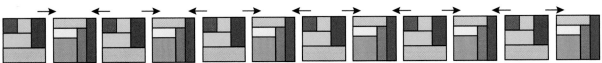

10

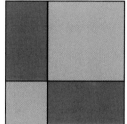
From the second black strip, cut two 57-in. top and bottom borders. From the remainder of the black strips, cut six 5-in. rectangles, two 7½-in. rectangles, and four 3-in. rectangles.

PIECED BORDERS
Select six A border blocks and six B border blocks and sew together in a row as shown, pressing the seams as indicated. Make four pieced border panels 5-in. x 54½-in. **10**

ASSEMBLE QUILT TOP
Arrange and sew the remaining parts of the quilt top into rows. Refer to the diagram on p. 190 for block and border orientation, as well as seam-pressing direction. To make the top and bottom pieced borders, sew in order, one B border block, one 1½-in. x 5-in. black rectangle, one 3-in. x 5-in. accent rectangle, one pieced border panel, one 1½-in. x 5-in. black rectangle, one 3-in.

x 5-in. accent rectangle, and one A border block. Repeat to make a second border.

To make the accent border, sew in order, one 3-in. x 5-in. accent rectangle, one 1½-in. x 3-in. black rectangle, one 3-in. x 57-in. accent strip, one 1½-in. x 3-in. black rectangle, and one 3-in. x 7½-in. accent rectangle. Repeat to make a second border. To make the black border, sew in order, one 1½-in. x 5-in. black rectangle, one 1½-in. accent square, one 1½-in. x 57-in. black strip, one 1½-in. accent square, and one 1½-in. x 7½-in. black rectangle. Repeat to make a second border. To make the quilt center panel, sew one pieced border panel, one 1½-in. x 54½-in. black strip, one 3-in. x 54½-in. accent strip, the quilt center, one 1½-in. x 54½-in. black strip, one 3-in. x 54½-in. accent strip, and one pieced border panel. Sew the pieced groups together and press seams as indicated. **11**

QUILT AND BIND
Layer the backing, batting, and quilt top; quilt as desired. Sew eight 2¼-in. binding strips together end-to-end using a diagonal seam. Press the connecting seams open, then press the binding in half lengthwise, wrong sides together. With raw edges aligned, sew the binding to the front of the quilt using a ¼-in. seam. Miter the binding at the corners (see page 46). Turn the folded edge of the binding to the back of the quilt, and hand stitch in place.

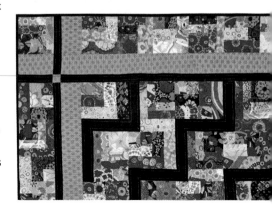

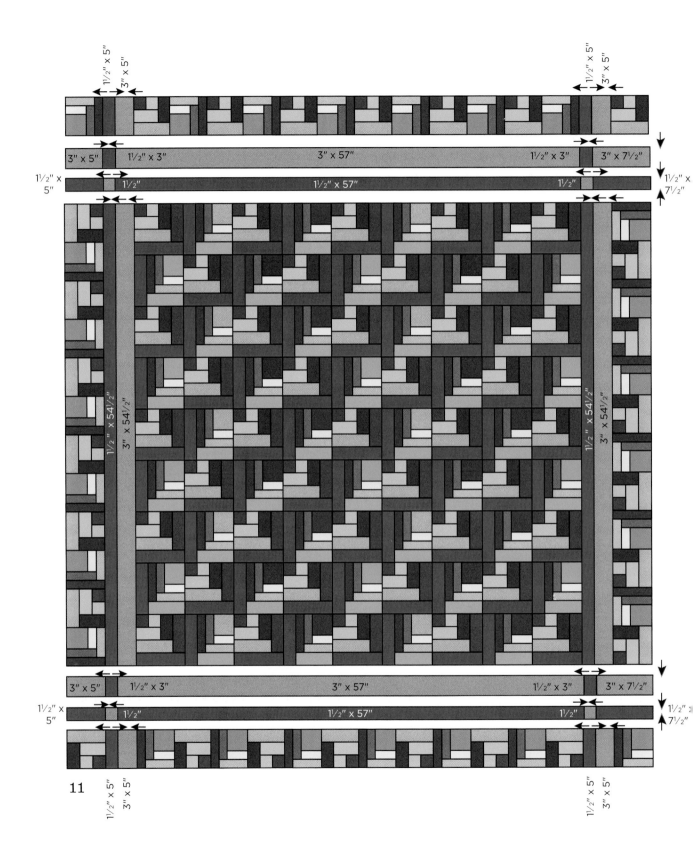

11

APPENDIX: QUILTMAKING BASICS

You probably already know the basics about quilting. You've made a quilt or two. Here, I'd like to offer insights into some of my favorite shortcuts, techniques, tools, and tips found referenced throughout the pages of this book.

BASIC INGREDIENTS

Every quilt starts with some basic ingredients: fabric, thread, and batting.

FABRIC

Use the best quality fabric you can afford—period. With scrap quilts, sometimes quilters feel obligated to use poor quality scrap fabrics inherited from various well-meaning sources. If the quality isn't there, the quilt won't stand the test of time, and all the creative effort to make a project can be wasted on fabric that's old and worn or has a loose weave. To get the most from your beloved hobby, thoroughly enjoy the touch and feel of every aspect of it.

There are two schools of thought on prewashing fabrics: prewash or don't. I'm a prewasher. It gives me one more excuse to handle my fabrics before digging in. Sometimes the fabrics reveal their purpose only after they've been washed and pressed. Be open to what the fabric has to "say."

Prewashing removes excess dye and chemicals from the printing and finishing processes. Since I tend to prewash, I don't wash the quilt once it's done. Every time a quilt is washed, the fabrics lose a little bit of color. I like to keep the quilt looking as new as the day it was made for as long as I can. Some fabrics, like precuts and fabric sold in kits, I don't

prewash. Not every piece of fabric that ends up in my scrap heap is prewashed, and I simply don't worry about it. If you don't like to prewash, consider throwing a color catcher sheet, found in the laundry aisle at the grocery store, in the washer along with the quilt on its first wash to prevent drak colors from bleeding into light.

To prewash quilting fabrics, first rinse in a basin of hot, steamy water with a little soap. Rinse with clean cold water. Spin in the washer. Dry in the dryer. Press and fold for cutting or storage.

THREAD

So many wonderful choices— cotton, polyester, rayon—in solid and variegated shades! In the end, I always seem to come back to cotton thread for one basic reason. Cotton thread ages at the same rate as the cotton fabrics used in the quilt. For piecing, I like a lighter weight thread. My favorites are 50-weight Mettler, Aurifil™, or YLI Soft Touch. For machine quilting, I prefer solid colors in 40- or 50-weight. I'm not a big fan of variegated threads for quilting— too many things are happening on a scrap quilt to add the variations in color from a variegated thread. For hand quilting, the glazed YLI Quilt-

ing Thread on wooden spools just can't be beat.

In the context of scrap quilts, consider using up all those partially used bobbins when piecing.

BATTING

Batting selection is often driven by how the project will be used. Washable wool is almost always my first choice. It has a beautiful hand, transitions seasons nicely, and drapes beautifully for a wall-hanging or bed. It's lightweight, and it makes the finished quilt feel silky smooth! Plus, wool batting can be machine washed in cold water and dried on a low setting. My second choice is cotton batting, especially for quilts intended for use by a child, as cotton will stand up to more frequent washing.

SEWING

PIECING ACCURACY

Trimming a completed block can create more problems than it solves. If a block isn't the correct size, it almost always comes down to three potential problems in the assembly of the block: precise cutting, accurate seam allowances, and proper pressing. By taking a closer look at the block, we can diagnose the problem area and make a correction (or two!).

With each step of quilt construction, tiny measurements that are off—a little bit here, a little bit there—can make a big difference in the final construction of the project. It's frustrating to spend hours working on something, only to find that blocks and borders don't measure up.

Cutting We discussed this in great depth in the ScrapTherapy steps. Let's just say that accurate cutting is important, but I realize cutting isn't the most exciting step in making a quilt. So let's see if we can't make it more fun and more accurate at the same time. Look for more details in Step 2, page 13.

Seam allowance Unless otherwise noted, use a scant $1/4$-in. seam allowance for piecing on any of the projects presented in this book. A "scant" $1/4$-in. seam is just one or two threads less than a true $1/4$-in. seam. Why a scant $1/4$ in.? That one- or-two thread width allows for the thickness of the fabric at the pressed fold. If you aren't certain of your seam allowance, always sew a test seam. I suspect you'll have some cut-up scraps now, so sew two 2-in. scraps together with a scant $1/4$-in. seam. Press the seam to one side and measure. The result should be a rectangle that is 2 in. × $3^{1/2}$ in. If the rectangle is any other size, adjust your needle position and test again.

Pressing Be meticulous about following seam-pressing directions on your projects. Unless I'm connecting fabric strips for borders, piping, or binding, I rarely press seams open.

As an avid machine quilter who does a lot of in-the-ditch quilting, I prefer to press seams to one side. When quilting in the ditch over seams that have been pressed open, threads can be severed by the quilting needle, weakening the quilt. When seams are pressed to one side, seams will be stronger and will nest together, creating accurate corners and reduced bulk at seam intersections.

SEWING MACHINE

Choose a machine that stretches your skills. Shop around and ask a lot of questions. The range is mind-boggling. Consider what you want to do on your machine as you evaluate your choices. Here are some features to think about:

For piecing and appliqué:
- Even straight stitches; test for nicely balanced tension
- Quarter-inch foot
- Needle up, needle down capabilities
- Adjustable needle positioning, so you can move the needle to the left or right
- Decorative stitch options, especially zigzag, satin stitch, and buttonhole stitches

For quilting:
- Large throat opening to make it easier to move the quilt around during quilting
- Walking foot or dual-feed option to allow the quilt to feed evenly through the machine
- Darning foot for free-motion quilting
- Hand (manual) controls, making it handier than keeping your foot on the foot control for the entire quilting process
- Adjustable upper thread tension and presser foot pressure

To maximize the enjoyment of your hobby, I encourage you to choose the best machine you can afford that has features that allow you to do what you want to do, whether it's a nice even stitch for piecing, or free-motion quilting. Over time, your improving skills may exceed the capabilities of your sewing machine. At that time, it may be time to consider an upgrade. The proper tools for any hobby, including quilting, can make all the difference in the enjoyment of your craft.

PINS AND NEEDLES

You can never have too many pins. Whether I'm securing small pieces, borders, or binding, I pin more than I think I need to. I use pins to secure every seam intersection, making sure the seams nest nicely by shifting the opposing seams between my thumb and index finger, then placing a pin across the seam intersection. On a longer seam, that means a pin is placed about every 2 in. or so to secure the seam for sewing.

If I have a quarter-inch foot with a guide, I place the pins with the points toward the seam, so the points stop just outside the $1/4$-in. seam allowance. That way I don't have to pull out pins as I sew, risking distortions in the seam from shifting fabric. I never run over a pin with the sewing machine needle if I can avoid it. It's bad for the sewing machine and could be dangerous for you if a pin breaks and becomes airborne.

At seam intersections, it's common to place a pin on both sides of the seam junction. Over the years, I've been in the habit of placing one pin

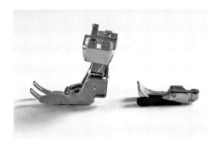

crosswise, catching both layers of seam allowances on either side of the seam intersection with one pin. This saves a little time, placing one pin instead of two, and I have found the results to be equally as accurate.

Another pin type I like is the appliqué pin. It is a very short, fine pin with a tiny head, perfect to hold a shape in place, but not so long that

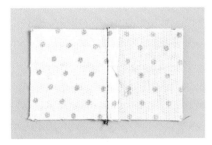

the thread gets hung up on it when you are hand sewing.

BLOCK AND QUILT CONSTRUCTION

The more you make quilts, the more you generate some favorite techniques. These suggestions for common construction elements pop up repeatedly in my patterns. Perhaps they'll become your favorites too.

FURLING SEAMS

Furling seams, so that the seam allowance is opened only where the two seams meet in the center, is a technique borrowed from hand-quilting. Once the center seam intersection is opened, all four seams rotate in one direction around the center. This technique is particularly nice on blocks where several seams come together in the center like pin-wheel blocks.

TO MAKE FOUR-PATCH BLOCKS WITH FURLED CENTER SEAMS

Sew two-patch units and press the seams consistently to one side, usually toward the darker fabric. Sew pairs of two patches with opposing fabric facing and seams nested.

Be sure to feed the four-patches into the sewing machine exactly the same each time, i.e., the light fabric first or dark fabric first.

Using a seam ripper, remove the last two or three stitches from the two-patch seam on each side of the four-patch unit. Stop removing stitches at the intersection with the longer four-patch seam. **1**

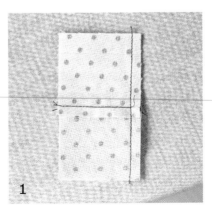

Press from the back so the seams rotate and the center intersection is furled. Note that only the center of the block seam section is open; the rest of the seams are pressed to one side, each rotating around the center. **2** Press from the front.

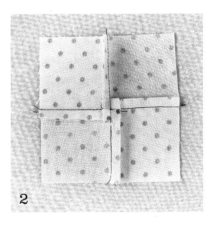

Seams can furl clockwise or counterclockwise. Also notice that a clockwise seam rotation from the back is counterclockwise from the front. The secret isn't that the seams furl one way or another, it's that they all furl in the same direction for the quilt construction.

When I teach this method in classes, some students get the seams furling in the opposite direction on a few of the blocks. I like to tell them that this isn't the end of the world. The seams are on the inside of the quilt. If blocks don't nest as you want them to, just use some extra pins to secure the "errant" seam intersection and sew as normal. No one will ever know!

CONNECTING STRIPS FOR BORDERS, BINDING, BAG HANDLES, AND OTHER APPLICATIONS

When connecting cross-grain strips end-to-end, I prefer to use a diagonal seam. A diagonal seam is stronger and less noticeable than a straight one. An exception: When connecting seams for a cross-grain border using striped fabric, I try to match the stripes using a vertical seam.

To sew a diagonal seam

1. Align the cut strips, right sides together, with ends perpendicular.
2. With a pencil, draw a line across the diagonal intersection.
3. Pin to secure and sew directly on the line.
4. Trim ends ¼ in. away from the seam.
5. Trim the point extensions.
6. Press the seams open. This is one of the few times I press seams open.

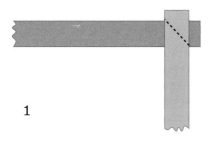

CHANGING QUILT SIZES BY ALTERING THE BLOCK NUMBERS

Sure! Do it!! But realize that some patterns have a symmetry created by an odd or even number of blocks in rows. If you change the size of the quilt by increasing or decreasing blocks in rows, consider that some quilts look better if the increase or decrease is done in increments of two blocks in a row, rather than one. Some quilts might require a bit more calculation for border and finishing elements when the block numbers are changed.

APPLIQUÉ

There are a million methods to do appliqué. Below are my favorites by hand or by machine.

I prefer hand appliqué to machine appliqué. My favorite method, the "back-basting" method, also known as the "template free" method, is attributed, to Jeanna Kimball in many circles.

Hand Appliqué

1. Trace the appliqué shape in reverse onto the back of the base fabric.
2. Cut the appliqué fabric piece slightly larger than the appliqué shape.
3. Pin the shape to the right side of the fabric, right side up so that the appliqué fabric covers the lines, plus at least ⅛-in. seam allowance. Hold the fabrics to a light source to be sure all lines plus seam allowances are adequately planned.
4. From the wrong side of the background fabric, pin-baste roughly around the shape using appliqué pins.

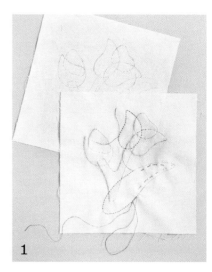

1

5. From the wrong side of the background fabric, using a heavy thread (like YLI Hand Quilting Thread) in a high contrast color, a thicker needle (I use a size 7 sharp), and a thimble if you wear one, sew a tight running stitch (about 10 stitches to the inch) directly on the line to secure the appliqué shape to the block. Don't knot the thread at the beginning or end of the running stitch, and stitch all the way around the shape.
6. From the front, trim the appliqué fabric about ⅛ in. from the running stitch. Leave the running stitch in place for at least an hour or overnight.
7. Working from the front, and using an appliqué needle (I like Clover Black Gold Appliqué Needles, size 10 or 11), a very fine cotton thread (I like YLI Soft Touch) in a color that matches the appliqué, and a thimble if you wear one, pull out a few of the running stitches. Bend the appliqué seam allowance under and secure the fold to the background fabric with short appliqué stitches that just catch the fold of the shape. The

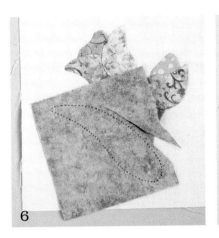

6

7

9

Machine Appliquéd Block

heavier needle and thread will have left a perforation in the appliqué fabric that will allow the seam allowance to turn under exactly where you want it. And the running stitch will also have left marks in the base fabric so you can see the outline of the shape.

8. Proceed around the appliqué shape, pulling out the running stitches about 1/2 in. ahead of where you are securing the appliqué.

9. Continue adding appliqué pieces, one layer at a time until the block is complete.

Machine Appliqué Using Light Fusible Web

Fusible webs come in a variety of weights, so check the package to be sure you have one compatible with the weight of your fabrics—it's better to go light and avoid stiffness in the appliqué area. If you have several types in your stash, try them on a scrap of the quilt fabrics and check for a feel you like.

Be sure the product is sew-through. No-sew fusible webs can damage your sewing machine.

1. Trace the appliqué shape in reverse on the paper side of the fusible web.

2. Cut out the shape roughly and press the adhesive side of the fusible web to the wrong side of the appliqué fabric following the manufacturer's instructions.

3. Cut around the shape, through paper and fabric, directly on the drawn lines.

4. Remove the paper and fuse the appliqué shape onto the right side of the base fabric.

5. Stitch around the edge of the appliqué shape with a zigzag, satin, or buttonhole stitch using matching or contrasting thread.

GLOSSARY

APPLIQUÉ BLOCK

A quilt element that incorporates fabric shapes sewn onto a background fabric. Appliqué may be done by hand or by machine using a variety of techniques.

APPLIQUÉ PRESSING SHEET

A heat-inert synthetic liner placed between the iron and the fabric as a barrier; heat will pass through the liner, but fusible glue will not adhere to the sheet.

BACK-BASTING

A type of appliqué technique. The arrangement of appliqué shapes is drawn on the back of the main block fabric, then the pieces are placed on the front of the block in layers and basted from the back. The shapes are trimmed, and seams turned under and sewn to the background fabric from the front to complete the block.

BACKSTITCH

A backward stitch or a stitch on top of an existing stitch to keep the thread from getting loose.

BASTE

An extra-long stitch by hand or machine to hold fabrics in place for the next step in the process, such as piecing or quilting.

BIAS

Fabric cut on an angle, as opposed to straight of grain. Fabric cut along the bias will be more stretchy than fabric cut along the lengthwise or crosswise grain. Also, the 45-degree line on an acrylic quilter's ruler.

BORDER STRIPE

A type of fabric print on which a decorative stripe typically runs along the length of grain of the fabric. It is often used for quilt borders.

CHAIN PIECING

An efficient method to sew block elements by machine. Sew two pieces of fabric together, make a few stitches in between, then sew the next two pieces of fabric together. The result can be a long "chain" of sewn units connected by threads in between units.

CORNERSTONE, CORNERSTONE BLOCK

A square of fabric placed between sashing strips. The square can be one piece of fabric or made from several pieces sewn into a small block used as a cornerstone.

DARNING FOOT

Sewing machine attachment used for free-motion quilting. The darning foot is often used with the sewing machine feed dogs in lowered position, allowing fabric to move freely under the foot to make curved quilting designs.

DIRECTIONAL PRINT FABRIC

A fabric print with design elements that face one or two ways. Depending on how the fabric is placed in a project, some elements may appear upside down.

DOUBLE BACKSTITCH

A short anchoring stitch, with a repeat of a stitch on top of itself in a series of running stitches.

DOUBLE-FOLD BINDING

A method of covering the raw edges of the finished quilt sandwich whereby a long strip of fabric is folded in half, attached to the quilt from the front with raw edges aligned, and the fold is sewn to the back of the quilt, typically by hand.

DUAL FEED

An integrated sewing machine feed device available on some sewing machine models that allows several layers of fabric to advance through the sewing machine with equal pressure from the top and bottom of the fabric. The dual feed operates similar to a walking foot.

FLANGE

An accent for a border or binding, usually made from a narrow strip of fabric folded in half lengthwise, then inserted, raw edges aligned, between two fabrics seamed together.

FLOAT

Blocks or block elements that do not extend to or touch the next design element, such as a border or sashing strip.

FLYING GEESE

A block element made from one quarter-square triangle and two half-square triangles. The resulting unit is a triangle within a rectangle that resembles the V-shaped formation made by migrating geese.

FREE-MOTION QUILTING

A quilting technique using a darning foot with the sewing machine feed dogs dropped below the bed. The quilt sandwich is moved under the sewing machine needle using smooth curvy strokes to create curved stitching patterns.

FURLING

A seam-pressing method for four-patch units. The center of the seam allowance is opened, allowing the remaining four seams to be pressed to one side, rotating around the center in a clockwise or counterclockwise direction.

FUSIBLE INTERFACING

A lightweight fabric similar to a stabilizer that has heat-sensitive glue. The interfacing may be printed with shapes for appliqué or piecing or may be unprinted.

FUSIBLE WEB

A heat-sensitive fabric adhesive that usually comes with a paper backing on one or both sides. Used for techniques like appliqué to adhere two pieces of fabric together without adding any additional fabric like interfacing.

HALF-SQUARE TRIANGLE

The right isosceles triangle that results from cutting a square in half diagonally.

HALF-SQUARE TRIANGLE RULER

A specialty ruler that facilitates making half-square triangle units from strips of fabric.

HALF-SQUARE TRIANGLE UNIT

The resulting square unit made from sewing two half-square triangles together.

HERA MARKER

A quilt-marking tool made of hard plastic. Used like a pencil, it produces an indent on the fabric as opposed to ink or pencil lead.

IN-THE-DITCH

Straight-line sewing to topstitch or quilt directly along the seamline.

LENGTH OF GRAIN

The direction along the selvage as it comes off the bolt. Also called lengthwise grain.

LOG CABIN BLOCK

A traditional block pattern that starts with a center or corner square, then increases in size as rectangular block elements are added to the sides of the block to create the pattern. The log cabin block has many traditional variations.

PIECED BLOCK

A section of a quilt made entirely from geometric shapes sewn together using $1/4$-in. seams. A quilt is usually made with several blocks sewn together in rows.

PRAIRIE-POINT BINDING

A finishing technique that incorporates squares that are folded in half twice. The raw edge of the folded triangle is incorporated in the seam, creating a jagged-edge appearance on the finished quilt. Prairie points may also be incorporated as a border embellishment.

QUARTER-SQUARE TRIANGLE

The resulting right isosceles triangles from cutting a square in half along both diagonals.

QUARTER-SQUARE TRIANGLE UNIT

The resulting square unit made from sewing four quarter-square triangles together.

RAIL FENCE BLOCK

A traditional quilt pattern that consists of several rectangles that, when sewn together in parallel lines, form a square. Rail fence blocks can be assembled by strip piecing a certain number of strips; then the pressed strips are cross-cut into blocks.

RUNNING STITCH

Equally spaced stitches made by rocking a threaded needle from front to back through one or more fabric layers. May be decorative as for quilting or embroidery or functional as for joining fabric pieces or making ruffles.

SASHING

Rectangular strips commonly placed between blocks in a quilt.

SAWTOOTH BORDER

A row of triangles sewn around a quilt center.

SEAM ALLOWANCE

The area between the stitching line and the raw edge of the fabric when two pieces are sewn together. Seam allowances are typically pressed to one side or pressed open to create a flat finished product.

SETTING TRIANGLE

Half-square and quarter-square triangles that complete the straight edges of a quilt when the blocks are set and sewn on-point or in rows that are at a 45-degree angle. Typically quarter-square triangles are used along the sides and half-square triangles on the corners. The triangles keep less-stretchy straight of grain along the outside or border edge of the quilt.

STRIP PIECING

A time-saving piecing technique of sewing two width-of-fabric strips together, which are then typically cross-cut into smaller sizes.

TOPSTITCH

Sewing through a few fabric layers, often to hold a fold compressed or to keep fabric from curling with use.

UNFINISHED SIZE

The width and length of a block unit, block, or quilt section that includes seam allowances, often provided at various checkpoints in a pattern to make sure piecing and seam allowances are accurate.

VALUE

The relative intensity or absence of color.

WALKING OR EVEN-FEED FOOT

A sewing machine attachment that works in conjunction with the feed dogs advancing the fabric from the top and bottom. Used for straight-line quilting or sewing through multiple layers of fabric.

WIDTH-OF-FABRIC OR WIDTH-OF-GRAIN

The crosswise, selvage-to-selvage direction as the fabric comes off the bolt. Quilting cotton fabrics are typically between 40 in. and 42 in. wide off the bolt.

RESOURCES

Visit these websites for additional information about products mentioned
in this book.

ALICIA'S ATTIC
Qtools Cutting Edge
www.online-quilting.com

AMERICAN & EFIRD
Mettler Thread
www.amefird.com

AURIFIL
Thread
www.aurifil.com

CEDAR CANYON TEXTILES
Shiva Paintstiks
www.cedarcanyontextiles.com

CLOVER NEEDLECRAFT
Black Gold Appliqué Needles
www.clover-usa.com

KATIE LANE QUILTS
Scallop Radial Rules & Handbook
www.katielane.com

MARY ELLEN PRODUCTS
Best Press Starch Alternative
(800) 977-4145
www.maryellenproducts.com

OLFA
Rotary Cutters and Mats
www.olfa.com

PATSY THOMPSON DESIGNS LTD.
Instructional Quilting Videos
www.patsythompsondesigns.com

PIECES BE WITH YOU
Piping Hot Binding Tool and Book
www.piecesbewithyou.com

QUILTSMART, INC.
Printed Fusible Interfacing
www.quiltsmart.com

RELIABLE CORPORATION
Digital Velocity Iron
www.reliablecorporation.com

SCRAPS OF TIME
Paper Pieced Label Patterns
www.scrapsoftimequilts.com

STUDIO 180 DESIGN
Wing Clipper and Tucker Trimmer
www.studio180design.net

SUPERIOR THREADS
Texture Magic
www.superiorthreads.com

YLI CORP.
Soft Touch and Quilting Thread
www.ylicorp.com

SCRAPTHERAPY
www.scrap-therapy.com
Log on for the latest patterns, tips,
and news on the ScrapTherapy
program.

INDEX

Note: Page numbers in *italics* indicate projects, and **bold** numbers indicate definitions.